LANGUAGE AND HISTORY IN AFRICA

Published in association with
THE AFRICAN LANGUAGE REVIEW

LANGUAGE AND HISTORY IN AFRICA

A VOLUME OF COLLECTED PAPERS PRESENTED TO THE LONDON SEMINAR ON LANGUAGE AND HISTORY IN AFRICA (HELD AT THE SCHOOL OF ORIENTAL AND AFRICAN STUDIES, 1967–69)

Edited by

DAVID DALBY

FRANK CASS & CO. LTD.

1970

Published by

FRANK CASS AND COMPANY LIMITED
67 Great Russell Street, London WC1B 3BT

ISBN 07146 2420 9

PRINTED IN GREAT BRITAIN BY HEADLEY BROTHERS LTD
109 KINGSWAY LONDON WC2 AND ASHFORD KENT

CONTENTS

CONTENTS

INTRODUCTION

THE *Language and History in Africa Seminar* was established at the School of Oriental and African Studies at the end of 1966, within the framework of the University of London Centre of African Studies. The expressed aims of the Seminar have been to explore the opportunities for collaboration between linguists and historians in the study of Africa, and to facilitate a dialogue between the two disciplines. A wide range of papers has been presented to the Seminar during its first three years, and eleven of these papers have been collected together to form the present volume. The School of Oriental and African Studies has provided an ideal forum for this Seminar in view of a unique concentration of fifty full-time Africanists among its academic staff (half of them linguists), and of an expanding postgraduate programme in African studies. This concentration of Africanists in London has not deterred the Seminar from inviting contributions from colleagues at other universities, however, and three of the papers in this volume were presented to the Seminar by visiting scholars (including two from American universities). The work of the Seminar is still in its early stages, and it is intended that increasing attention should be devoted in its future programme to the historical interpretation of the contemporary language-map of Africa, and to the study of the processes of linguistic change and interaction in different parts of the continent. Specialized working-groups have also been set up to deal with long-term research and discussion in two specific areas, Comparative Bantu and the investigation of Cattle-keeping in Africa, and meetings of these working-groups—together with the plenary sessions of the Seminar—will be open to interested scholars and students from any university. It is hoped in particular that an increasing number of postgraduate students will become associated with the work of this Seminar, either in preparation for advanced London degrees or as part of their course-work for degrees at other universities.

It would be presumptuous to overlook the fact that historians have already accomplished a great deal in facilitating interdisciplinary collaboration within African studies: it is, after all, the professional task of the historian to assemble data from every relevant field. The present Seminar, however, has been able to view the subject of interdisciplinary collaboration from the standpoint of the linguist as well as from that of the historian, and has been able to spotlight not only the advantages, but also the dangers, of co-ordinating the aims and methodologies of the two disciplines. These dangers may be avoided, as they have not always been avoided in the past, if linguists and historians remain aware of the differing objectives and principles of their two disciplines, and it is the intention of the present volume to contribute towards this mutual understanding. In particular, it is important that we should acknowledge the different *types* of task facing the linguist and the historian in Africa. Whereas the linguist's primary concern is with the verifiable recording of the present-day languages of the continent, so the historian is concerned with the often tentative reconstruction of its largely undocumented past. At the level at which linguistic facts are used for historical purposes, success will depend to a large extent on the degree to which each discipline is able to understand—and also scrutinize—the differing aims and procedures of the other.

Despite their formal differences, the fields of linguistic and historical study are dominated alike by two salient features of the African scene. One of these is the dearth of primary documentation of any historical depth, either about sub-Saharan Africa or in the languages of Africa. The other, perhaps a cause of the former, is the extreme ethno-linguistic fragmentation of the sub-Saharan continent, a feature which has impeded the development not only of African societies but also of African studies. This fragmentation of language has formed a barrier to communication within Africa and to knowledge about Africa, and has also stood in the way of an equal dialogue between Africa and the outside world. White intruders, deterred by the multiplicity of African languages from the task of learning even one, have often been content to judge African cultures from a position of relative ignorance, and it is still the African who has to shoulder the main burden of communication with the outside world. African speakers of European languages continue to outnumber Western speakers of African languages by a thousand or more to one, and even among professional Africanists there are relatively few who acquire more than a smattering of any African language.

On the other hand, the very complexity of the African language-map and the lack of historical data on or in its languages have served as a stimulus to scholarly curiosity. Western philologists have been endeavouring to unravel the historical relationship of African languages since the beginning of the nineteenth century, and it is a measure of the magnitude of this problem that there should still be widespread disagreement about its solution. At the same time, *one* aspect of the African language-map has become especially clear, and it is important that both historians and linguists should bear this in mind: the remoter levels of linguistic relationship have often proved easier to determine than the intermediate levels. It can hardly be denied, for example, that some kind of distant historical relationship lies behind the so-called Niger–Congo languages (or a large part of them), or behind most of the so-called Erythraic or Afro-Asiatic languages. There can be far less certainty, however, about the historical sub-classification or precise limits of either of these apparent 'families'. Even in the case of Bantu, where comparative study is now on a level exceeded perhaps only by Indo-European, there is still doubt as to its precise historical relationship to other Niger–Congo languages, and we are still without a detailed historical sub-classification of Bantu. Such a situation calls for caution from both linguists and historians. For comparative linguists, the demonstration of intermediate levels of relationship remains a major task. For historians, any proposed linguistic groupings beyond the most immediate and obvious level need to be evaluated alongside other forms of prehistorical evidence, rather than being accepted as the basis for further hypotheses.

Probably no scholar, either linguist or historian, would disagree with this plea for caution in historico-linguistic research. On the other hand, Africanist linguists in Britain have sometimes been regarded by historians and linguists elsewhere as being *over*-cautious and unduly negative in their attitude to comparative and historical research, and it is pertinent for us to examine the substance of this criticism. Daniel F. McCall of Boston University gave voice to this impatience with British linguists in his stimulating volume *Africa in Time Perspective*:[1]

> For just over a decade, the classification [of African languages] which has occupied the centre of attention is that of Greenberg. It is accepted in its general outlines without demur by other American linguists and seems to have had a quite extensive acceptance on the continent of Europe, but is generally rejected by British linguists.
>
> One objection is that this classification has not yet resulted in the elucidation of regularities similar to 'Grimm's law' . . . and that to demonstrate the presence or absence of these regularities requires further analysis, some of which would be dependent on the collection of more complete descriptive data. Thus this criticism cannot be definitive unless and until it is established that it is *impossible* to derive such correspondences from this classification.
>
> One is tempted to ask if this disagreement is deeper than the immediate issue, if it is not due to a difference in orientation . . . to the previously mentioned 'lost unity of linguistics'? . . . In this case the lack of agreement is particularly disturbing because British linguists constitute an important part of the language specialists who have given attention to African languages and whose talents will not be directed to any work useful to historians until these linguists have some classification acceptable to them.
>
> The linguists can go on working on non-historical problems and

1. Daniel F. McCall, *Africa in Time-Perspective*, Boston and Legon, 1964, pp. 68–9.

be less disturbed by the failure of their colleagues to arrive at a consensus; but the historian, in so far as his work touches language, is stymied if he has no classification. What he asks from the linguists is a reasonable degree of agreement upon an existing classification—or if this is impossible, serious attempts to achieve an improved classification. There has not been much evidence of such work on classification by the critics, and so it is not surprising that some historians are using Greenberg's classification, even if they may consider it only *faute de mieux*. The results obtained by a number of linguists who do accept this classification and are carrying out further linguistic work upon this basis will also be welcomed by historians.

McCall's statement that Greenberg's classification is 'generally rejected' by British linguists is only partially true, but in assessing the reasons for this partial rejection he reveals a number of misconceptions which historians have sometimes harboured about the nature and use of linguistic evidence. The reference to the 'lost unity of linguistics' relates to the post-Saussurean dichotomy between the synchronic and the diachronic study of language,[2] a dichotomy which is of methodological value in the African field no less than any other. The two branches of linguistics are by no means mutually exclusive, however, and—in the absence of adequate historical documentation—diachronic conclusions about African languages can be based only on the sound synchronic description—and synchronic comparison—of those languages. The building up of primary descriptive data is thus vital to any subsequent historico-linguistic study, and McCall appears to misjudge the ultimate interests of his own discipline in suggesting that the 'talents' of British linguists, who have been admittedly more concerned with description than with classification, 'will not be directed to any work useful to historians until these linguists have some classification acceptable to them'.[3]

That linguistic research may contribute to the study of African history in many fields apart from classification is evidenced by the present volume. The papers which follow cover only a sample of the subjects which have been considered by the London Seminar, but they are a representative sample, and their main collective purpose is to stimulate further enquiry and research. Each of them was compiled originally as a basis for oral discussion, and—in an inter-disciplinary field which is still in its infancy—it is appropriate that

2. Cf. Ferdinand de Saussure, *Cours de Linguistique Generale*, 4th edn., Paris, 1948 (1st edn. 1915), pt. I, chap. III.
3. Although McCall (op. cit., p. 69) looks forward nevertheless to the publication of Malcolm Guthrie's Proto-Bantu starred forms ('which should extend our vista considerably'). For a fuller discussion of classificational issues, see David Dalby, 'Reflections on the classification of African languages', *African Language Studies*, XI, 1970, pp. 147–171.

they should retain this introductory character. None of them claims to be the last word on any topic, but it is hoped that each of them will encourage further collaboration between historians and linguists. While comprising a healthy diversity of views, the eleven papers serve also as a group to highlight some of the principles and priorities which must underlie such collaboration, and it will be worthwhile for us to consider these briefly here.

By its very universality, the subject 'Language and History in Africa' should not be confined to linguists and historians, and its adequate study will be dependent ultimately upon collaboration among all disciplines relevant to the study of past and present societies in Africa. In a continent so lacking in direct historical sources, inferences made from modern data become especially important. To arrive at these, synchronic data must first be collected and synchronic comparisons made. The diachronic implications of these comparisons can then be compared with, and checked against, any available sources of relevant historical or prehistorical data. The first operation involves descriptive and comparative work by linguists, sociologists, cultural and physical anthropologists, and human geographers. The second operation relates to direct historical data, either documented or oral, and to prehistorical data assembled by archaeologists, ethno-botanists and palaeo-climatologists. The increasing technicalities and literature in each of these specialized fields leave little place for the inter-disciplinary 'Jack-of-all-trades', who was one of the main pillars of African studies in the nineteenth century. Today, any such collaboration must involve individual members of each discipline, and its success therefore rests upon the availability of adequate means of communication among the disciplines. One approach is for each discipline to concern itself exclusively with its own data and to present its resulting conclusions for the perusal of scholars in other fields: this mono-disciplinary approach is followed and advocated in this volume by Malcolm Guthrie,[4] and would seem to be the most suitable foundation for comparative studies on a continental scale. In the investigation of individual cultures or geographical areas, however, an alternative approach would seem desirable, whereby members of adjacent disciplines work in close collaboration throughout: the advantages of this team-approach are discussed by Desmond Clark.[5]

Although it is not possible for the individual Africanist to master the techniques and data of all adjacent disciplines, collaboration with those disciplines must inevitably make demands upon him. He needs to understand the objectives and principles of those disciplines, and must likewise be able to present a digest of the aims and principles of his own discipline to his colleagues from outside. And it

4. See Guthrie, pp. 20–49 below.
5. See Clark, p. 17 below.

is at this theoretical level that some of the most fruitful exchanges can occur. The world of Africanist scholars is a relatively small but fast-growing one, and in this developing situation it is important that the aims and methodologies of each disciplinary group should be kept continually under review. There is no better way of doing this than by subjecting them to the examination of colleagues in other fields, and by pooling the experiences of each field. From this point of view, it has been valuable for the Seminar to have had a review of interdisciplinary collaboration by an archaeologist, and to have been made aware of the similarity of his problems to those of the linguist and the historian, despite the quite different technical nature of the three fields. For this reason, Desmond Clark's paper has been chosen as the opening contribution in the present volume, and the reader will observe that many of the theoretical issues which he raises recur in the following papers. On a cautionary note, Clark emphasizes the dangers inherent in fragmented data and in the uneven spread of field-research (as often determined, of course, by former colonial boundaries); he touches on the problem of physical hybridization (comparable to the problems of cultural and linguistic hybridization) and on the need to avoid any rigid categorization in distinguishing different periods of African prehistory. On a programmatic note, he outlines the basic need for interdisciplinary checking and confirmation of findings (as between archaeology and oral tradition or comparative linguistics, for example), for the application of quantitative—i.e. measurable and verifiable—techniques, and for the use of seriation techniques in unravelling layers of culture[6]; his call for the study of cultural—and associated linguistic—'assemblages' (rather than of isolated artifacts and words) provides us with a useful conceptual term in the study of cultural vocabulary. We are also shown how archaeologists may work from a knowledge of the ethnographic present towards an interpretation of the past record, just as comparative linguists and historians will need to have a sound knowledge of the sociolinguistic present and recent past of Africa, if they are to attempt any interpretation of Africa's linguistic prehistory.[7]

At this point, and before considering some of the specific priorities suggested in this volume, one should mention briefly two or three further theoretical issues which have been broached here. The most important of these is expressed by Shula Marks and Anthony Atmore in their warning that 'linguistic, racial and cultural traits are independent variables'.[8] This is an obvious principle, but one which has been repeatedly infringed in writings about African peoples and

6. Cf. Edgar A. Gregersen, 'Linguistic seriation as a dating device for loanwords, with special reference to West Africa', *African Language Review*, 6, 1967, pp. 102–8.
7. Cf. Bynon, p. 65 below.
8. See Marks and Atmore, p. 127 below.

cultures—witness the numerous, and frequently unfounded, inferences which have been made from 'race' to language or from language to 'race'. Linked with the infringement of this principle is the subsidiary danger of using modern ethnic and/or linguistic names diachronically, as exemplified by the confused use of *Nguni*, for example, and as discussed here also by Paul Hair.[9] Even more important, however, is the danger of telescoping time-depths and differing degrees of relationship in any assessment of languages, peoples and cultures.[10] This particular danger is perhaps most evident in the comparative study of languages, where—with greater remoteness of time—it becomes increasingly difficult to distinguish between historical layers within individual languages[11] or between different levels of relationship among these languages.[12] This is why so much circumspection is required in drawing diachronic conclusions from some of the remoter linguistic groupings postulated by comparative linguists, for which degrees of relationship often vary widely at the same 'level' of classification, and for which the evidence—as Babatunde Lawal has so aptly phrased it—has been 'viewed from so high an altitude that the Silk-Cotton tree, the Mango tree, the Baobab and even shrubs have all looked alike'.[13] Circumspection is likewise called for in considering the claims of lexico-statistical dating or 'glottochronology', based on the dubious assumption that certain vocabulary in a language changes at a more or less predictable rate.[14]

At more immediate levels of prehistory, as reconstructed from oral tradition in particular, attention has also been drawn in this volume to the pitfall of confusing 'dynastic shuffles with ethnic migrations'.[15]

In considering the main priorities for future research, the Language and History in Africa Seminar has been faced with great difficulty. On the one hand, there are pressing needs for new research in almost every direction, but on the other hand funds and personnel are grossly inadequate for attending to these. It seems likely, for example, that less—rather than more—financial support may be available to Africanist researchers in the nineteen-seventies than in the previous decade, on both sides of the Atlantic. In this situation, it behoves us to be as economical as possible in the application of research, and to take every opportunity to co-ordinate and integrate our investigations. Research students would benefit, and the subject would benefit, if groups of doctoral theses could be centred

9. See Marks and Atmore, p. 120 f. below; and Hair, p. 60 f. below.
10. See Hair, pp. 58–60 below.
11. Cf. Bynon, p. 70 below.
12. Cf. David Dalby, 'Levels of relationship in the classification of African languages', *African Language Studies*, VII, 1966, pp. 171–9.
13. Unpublished term-paper on African language classification (Indiana University, 1969).
14. Cf. Bird, p. 148 f. below.
15. See Hair, p. 55 below.

around common themes—as is the custom in many of the natural sciences.

The emphasis during the nineteen-sixties has been on expanding the volume of field research in Africa, throughout all the relevant disciplines. It is to be hoped that this trend will not be reversed, but even if it is only halted—either through a shortage of funds or through other practical difficulties—then we should not lose the opportunity to explore other avenues of Africanist research. One of the most important of these will be the investigation and co-ordination of existing documentary material, both published and in manuscript, relating to the languages and peoples of Africa. With the development of more sophisticated descriptive techniques during the twentieth century, linguists in the African field have often disregarded any earlier linguistic data which has not measured up to their own modern standards; meanwhile, Africanist historians have sometimes been more preoccupied with the analysis of oral traditions, as they survive today, than they have with the detailed analysis of the ethnolinguistic evidence contained in many early European and early Arabic sources on Africa. This bias in both disciplines is already being rectified, and it is to be hoped that the coming decade will see a marked increase in the amount of edited historical data available on the individual peoples and languages of Africa.[16] Paul Hair points out how the failure to take these data seriously in the past has resulted, among other things, in bibliographers neglecting even to note the occurrence of African linguistic material in early manuscript sources, and in lexicographers remaining ignorant of the origins of many African loan-words in European languages.

There is one important field of historico-linguistic research where initial efforts need to be devoted in any case to a survey of existing documentation, and this is in the comparative study of certain cultural and linguistic 'assemblages' (to use Clark's term). Two of the most important of these for the culture-history of Africa are the assemblages associated with iron and iron-working and with cattle and cattle-keeping: in both cases, any satisfactory comparative study will need to cover the whole continent (and sometimes beyond) and to embrace technological and ecological as well as linguistic, ethnographic and archaeological data. Only when an adequate survey has been made of the available documentation in all these areas will it be possible to determine how much further field research will be required, and the forms which it should take. As already mentioned, the present Seminar is now embarking on an investigation into Cattle-keeping in Africa, by means of an interdisciplinary working-group, and the first task of this group will be to initiate the necessary survey of this complex subject. Members of the Seminar have already devoted careful attention to two recent papers by

16. Cf. HAIR, p. 50 f. below; WANSBROUGH, p. 89 f. below; and HUNWICK, p. 102 f. below.

Christopher Ehret on cattle-keeping and sheep-keeping in Africa,[17] in which prehistorical conclusions have been drawn from selective linguistic data. Although the data are insufficient to substantiate Ehret's hypotheses, the endeavour has provided a useful test-case in methodology. It has confirmed not only the need for disciplined comparative techniques, but also the difficulty of evaluating isolated linguistic terms without an adequate study of their extra-linguistic environment and of the total linguistic assemblages of which they form part.

An important corpus of data for the historical study of cultural vocabulary has become available with the current publication of Malcolm Guthrie's *Comparative Bantu*,[18] and the present volume includes a sample of the results which may be anticipated from these data.[19] The philological procedures involved in establishing this corpus form a technical subject for discussion among linguists, but the historical interpretation of the data requires an interdisciplinary forum. Guthrie has been concerned with the isolation of material which is common to a relatively large part of the Bantu field, and which may best be accounted for by common origin in a postulated Proto-Bantu language. On the other hand, this material represents a comparatively small proportion of the lexicon of any individual Bantu language, as Guthrie has himself pointed out, and it is imperative that the further study of common Bantu features should proceed alongside the study of features with more limited geographical extension.[20] Some material in this direction has already been produced as a by-product of Guthrie's main comparative study,[21] and will need to be supplemented as the detailed study of each specific area of vocabulary proceeds. At this level we shall be concerned with the totality of existing vocabulary, regardless of its provenance, and shall be concerned as much with the study of loan-words, discussed in this volume by Jan Knappert,[22] as we shall with the study of commonly 'inherited' material. Each language includes a body of inherited material which has been conveyed diachronically through a long line of speakers, but the proportion which this material represents of the whole modern language is dependent on the relative time-depth against which we choose to judge it: a much higher proportion of the modern French language can be traced back to Common Romance, for example, than to Common Indo-European. One may thus visualize a 'core of direct

17. Christopher EHRET, 'Cattle-keeping and milking in eastern and southern African history: the linguistic evidence', *Journal of African History*, VIII, 1, 1967, pp. 1–17; 'Sheep and Central Sudanic peoples in Southern Africa', ibid., IX, 2, 1968, pp. 213–21.
18. Malcolm GUTHRIE, *Comparative Bantu*, Farnborough, 1967 ff. (in progress).
19. See GUTHRIE, p. 27 f. below; and MANN, p. 133 f. below.
20. Cf. HAIR, p. 59 and p. 63 (note 19) below.
21. Cf. GUTHRIE, p. 31 below (Diagram 15).
22. See KNAPPERT, p. 78 f. below.

retention' in every language, which—viewed against a relatively short time-scale—may embrace the majority of elements in that language. As one's diachronic view increases, however, this core grows inevitably narrower, accounting for an ever-decreasing proportion of the modern language as time-depths recede, and becoming increasingly difficult to trace. It will thus be seen that classifications based on cores of direct retention (even assuming these to have been accurately isolated) will become of less and less significance historically as their depth increases. If we are using linguistic evidence to trace the pre-history of a particular modern people and their culture, and of their physical ancestors and cultural donors, then we need to make an assessment of the diminishing core of direct retention and of the conversely *increasing* 'lines of accretion' in their language (involving innovation and borrowing) as we set our sights further back in time. If, on the other hand, we are using linguistic evidence to trace prehistorical developments within a particular cultural sphere, then we need to make an assessment of the whole area of vocabulary involved, in all the languages involved, in order that we may reconstruct lines of accretion passing from language to language, and cores of direct retention converging on presumed ancestral languages.

Such a programmatic statement is easier to formulate than it is to implement, and the diagrammatic analogy is in any case an over-simplified one. On the other hand, there is one linguistic approach which promises to contribute much to the comparative study of African languages, and to the historical assessment of the vocabulary in each language. This topological approach, discussed here by Michael Mann[23], involves the study of the distribution (including mapping and statistical quantification) of vocabulary or other linguistic features over a given geographical area. Guthrie has provided us with some useful examples, but his own data alone would yield hundreds of further maps of the Bantu field, quite apart from the thousands of maps which could be constructed from other available data, either for specific areas or for Africa as a whole. Clearly, there will be need for selectivity in this task, and for concentration on certain key semantic areas such as iron-working and cattle-keeping: these linguistic maps will be amenable for correlation with other cartographic data, such as archaeological and ecological maps.

This brief introduction may be concluded by reiterating that the topic 'Language and History in Africa' is not a subject for discussion by linguists and historians alone, and that its adequate study will be dependent ultimately upon collaboration among all disciplines relevant to the study of past and present societies in Africa. In the future concern of the Seminar with the historical interpretation of the contemporary language-map of Africa, our aim will be to establish

23. See MANN, p. 133 f. below.

a dialogue between comparative linguists and historians on the one hand, and social anthropologists and socio-linguists on the other. At the level of historical interpretation, comparative linguistics should be a form of diachronic socio-linguistics, in which extrapolations about the remoter past need to be based on a sound knowledge of the socio-linguistic present and recent past.

David Dalby

African Prehistory: Opportunities for Collaboration between Archaeologists, Ethnographers and Linguists

J. DESMOND CLARK

TEN years ago, while there was a general feeling among Africanists that some of their colleagues in fields other than their own might be able to help clarify problems that their own discipline could do little to solve, it is my impression, at least from the literature, that collaboration between scholars in different spheres was the exception rather than the rule. In some fields, of course (economic anthropology, nutrition and ecology, for example), the interdisciplinary approach was both obvious and productive but, in general, social scientists had little to say to natural scientists. The same was equally applicable among the different disciplines and sub-disciplines within the social sciences and there was little common meeting ground between social anthropologists and archaeologists or between archaeologists, linguists and historians. Far from collaborating, each tended and, perhaps, still tends to view the findings of the other, where they impinge on his own field, with veiled suspicion, especially where they run contrary to his own data and interpretations.

In fact, as Alexander Pope put it, ' 'tis with our judgements as our watches, none go just alike, yet each believes his own'.

There is no doubt that a very different situation exists or is emerging today, especially among those who are concerned with the peoples and cultures of Africa, present and past. This situation is due to a number of factors—overall broadening of the background training and a more general understanding of what others have to offer; a more realistic appreciation by the scholars themselves of the limitations of their own respective fields; the compilation and availability of a large corpus of taxonomic data and the present swing towards using this as a basis for the study of behaviour and change; and the development of physical, chemical and other methods of measuring change chronometrically. The realization that archaeologists, linguists and cultural anthropologists or ethnographers are faced with many of the same problems and that the best way of solving them is by interdisciplinary teamwork, is one of the most encouraging and exciting factors in African studies today.

It is of the directions in which collaboration for culture-historical studies in subsaharan Africa can advantageously develop that I would like to say something in this paper. If I do so largely from the viewpoint of the archaeologist this is because it is my own field: I wish to point to some of the ways in which the findings of the archaeologist can contribute to a closer understanding of African culture history and, also, to stress some of the shortcomings of his data and the ways in which these may be hopefully lessened, and perhaps overcome, by the evidence of the oral historian, the linguist, the agronomist and the ethnographer.

The greater part of my own research has been concerned with man's physiological and cultural development during the three million years or so that comprise the Pleistocene and the following eight thousand or so of Recent time. During this time range it is the exception to find very much more than the most imperishable evidence of human activity—stone implements and fossil bones of animals and, occasionally, of man himself. By themselves such remains can tell us little about the abilities and behaviour of the men who used and scattered the implements and the food waste. Viewed in the context of the palaeo-environment and of the associations and patterns made by these remains on the undisturbed camping places, a whole new range of possibilities for reconstruction begins to open up. Of necessity, therefore, there has developed a close relationship—which has been in existence for some while—between the prehistorian and colleagues in the natural sciences (geologists, pedologists, palaeontologists and many others). More recently, physicists have evolved methods of chronometric dating that have revolutionized knowledge of rates of biological and cultural change. Chemists and bio-chemists are now constructing a further range of highly promising analytical processes and techniques—trace element analysis, for example—that are providing a mass of new data concerning diet, settlement patterns and trade relationships. These data will enable us to determine the nature of the subsistence base and give us some idea of population density, even if, at that far distant period of time, they can do little to throw light on the social structure beyond the broad nature of the unit.

In the case of all time before about 35,000 years ago the problem is further complicated since it was only at that time that modern man—*Homo sapiens*—made his appearance. Thought processes, technical skills and behaviour generally among the earlier Hominines may have been very different from our own and probably lay somewhere between those of present-day hunter-gatherers and the African great apes. It is refreshing, therefore, to turn to later times, because the possibilities for reconstruction of past culture patterns are so much greater for the past 2,000 years in Africa, where many of the existing patterns of behaviour, language and ethnic grouping are of long standing and find direct or indirect expression in the archaeological record, when we are able to read and interpret this correctly. Subsaharan Africa provides a unique record of many different social and economic patterns in many varied habitats, but as yet much of the kind of data the archaeologist needs from these still remains to be collected, callibrated and correlated with the physio-chemical, chronological, climatic and purely archaeological evidence, in order that they may be distinguished apart in the archaeological record.

Iron Age archaeologists have the inestimable advantage of being able to start from the present and work back into the immediate past and so to the more remote time when food production and metal technology become apparent in the record at the beginning of the present era. Only comparatively recently have the importance and possibilities of the existing ethnographic data been realized, so that few attempts have so far been made to collect and use it. Pioneer studies such as those by Richard Lee on camping sites of the Central Kalahari Bushmen (Lee, 1968), by Richard Gould on the Bindibu of western Australia (Gould, 1968), or by Peter White on groups in the New Guinea highlands (White, 1968), are concerned with stone using hunters and collectors. The time is now ripe to make similar studies for food producing communities in Africa—the return, since the culture is both richer and more complex, will be so much the more rewarding. Ethnography with an archaeological slant can greatly increase the possibilities of the interpretation of the remains that survive in archaeological context since we may infer that human reactions within similar cultural and ecological parameters are likely to have been the same or very similar in the past as in the present, in particular as regards the present era.

'The elements of scarcity and choice are the outstanding factors in human experience', to quote Mel Herskovits (1952, p. 1), and the ways in which these are dealt with are determined by environment and tradition. If, therefore, we know the needs and the technological level of a present day population and the carrying capacity of its habitat, we have a means of comparison and a basis for determining those of a prehistoric population in the same locale.

Moreover, by working from the ethnographic present back into the past, the existing material culture (especially the less perishable elements such as pottery, metal or bone objects, for example), the nature of dwelling and settlement patterns and technology generally can, through seriation and other studies, show to what extent the prehistoric aggregates and patterns represent continuity or change. By this means more substance will be given to archaeological interpretation of the communities and settlements of the remoter past.

Much valuable data already exist in historical records or in the writings of anthropologists, but they need to be extracted and correlated. George Kay's study of the economic life of an Ushi village (Kay, 1964) or Audrey Richards' account of subsistence in a Bemba village (Richards, 1939) provide an invaluable source of data on diet, nutrition and land use and many more such studies are available. A wide variety of data is involved: air-surveys of changing settlement patterns, surveyed village plans showing structures, activity areas, waste disposal areas, relationship of settlements to field systems, water resources, hunting and wild relish areas, work apportionment and time spent on these various activities, length of occupation of a settlement site under different environmental conditions, seasonal activities and camps, decay rates of materials on abandoned village sites, survival rates (what stays and what disappears), and records remaining in the soil that can be detected by various chemical tests (for instance, calcium and phosphate analysis, determination of pollen and, perhaps, protein types, etc.). These last have long survival rates and the potential thus exists for being able to reconstruct diet. Some sources of these types of data are already available in the literature; much is not and to obtain it calls for a new approach by the enthnographer or the archaeologist, preferably by both.

Knowledge of material culture is surprisingly deficient for subsaharan Africa and this is especially the case where it comes to one of the archaeologist's main tools—pottery. There are very few good studies of modern pottery. Moreover, the emphasis has tended to be on the artifacts themselves and not on the artifacts in their functional context in relation to the culture of the community as a whole. Thus, when we find relish bowls, or arrowheads, iron gongs or gold or glass beads, we need to know to what extent, on the basis of the numbers in which they occur, they can be taken as representative of certain activities and relationships.

Single artifacts are rarely indicators of culture levels or associations as those people soon found out who tried to link Zimbabwe with the Phoenicians, Sabaeans and other classical peoples on the basis of the inferred similarities of isolated traits. Only where we are dealing with an assemblage of traits are we on sure ground. But considerably more can be learned from an archaeological assemblage if we have the precise record of an ethnographic assemblage for comparison. For example, we need to know the range of materials, artifacts, waste products and structures associated with various activities, such as iron working, fishing, hunting or warfare.

Much of this type of information already exists, especially in regard to social relationships, but much still remains unrecorded and a whole range of activities needs to be sampled and their relationship determined to various structures about the village—for instance to dwelling-huts or stock-pens, paths, storage structures, etc. At the same time the environment should be studied by an ecologist. The importance of this needs no further stressing. Also, where we are concerned with the change from the collection to the production of food, an agronomist and plant ecologist would have a natural interest and the productivity values for different soil and vegetation types would need to be known. We need more of such classic studies as those of Trapnell and Clothier (Trapnell and Clothier, 1953; Trapnell, 1957) and of William Allan (Allan, 1965) in Zambia. These and similar lines of approach, relating environment, the needs of the community and the artifacts it uses to satisfy these, can be expected to provide much additional data for interpretation of economic patterns and, to a lesser degree also, of social structure and ethics in the past.

Such an ethnographic interpretation of the archaeological aggregate in primary context can be made more precise and meaningful if it is combined with the evidence from oral history and tied into a chronology based on radiocarbon or other dating methods. Not only does this provide, on the one hand, the time-depth necessary to interpret oral tradition and the events it records but it forms an invaluable check upon the subject matter where this speaks of changes—either by diffusion, population movement, or economic or political necessity.

One of the best examples known to me of the use of archaeology for substantiating oral tradition is that of Bweyorere, one of the former capital sites of the kings of Ankole (Posnansky, 1962). The location was found from tradition by Professor Roland Oliver and, after it had been excavated by Merrick Posnansky, it completely substantiated the tradition that spoke of two occupation periods at the site. In other instances the archaeological record can help interpret puzzling parts of the traditional history, as, for example, in the case of the individual who established chieftainship among the Inamwanga of northeastern Zambia some two to three hundred years ago and who is said to have introduced iron smelting. We know that this is not so because we have evidence of much older dated early Iron Age sites in the district. It is likely, therefore, that it was not the basic technique but improved methods of working iron that were introduced at this time (Wilson, 1958, p. 21).

The shortcomings of the archaeological evidence are, of course, many and some of these I will mention briefly here. To begin with there are few parts of the continent where coverage is sufficiently complete for geographical distribution patterns to be very meaningful (but for Stone Age cultural distributions related to ecological data, see the series of overlays and base maps in Clark, 1967(*a*)). Secondly, there have been very few, if any, investigations in depth that give anything like a clear picture of subsistence patterns, technology and social structure. A few elephant bones and fragments of tusk are hardly sufficient basis on which to postulate the existence of a regular trade in ivory, and one could quote a number of other examples where, although suppositions are being made, the data to substantiate them still remain to be collected.

Apart from the work on the Rhodesian stone ruins, practically nothing has been done to recover settlement patterns and to study the archaeological component in relation to natural resources and land use. Mostly our work has been confined to small scale test excavations to recover sequences of pottery wares which can be classified in relation to other pottery traditions and not infrequently dated by the radiocarbon method. Even here considerable caution is necessary in assessing the significance of these results and far too great an emphasis has been placed on isolated radiocarbon dates. Runs of such dates are the only reliable indication of time relationships. Recovery of settlement plans by magnetometer or resistivity methods are not yet used—with one exception, at Tarruga in Nigeria (Fagg, 1965).

Again, little attempt has been made by seriation to show relationships between pottery wares or to relate them, using quantitative methods, to the appearance or disappearance of other technological traits as expressed by the surviving material culture. While we may claim to have established the basis for a classification of pottery for some areas—for example, in Rhodesia (Summers, 1966), Zambia (Phillipson, 1968), Uganda (Posnansky, 1967) or Rwanda (Hiernaux, 1960)—we cannot even do that for most other regions. If the more than one hundred graves in the Lake Kisale area in Katanga (Nenquin, 1963) have produced a magnificent record of pottery and metal wares, we have not the least idea of what the settlements were like or of the subsistence pattern, though fishing was of obvious importance. No dwellings or activity patterns are known, neither is the time relationship of the three wares found in the graves. All in all, however, we are better off here than in many other areas and I would like to stress that a tremendous amount of *new* archaeology needs to be done that will provide just this kind of economic and demographic data. This must then be subjected to critical analysis using the new ethnographic evidence that should be forthcoming. With this as the basis for reconstruction, interpretations can then be more precise and more meaningful.

Clearly, for any systematic study of the culture history of a region or people, it is now essential that the oral history be collected at the same time as or prior to any archaeological work and that this be carefully analysed to determine the important localities which should then be pin-pointed on the ground as was done by Roland Oliver in Ankole and by Jan Vansina in the Lower Congo (Vansina, 1966, pp. 35, 103). In Rhodesia the work of Robinson (Robinson, 1966), Summers (Summers, 1967) and Abraham (Abraham, 1961) in linking oral tradition with archaeological sites has gone a long way to providing a better understanding of the events, political and social structure and the economy of the Monomatapa period and Zimbabwe Industrial Complex (Summers, *et al.*, 1961). The same is true for the tradition that links the origins of the Luba empire with the region of Lake Kisale where archaeology has proved the existence of a large population and a rich culture that—one can hypothecate, though not, as yet, prove—was built up on a fishing and trading economy in the eighth to ninth centuries (Vansina, op. cit. p. 11). When archaeological work is initiated in the Barotse valley in Zambia it may be expected that the traditional capital sites, which are readily identifiable, will provide some of the best evidence for interpretation and reconstruction of Lozi culture history and, as in all joint studies of this kind, will provide some varying degree of control over bias in the traditional oral record.

It might be considered that studies of skeletal remains by physical anthropologists would be definitive in deciding the ethnic composition of the prehistoric populations of a locality or region and in showing when these change. If there had been no genetic grading—hybridization, as it is often called—between populations, then clear-cut classifications in the old manner would have some meaning. Today, however, physical anthropologists are less and less prepared to commit themselves on bones alone and, while it is still possible to separate out those at one end of the spectrum, as it were, from those at the other, this is not the case for the greater part of the material which falls in the intermediate ranges. Few would doubt, however, that there have been changes in the genetic pattern of the human populations of south-central and south-eastern Africa since the initiation of food production and a metal technology, though these changes may not have been of the sudden and rather dramatic kind that is usually believed. Although, at this time, the economy and culture underwent considerable changes, the physical changes in the population were, it would seem, not so much the result of replacement as of modification, through the introduction of negroid genes by migrants who initially were comparatively few in number but who multiplied rapidly, and through later selection for these desirable genes by the autochthonous stock. Such a pattern of ethnic and culture change is clearly apparent in later Iron Age times from tradition and archaeology and can be postulated for the earlier period also.

Linguistic data are also providing a record of ethnic movements in prehistoric times as well as demonstrating the antiquity of the languages of Africa. These data are not only extremely precise but, when they are correlated with the archaeological evidence and oral history, should be able to provide ethnic and cultural affiliation for languages far back into the past, of a kind that can never be obtained from archaeology alone.

Of special interest to those of us working in subsaharan Africa are the reconstructions of the prehistory of the Bantu language family made by Greenberg (Greenberg, 1963, pp. 6–38) and Guthrie (Guthrie, 1962; 1967 ff.; and this volume, p. 20 ff. below). Both stress the relationship between Bantu and the Negro languages of West Africa and the magnitude of the time-depth since their separation. For both, the homeland of the Pre-Bantu speakers was probably in the region of the Benue/Chad. Based upon a comparative study of over three hundred Bantu languages, including twenty-eight 'test languages' studied in considerable depth, Professor Guthrie's evidence suggests that a nuclear centre of 'Proto-Bantu' speakers existed in the southern part of the Congo basin, from where the language and culture spread in most directions at different times. The evidence also indicates the existence of two main sub-divisions of these languages—reflecting western and eastern proto-dialects—separated approximately by the line of the western Rift. These are well attested facts and it is, therefore, not the facts themselves but their meaning in terms of culture history and time that needs clarification. For example, to explain the findings it is necessary to suppose a movement of Pre-Bantu speakers either through the Congo forest from the Cameroons and Central African Republic to the Katanga or else round the forest to the east (or west) to the new homeland in the south. Which is correct? This is one instance where archaeologists and linguists can profitably work closely together to solve a prehistorical problem, and it might be of interest to digress here to speak of the archaeological evidence (or lack of it) for a possible migration into and movements within the basin of the Congo.

The proto-historic archaeology of the Congo basin is almost unknown with two or three spectacular exceptions. For the areas in question in the north and west we have only a few scattered surface indications. One essential, therefore, is some systematic team survey of key areas in the Cameroons, Central African Republic, Gabon and the Congo Republic. In the first three of these countries work is possible now and is already under way in the Cameroons (David, in press) and Gabon (Blankoff, 1965); but, except in the Lower Congo, such a survey is not practicable at present in the Congo Republic and knowledge rests on the pioneer work of van Moorsel (van Moorsel, 1968) and earlier investigators. I would stress that such surveys need to be of carefully selected areas and should be in some depth and detail so that the results can be quantified and checked for significance.

Recovery of settlement patterns and artifact assemblages will provide the archaeologist with data on activities, technology, economic level, food supplies and social groupings and can be tied into the ethnographic present by such methods as I have already outlined. In this way one may expect to cover perhaps the greater part of the second millennium A.D. Earlier than that the linguistic evidence becomes even more important. Here it seems to me that this linguistic evidence would acquire even greater significance if groups of words or roots related to some specific trait or complex were studied and compared in the same way, since it is the associations of artifacts rather than individual tools that are the significant factors in an archaeological context. In the same way that linked traits are a much better indicator of diffusion than are individual traits, so greater significance would, I feel, attach to the presence of such linked words or roots. Where an assemblage of cognate words or roots covering, for example, smithing or iron smelting equipment and techniques, is present in two related languages, this would constitute sound evidence for these activities' having been practised at the time the languages separated.

If, as Guthrie has postulated (Guthrie, 1962, p. 280; cf. also Guthrie, p. 29 below), the Proto-Bantu people were culturally advanced and later possessed a knowledge of iron working, then iron should be present in the archaeological record coincident with a time at which we would be justified in believing that Proto-Bantu was being spoken in the nuclear area to the south of the forest. It is certainly present in the eighth century 'statelets' on the Lualaba, but how much earlier can it be taken back? This we have at present no means of knowing so far as the Bantu 'nuclear area' is concerned. Iron appears, however, to have been present in Rhodesia, Zambia and East Africa by the second and third centuries A.D. (Struiver and van der Merwe, 1968) and in Nigeria between the Niger and Benue by the fourth century B.C. (Shaw, 1968; Fagg, op. cit.). Radiocarbon dates in the first half of the first millennium B.C. from the Congo Basin show that, until at least that time, stone continued as the most important raw material for tools (Clark, 1968). It would, therefore, seem that the introduction of metallurgy must have taken place sometime between 500 B.C. and 500 A.D. in the Congo Basin. Other evidence (Clark, op. cit. pp. 142–8) suggests that it was about 0 A.D. that this event occurred. If the Proto-Bantu had a knowledge of iron-working when they migrated, then this would date the migration. If they did *not* possess this knowledge, the movement to the Katanga could have been earlier, though still, presumably, by a people with knowledge of cultivation and water transport. Linked words concerned with the cultivation of domestic plants might throw light also on the spread of cultivation methods and of certain food plants for these times.

The archaeological evidence, slight as it is, lends some support to the belief that iron-working may have been diffused to an already sedentary and cultivating Proto-Bantu in a somewhat more extended region than Professor Guthrie's 'nuclear area'. Village sites in the south of the Lake Chad basin indicate a long period of uninterrupted

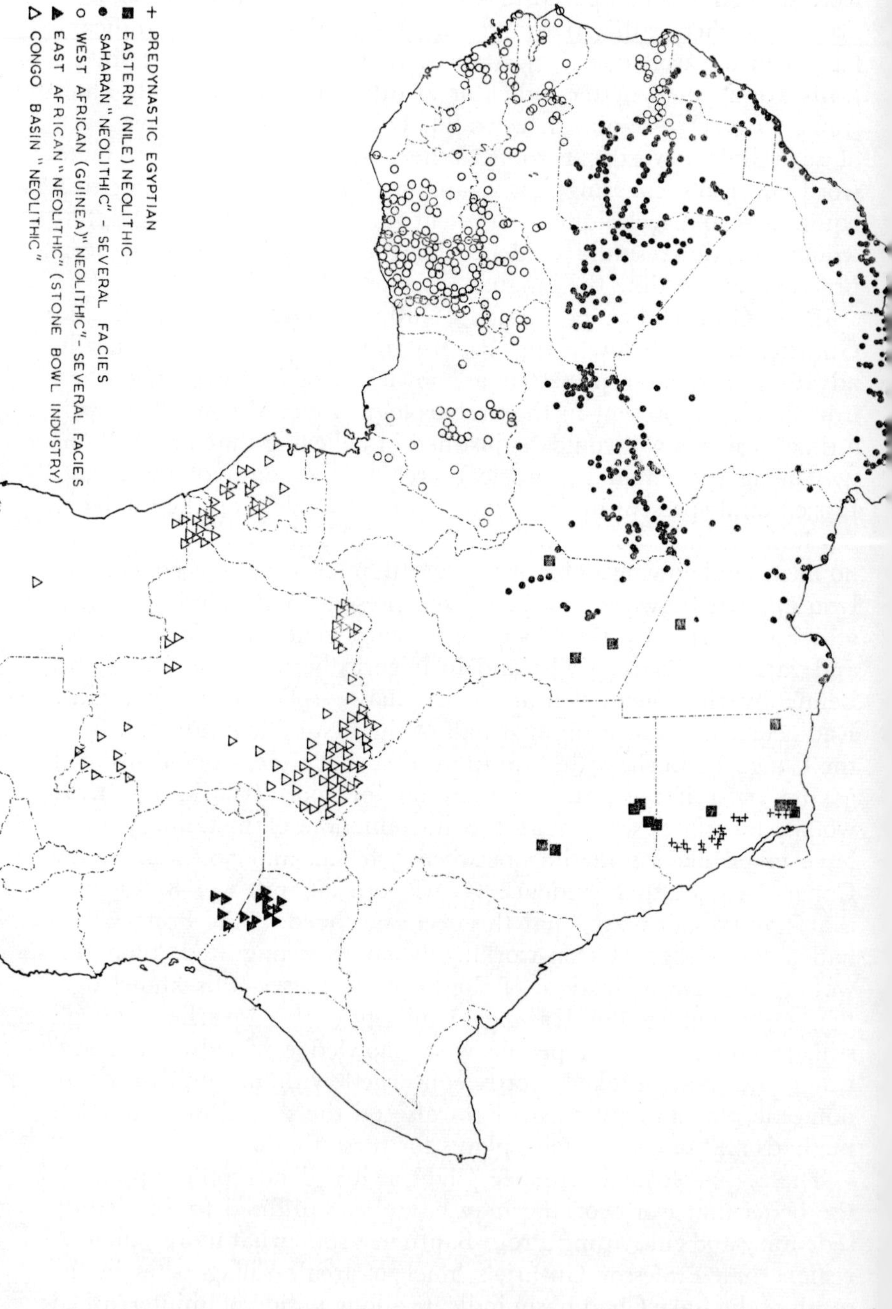

Fig. 1. Distribution of 'Neolithic' occurrences. (After Clark, 1967(*a*), Overlays 23 and 24.)

occupation. Of great significance in this connection is the excavation by Graham Connah of the Daima mound in Bornu (Connah, 1967). This has yielded a record of a cultivating and stock-raising tradition, initially Neolithic with bone and stone artifacts and pottery, dating to more than 500 B.C. at the beginning but grading into a full Iron Age which began about 400 A.D. To the north in Chad and to the west in Ghana there is evidence of Neolithic stock-raisers in the third millennium B.C. (Clark, 1967(*b*)) and the same is the case also in the forest zone of West Africa (Davies, 1966). If the artifacts are valid indicators, there developed two very distinct traditions in West Africa and it is most probable, though we do not as yet have the evidence to prove it, that the northern one was confined to the steppe and savannah and was based upon cereal crops—sorghums, millets, fonio, etc.—and animal husbandry, while the southern one in the forests was based on plant cultivation, perhaps yams, dry rice and the oil palm. The latter made its appearance in southern Nigeria sometime after 3000 B.C. and it would be of interest to know if it also extended south into the Congo Basin.

I have always considered that it did not and that the examples of polished and ground stone axes and pottery that are found in the Lower Congo (van Moorsel, op. cit.), Gabon (Blankoff, op. cit. pp. 196–7) and Oriental Province of the Congo Republic (van Noten, 1963) were elements of an early Iron Age component. Most of this material comes from surface sites and no stratified or excavated Neolithic assemblage exists from anywhere south of Nigeria, except from Fernando Po (Martin del Molino, 1965) where an early stage has been carbon dated to 680 A.D. and a later stage to the early fourteenth century A.D. (1320). However, if we look at the distribution map of these 'Neolithic' elements in the Congo (Fig. 1) we can see concentrations in two main areas—in the Lower Congo and Gabon and in the Ubangi/Uele basins in the northeast (Clark, 1967(*a*), Overlay 23). That the fine haematite axes from the latter region were still being made until fairly recent times is shown by the evidence of Calonne-Beaufait (Calonne-Beaufait, 1921, p. 145), but this does not invalidate the possibility that an earlier, pre-iron, and stone-using tradition was already present in both these regions before iron-working was initiated in the early centuries A.D. The Gabon is certainly not today the impenetrable forest one was always led to suppose and, though the attenuated forest distribution of the present day is, no doubt, due to a long period of cutting and burning for cultivation, the main access routes into the basin of the Congo proper in the west must always have been along the savannah of the tributaries and the major valley of the Ogooue, perhaps between 2500 and 500 B.C. when there is evidence for an arid climate in the Sahara and Chad (Butzer, 1967). If this is later substantiated by stratified evidence, it shows two routes of penetration of the Congo

Basin—in the north or northeast from the Central African Republic and in the northwest from the Niger/Benue via the Cameroons.

Ground stone axes are absent from the Kasai as they are from Lunda, but this could be explained by reason of most of its solid geology's having been covered by the Kalahari Sands so that a digging stick would be all that was necessary in the light, sandy soils of the savannah of the interfluves. The axes/adzes in the Katanga are surface finds but are similar to others dated with the Later Stone Age industries of Zambia to several millennia B.C. (Miller, in press). Perhaps this absence of neolithic elements in the 'nuclear area' of Bantu may be explained by the obvious pre-occupation with fishing and hunting in these regions. Consideration should, however, be given to the validity of the supposition made from the linguistic data that, because the greatest number of common elements is found in a particular region this is likely to be the centre of origin and dispersal. Areas of chromosome complexity in domesticated plants have been shown to have nothing necessarily to do with the areas of original domestication. Might the same not also be the case with the linguistic data? Clearly, to elucidate the matter further, archaeologist and linguist will need to work together closely.

The linguistic evidence suggests also that the western and eastern dialects of Bantu developed within Proto-Bantu and that the western separated from the parent stock appreciably before the appearance of the eastern dialect (Guthrie, op. cit. p. 280). This implies a first stage of expansion within the Congo Basin itself from a savannah or savannah forest mozaic environment, penetrating the primary forest. The efficacy of stone equipment for subsistence agriculture in hardwood, tropical forest is really unknown but, although some experiment is needed here, stone used in conjunction with fire is probably more efficient than is usually thought. The important factor here is that the population density for the achievement of regular and effective cutting and burning and cultivation of mound gardens in forest must be sufficiently great. There is still little doubt that iron axes and machetes would have been considerably more efficient, however, and, as Christopher Wrigley (Wrigley, 1960, p. 203) has stressed, the iron spear and arrow point would have significantly increased the hunting potential. It still needs to be shown that sorghum and millet were able to grow in the Lower Congo (for example, at the time the Portuguese entered) and that these were old staples there and in the basin generally. The environment today does not favour the cereals and the only areas where these crops are grown are in the northeast and southeast where they are minor crops. Whether or not they were at one time more extensively grown still remains to be proved, as also does the identity of the root crop (or crops) that was replaced by cassava;

this may have been an indigenous yam and/or the Livingstone potato. Again, taro (or cocoyam) (*Colocasia antiquum*, one of the Asian food plants) is still grown in isolated patches in the forest in Kuba country (Vansina, op. cit. p. 21). Another such area where taro is grown is in the east among the Nyakyusa at the north end of Lake Malawi, and a wild relict occurs at the bottom of the Kalambo Falls on the Zambia/Tanzania border. The plant occurs wild also along the stream courses in the Shire Highlands in Malawi where it is sometimes dug up and replanted close to the villages (personal observation). Is it possible that, as with yams, there may have been an indigenous African plant belonging to this genus that was equally amenable to domestication? In this connection it is of interest that Allan considers the old cocoyam *Colocasia esculentum* in Ghana to be also a probable indigenous cultigen (Allan, 1964, p. 226). There is a need for research to determine the precise nature of the subsistence crops in the higher rainfall areas of the Congo Basin prior to the introduction of the Asian and American crops which form the staples there today.

If it should be shown that cultivation of the sorghums and millets was and is, as generally believed, confined to the drier and more rapidly drained areas on the periphery of the basin, then it is unlikely that these plants were carried from the north across the basin by the ancestors of the Proto-Bantu. It seems more probable that these cereals, together with iron, reached the Proto-Bantu at a later date than the initial migration, by way of the northwestern route, on the one hand, and down the high country east of the forest, on the other. This latter route was country which, at the same time, would probably have been free of tsetse (Fig. 2) and so would have favoured stock-raising (Clark, 1967(*a*), Overlay 4). Pastoral stone-using peoples were occupying the high grasslands of the eastern Rift and the Victoria Basin by the first millennium B.C. and continuing into at least the first few centuries A.D., and it would seem that iron did not reach here until the sixteenth century A.D. (Sutton, 1966, p. 43).

Outside West Africa, the earliest iron working communities of which we have record are present in Guthrie's eastern Bantu region on both sides of the western Rift in Uganda, Rwanda, Burundi, Kenya and northern Tanzania and even in northern Zambia, with one isolated occurrence in the southern Kasai. This is the Dimple Based pottery tradition and the related Channel Decorated tradition from the Kalambo Falls. It is associated with a fully developed iron technology without the slightest sign of any ground stone equipment's having been associated. The only settlement site of this time (3–400 A.D.) to have been even partially excavated is at Kalambo Falls, but here, although there are what appear to be grave shafts and grave goods, there are no bodies, so

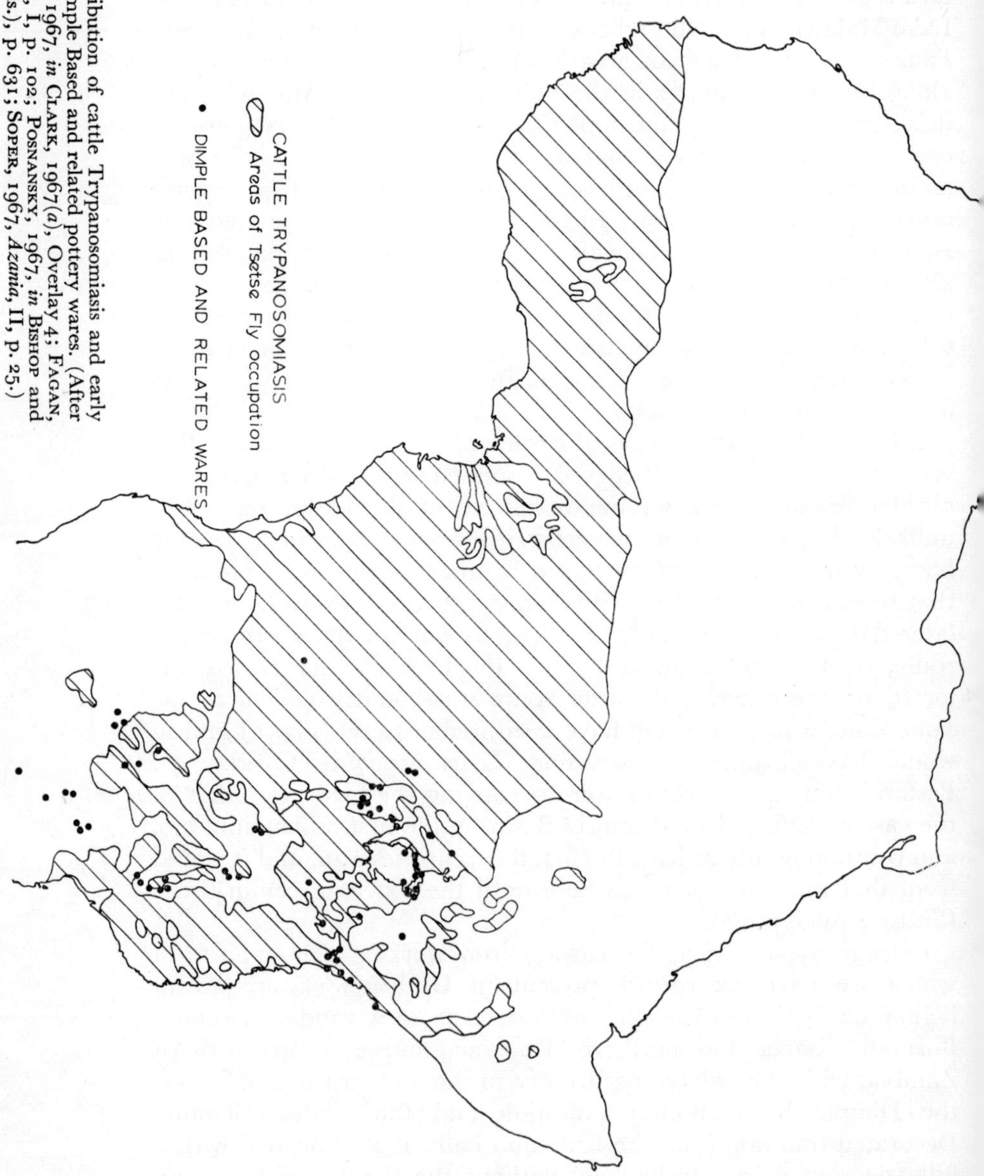

FIG. 2. Distribution of cattle Trypanosomiasis and early Iron Age Dimple Based and related pottery wares. (After LAMBRECHT, 1967, *in* CLARK, 1967(*a*), Overlay 4; FAGAN, 1966, *Azania*, I, p. 102; POSNANSKY, 1967, *in* BISHOP and CLARK (eds.), p. 631; SOPER, 1967, *Azania*, II, p. 25.)

that we have no information on the physical appearance of the population. Also, no skeletal remains are as yet known from a Dimple Based Ware context so that we do not know whether, for example, the people were Nilotes or Negroes. As known at present, the distribution of sites (Fig. 2) is suggestive of a migration of population, not necessarily in large numbers, southwards down the high country on either side of the Rift from the Central African Republic and the southern Sudan as well as eastwards through Kenya to the coast at the same time (Soper, 1967). If, as seems more probable, this latter movement is related to the spread of Bantu-speaking peoples, then we would expect to find the Dimple Based pottery in the Bantu 'nuclear area'. There is, indeed, one such site at Lupemba, near Tshikapa in the southern Kasai, but it is inadequately known (Nenquin, 1959). Although one swallow does not make a summer, it definitely makes us sit up and take note that one of the most pressing archaeological needs is a systematic survey of the 'nuclear area' in the southern Congo tributaries, as well as a survey of the Lower Congo round Stanley-Pool. However, if this spread is connected with Bantu, it is coming from the wrong direction.

It is important to know the significance and antiquity of traits concerned with the cattle complex and sheep/goat herding, cereal crops and iron working in Guthrie's eastern region, since, if I am not mistaken, it is in this region that most of the Dimple Based and Channel Ware sites occur. If this tradition is associated with the Bantu, and dates, as from the archaeological record it appears to do, from between 200 and 800 A.D., then the dialect of the western region separated from Proto-Bantu before about 200 A.D. and the ancestors of the Proto-Bantu settled in the Katanga even earlier still. It is likely that they were cultivators of root crops and possessors of what is generally conceived of as a neolithic technology which may have been present in the Congo in the first millennium B.C. On the other hand, we have now also to consider the possibility that Proto-Bantu may have been spoken by the 'Later Stone Age' hunting and collecting peoples of the region. If this were the case then the movement from the Pre-Bantu area may have taken place several millennia B.C. This gives new significance to the various phases of the 'Later Stone Age' Tshitolian industry (Fig. 3) with its many bifacial points and tranchets and the meaning of the large concentrations of lithic elements on sites in the Congo Basin that overlook the stream courses from the closing stages of the Pleistocene (Bequaert and Mortelmans, 1955; Clark, 1963, p. 152). It also shows the absurdity of thinking that what have come to be considered as 'Stone Age archaeology' and 'Iron Age archaeology' can be studied separately. Culture and population in subsaharan Africa form a continuum to which new elements have from time to time been added while old ones have been superseded.

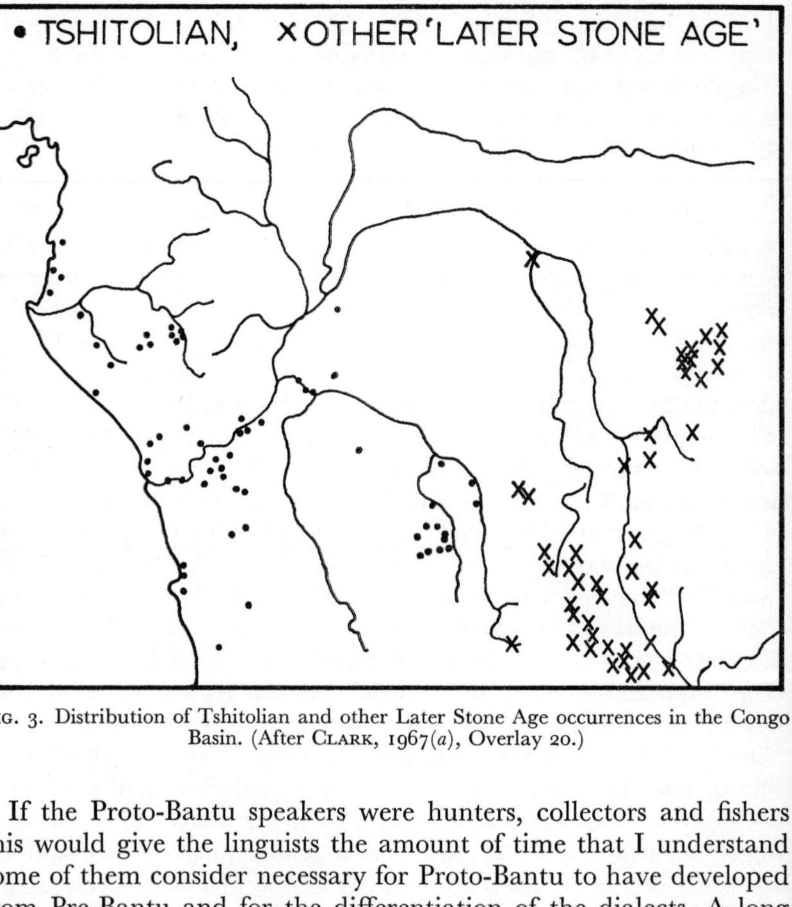

FIG. 3. Distribution of Tshitolian and other Later Stone Age occurrences in the Congo Basin. (After CLARK, 1967(*a*), Overlay 20.)

If the Proto-Bantu speakers were hunters, collectors and fishers this would give the linguists the amount of time that I understand some of them consider necessary for Proto-Bantu to have developed from Pre-Bantu and for the differentiation of the dialects. A long chronology would also probably be more favourable for the appearance of the sickling mutation. This would, perhaps, not be so acceptable to the archaeologists, however, since it would then be necessary to find some explanation for a sustained movement over such a long distance—unless the group was the possessor of more efficient and desirable cultural traits than are usually associated with a hunting and gathering economy, or unless Pre-Bantu was a very widely spoken language.

All this is, of course, mostly speculation at present, using the very incomplete evidence at our disposal, and I have discussed it simply as an example of where collaboration between linguists and archaeologists could have most promising possibilities. By a systematic, interdisciplinary survey and excavation programme in the two key areas—to the north of the forest in the Central African Republic and south of it in Katanga and the Kasai—it should be perfectly possible to select the right answer from several alternatives. The same is true for most other regions of tropical Africa and time levels back over the past 2000 years. There is now a sufficient common interest among scholars in research into the history of the indigenous African peoples that the time has come for joint action—not simply an interdisciplinary study in name only in which several colleagues may contribute to write a book following from their own independent investigations, but a closely co-ordinated programme of collaboration in the field with consultation at all stages along the line from the initial surveys through to the analysis and interpretation of the evidence each of the different disciplines and sub-disciplines has been able to contribute. It will not be easy to interpret with well documented authority the surviving incomplete archaeological evidence. Methods and techniques will have to be developed as a result of new ethnographic studies, archaeologically orientated, together with close attention to oral traditions and to comparative language studies. In this way the relative importance for any one region of agriculture and domestic plants, hunting and fishing, metallurgy and livestock raising will become apparent, as also will the *time* at which each of these traits became important. Working from the present back into the past is, after all, what our colleagues in the earth sciences have been doing for many years, since the days of Sir Charles Lyell. It behoves us now, certainly those of us who are archaeologists, to take a leaf out of the geologists' book and to apply to archaeology some of the precise and quantitative methods which they use, and which can form the only firm basis for the study of prehistoric times.

BIBLIOGRAPHY

D. P. ABRAHAM, 'Maramuca: An exercise in the combined use of Portuguese records and oral tradition', *Journal of African History*, II, 2, 1961, 211–25.

W. ALLAN, *The African Husbandman*, Edinburgh, 1965.

M. BEQUAERT and G. MORTELMANS, 'Le Tshitolien dans le bassin du Congo', *Acad. roy. des sciences coloniales*, Mem. in-8°., New Series, II, 5, 1955, 39 ff.

B. BLANKOFF, 'Quelques découvertes préhistoriques récentes au Gabon', *in* L. D. CUSCOY (ed.), *Actas del V. Congreso Panafricano de Prehistoria y de Estudio del Cuaternario*, Museo Arqueologico, Santa Cruz de Tenerife, I, 1965, 191–206.

K. W. BUTZER, 'Climatic changes in the arid zones of Africa during early to mid-Holocene times', *in* J. S. SAWYER (ed.), *World Climate from 8000–0 B.C.*, Royal Meteorological Society, London, 1967, 72–83.

A. DE CALONNE-BEAUFAIT, *Azande. Introduction à une ethnographie générale des bassins de l'Ubangi-Uele et de l'Aruwini*, Brussels, 1921; xxxi, 276 pp.

J. D. CLARK, *Prehistoric cultures of north-east Angola and their significance in tropical Africa*, Museu do Dundo, Publicações culturais no. 62, Lisbon, 1963.

—— (ed.), *Atlas of African Prehistory*, University of Chicago Press, Chicago, 1967(*a*).

——, 'The problem of neolithic culture in subsaharan Africa', *in* W. W. BISHOP and J. D. CLARK (eds.), *Background to Evolution in Africa*, University of Chicago Press, Chicago, 1967(*b*), 601–27.

——, 'Observations on forest destruction in the Congo Basin in prehistoric times with special reference to northeast Angola', *in* J. D. CLARK, *Further Palaeo-Anthropological Studies in Northern Lunda*, Museu do Dundo, Publicações culturais no. 78, Lisbon, 1968, 125–66.

G. CONNAH, 'Radiocarbon dates for Daima, northeastern Nigeria', *Journal of Historical Society of Nigeria*, III, 4, 1967, 741–2.

N. C. David, 'An archaeological reconnaissance in Cameroon and the Iron Age site of Nassarao I, near Garoua', *C.R. VIe Congrès pan-africain de Préhistoire et de l'Etude du Quaternaire, Dakar, 1967*, Dakar (in press).

O. Davies, Comment on 'The Iron Age in subsaharan Africa', *Current Anthropology*, 7, 4, 1966, 470–1.

B. E. B. Fagg, 'Carbon dates from Nigeria', *Man*, 65 (8), 1965, 22–3.

R. Gould, 'Living archaeology: The Ngatatjara of western Australia', *Southwestern Journal of Anthropology*, University of New Mexico, Albuquerque, 24, 2, 1968, 101–22.

J. H. Greenberg, *Languages of Africa*, The Hague, 1963.

M. Guthrie, 'Some developments in the prehistory of the Bantu languages', *Journal of African History*, III, 2, 1962, 273–82.

——, *Comparative Bantu*, Farnborough, 1967 ff. (in progress).

——, 'Contributions from comparative Bantu studies to the prehistory of Africa', pp. 20–49 below.

M. J. Herskovits, *Economic Anthropology*, New York, 1952.

J. Hiernaux and E. Maquet, *1960, Cultures préhistoriques de l'âge des métaux au Ruanda-Urundi et au Kivu (Congo belge)*, Acad. roy. des sciences d'Outre-Mer., Mem. en-8°., New Series, X, 2, 1960, 6–102.

G. Kay, 'Chief Kalaba's village: A preliminary survey of economic life in an Ushi village, Northern Rhodesia', *Rhodes–Livingstone Papers*, 35, Manchester University Press, 1964.

R. Lee, 'What "hunters" do for a living or, how to make out on scarce resources', *in* R. B. Lee and I. De Vore (eds.), *Man the Hunter*, Chicago, 1968.

A. Martin del Molino, *Secuencia cultural en el Neolitico de Fernando Poo*, Trabajos de Prehistoria, Instituto Español de Prehistoria del Consejo Superior de investigaciones cientificas, XVII, 1963, 53 pp.

S. F. Miller, 'Archaeological sequence of the Zambian Later Stone Age', *C. R. du VIe Congrès pan-africain de Préhistoire et de l'Etude du Quaternaire, Dakar, 1967*, Dakar (in press).

J. Nenquin, 'Dimple Based Pots from Kasai, Belgian Congo', *Man*, 59, 1959, 242.

——, *Excavation at Sanga, 1957. The proto-historic necropolis*, Musée roy. de l'Afrique centrale, Tervuren, Ann. Series in-8°, sciences humaines, no. 45, 1963.

D. W. Phillipson, 'The early Iron Age in Zambia—regional variants and some tentative conclusions', *Journal of African History*, IX, 2, 1968, 191–211.

M. Posnansky, 'Some archaeological aspects of ethnohistory in Uganda', *in* G. Mortelmans and J. Nenquin (eds.), *Actes du IVe Congrès panafricain de Préhistoire et de l'Etude du Quaternaire*, Musée royal de l'Afrique centrale, Tervuren, Ann. Series in-8°, Sciences humaines, No. 40, 2, 1962, 375–9.

——, 'The Iron Age in East Africa', *in* W. W. Bishop and J. D. Clark (eds.), *Background to Evolution in Africa*, University of Chicago Press, 1967, 629–49.

A. I. Richards, *Land, Labour and Diet in Northern Rhodesia*, O.U.P., 1939.

K. R. Robinson, 'The archaeology of the Roswi', *in* E. Stokes and R. Brown (eds.), *The Zambesian Past: Studies in Central African History*, Manchester University Press, 1966, 3–27.

T. Shaw, 'Radiocarbon dates in Nigeria', *Journal of the Historical Society of Nigeria*, 4, 1968.

R. Soper, 'Kwale: An early Iron Age site in southeastern Kenya', *Azania*, II, 1967, 19–36.

M. Struiver and N. van der Merwe, 'Radio carbon chronology of the Iron Age in sub-Saharan Africa', *Current Anthropology*, 9, 1, 1968, 54–8.

R. F. H. Summers, 'Rhodesian prehistory re-examined: Part II, the Iron Age', *Arnoldia (Rhodesia)*, 2, 17, National Museums of Southern Rhodesia, 1966, 1–11.

——, 'Iron Age industries of southern Africa with notes on their chronology, terminology and economic status', *in* W. W. Bishop and J. D. Clark (eds.), *Background to Evolution in Africa*, Chicago University Press, 1967, 687–700.

R. F. H. Summers, K. R. Robinson and A. Whitty, 'Zimbabwe excavations, 1958', *Occasional Papers of the National Museums of Southern Rhodesia*, 3, no. 23A, 1961, 1–332.

J. E. G. Sutton, 'The archaeology and early peoples of the highlands of Kenya and northern Tanzania', *Azania*, I, 1966, 37–57.

C. G. Trapnell, *The Soils, Vegetation and Agricultural Systems of North-Western Rhodesia*, Government Printer, Lusaka, (2nd ed.) 1957.

C. G. Trapnell and N. Clothier, *The Soils, Vegetation and Agriculture of North-Eastern Rhodesia*, Government Printer, Lusaka, 1953.

H. van Moorsel, *Atlas de Préhistoire de la Plaine de Kinshasa*, Université Lovanium, Kinshasa, 1968.

F. L. van Noten, 'Une typologie des outils polis appartenant à l'Uelien', *Bull. Soc. belge Anthrop. et Prehist.*, 73, 1963, 155–95.

J. M. Vansina, *Kingdoms of the Savanna*, University of Wisconsin Press, 1966.

J. P. White, 'Ethno-archaeology in New Guinea: two examples', *Mankind*, official Journal of Anthrop. Societies of Australia, 6, 9, 1968, 409–14.

M. Wilson, *The Peoples of the Nyasa–Tanganyika Corridor*, Communications, School of African Studies, University of Cape Town, New Series, no. 29, 1958.

C. Wrigley, 'Speculations on the economic prehistory of Africa', *Journal of African History*, I, 2, 1960, 189–203.

Contributions from Comparative Bantu Studies to the Prehistory of Africa

MALCOLM GUTHRIE

THE study of the prehistory of Africa, which has become a preoccupation of an increasing number of scholars during the past twenty years, is by no means a recent development. It is worth recalling that various contributions to the subject have been made since Africa south of the Sahara began to be a focus of interest just over a hundred years ago. One major change that has taken place in recent years, however, is that the study of African prehistory has come to be regarded as a subject in its own right with which historians may properly concern themselves. In addition, it is proving necessary to enlist the co-operation of specialists from such fields as palaeo-climatology and palaeo-botany, to say nothing of the various fields usually grouped together under the all-embracing heading of archaeology. In the earlier period, most of the work was based on ethnological or linguistic observations, and in general it seems fair to say that the broad pictures which were drawn were in fact based on rather inadequate evidence interpreted no doubt with some flair but also with considerable imagination.

It is to be anticipated that it will ultimately be possible to build up a picture of the prehistory of Africa on the basis of inferences provided by the relevant branches of enquiry, but if the ultimate synthesis is to be valid, it is necessary in the first place for each of the lines of investigation to be pursued separately by specialists. Only when this has been done can the final stage be undertaken, and from this two things follow. In the first place it is unrealistic to expect quick results, since in each field the collection and analysing of the data can be tedious and exacting. In the second place, no one person can be in a position to vouch for the validity of all the conclusions. Competent specialist prehistorians in each field should be able to discuss the relevance of the inferences drawn by their colleagues in other fields, but they are rarely likely to be in a position seriously to challenge the substance of such inferences. In fact one must be prepared to cope with awkward indications from other fields, and to accept them, however incompatible they may be with the conclusions reached from evidence in one's own field. And these are the basic presuppositions that underlie my investigations of the material that is to be found in the Bantu languages. In other words, my comparative study of these languages has been carried out without taking into account the contributions to the prehistory of Africa from other lines of investigation. I have simply had the specific intention of providing an answer to the question: 'what does the linguistic evidence show about the probable prehistory of the ancestors of the speakers of Bantu languages?'

It is probably unnecessary to discuss the reasons for assuming that languages spoken today contain certain data that reflect features in prehistory, since, although this is an assumption that is widely made, it is for me simply a working hypothesis. In fact, when commencing my comparative study of the Bantu languages over twenty years ago, I had no certainty that I would be able to reach any clear conclusions different from the general hypotheses advanced by Carl Meinhof. As this paper illustrates, my investigations do seem to have produced some interesting results, but in the event they might not have done so.

At this point it may be useful to emphasize that there are two different ways in which investigations of this kind can be undertaken. On the one hand one can apply simple commonsense procedures so as to get quick results, or on the other hand one can work closely over the data in order to discover by experiment which is the most satisfactory way to extract the kind of information one is seeking. This second method can consume a great deal of time and energy, some of which is apparently lost by following false trails. Nevertheless, it seems to be justified by the fact that any conclusions can be demonstrated as valid on the basis of the data, albeit the verification may not be readily understood by a non-specialist. Perhaps I may usefully draw an analogy from the way observations can be made about physical types. In my travels in different parts of Africa I have often been aware of physical correspondences between the inhabitants of widely separated places, and that this is not an entirely subjective judgement could be demonstrated by the simple device of appealing to the powers of observation of others to whom the determining factors could be pointed out. Nevertheless, nothing of value could be built on observed correspondences of this kind, since they can be neither verified nor falsified. If, however, a skilled physical anthropologist, making use of say twenty parameters, takes measurements of a wide sample of the two populations, and then after suitable processing his data indicate that there is indeed a correlation in the physical characteristics of the populations in the two areas, his conclusions are of value for prehistory, in a way that subjective observations are not.

One of the difficulties that confronts anyone who embarks on a detailed investigation of the kind described here is that interim conclusions are rarely possible, and one has to plod on without being able to comment on other current theories based on simpler procedures. I refer specifically to the widely accepted ideas associated with the name of Joseph Greenberg, which seem to me to be based on penetrating observations rather than on verifiable techniques, and which therefore cannot be synthesized with the conclusions of, say, palaeo-botany. In many respects, I feel that the method of lexico-statistical dating used in glotto-chronology suffers from the same defect, since one of its premises cannot be verified in a wholly preliterate area, namely that a given section of the lexicon will display a regular rate of decay. The results of applying such a method may be rapid, but since they are based on an aprioristic assumption, they cannot be put alongside say the information obtained by radio-carbon dating of archaeological material. What I have just said will explain why I shall refrain from any further comment on either of these types of study, since they lie outside what I understand to be the basic investigations on which the prehistory of Africa should be built up.

Turning to the substance of my own work, it would not be appropriate here to launch into a detailed technical description. What I propose to do is to explain in broad terms what the data I collected consist of, and how they were treated, and then to summarize a few of the interesting conclusions that it has been possible to reach.

The basic feature of my method has been the examining of all the available data for evidence of any kind that might prove to be relevant for linguistic prehistory, without prejudging the value of any information that emerged. This has involved a considerable amount of experimenting to discover the most efficient techniques for handling the data, and at the same time a readiness to take into account items of data that seemed not to fit in with the main bulk of the information. In practice it was necessary to adopt the rather rigid procedure of collecting and working over the data for a number of years without having any clear idea of the kind of results that might ultimately be achieved. Although this called for a rigorous control of curiosity, it had one very great advantage in that it removed the temptation to devise ways of processing the data that might imply what I was trying to prove.

Briefly, the bulk of my data consists of material from some 350 languages and dialects, representing over five-sixths of all the Bantu languages; while in no fewer than 150 of these the total range of the available material is considerable. From these 350 languages items have been collected into what are termed 'sets of cognates', each set being held together by completely regular rules of phonological correspondence of the type required in the discipline of comparative philology. In fact one of the ways in which this procedure is more precise than certain other comparative studies in the African field is that any apparent cognate that displays some irregularity is not included in the set. Instead, these indirect cognates, as I term them, are merely noted, since their existence may provide useful indications of another kind later on. Over 2,400 sets of cognates have been constructed from some 21,000 regular items, while more than 4,000 irregular items have also been noted. By way of a simple illustration two different sets may be cited here.

(1) Shambaa *|zunde* 'cloud'
Makua *ni|hute* 'cloud'
Umbundu *e|lende* 'cloud'
[Mpoto *lį|hụndi* 'cloud']

(2) Tetela *ẹ|düva* 'pool'
Songe *ki|ʃiba* 'pool'
Herero *oci|ðeβa* 'pool'

(Nyankore *e|ziβa* 'well')
[Bali (Teke) *i|dzia* 'pool']

Each of the items in the first set differs from the others in a way that occurs also in other sets, both as to stem and prefix, which are separated by a vertical line. The Mpoto word cannot be included in the set because it ends in *i* and not in *e* and can therefore be no more than an indirect cognate. The three items in the second set similarly are completely regular, but the Bali word cannot be regarded as a direct cognate because there is no *b* between the *i* and the *a*, while the Nyankore word also cannot be included since its meaning is not the same, although it could be regarded as an indirect cognate involving some change of meaning.

It is the total collection of material of this kind that gives rise to the presumption of some kind of genealogical relationship among the various Bantu languages, but it would be an oversimplification of the problem to decide outright that therefore all the Bantu languages should be treated as direct descendants of a single ancestor language. It may not be out of place here to consider for a moment the significance of a family tree as a representation of the inferred prehistorical development of various languages from a common ancestor. Sometimes several languages are shown as all being genealogically related to a single parent language, but this could in fact be a considerable over-simplification. The most straightforward case is where an earlier language can be regarded as having differentiated into a number of dialects, each of which is a former state of one of the present-day languages. Nevertheless it cannot be assumed that such a uniform development has in fact taken place, since the intermingling of dialects could easily give rise to a more complex type of relationship, while the mere juxtaposition of two languages, both ultimately with the same origin, could result in such contamination that their genealogical relationship would be no longer simple. A still more involved situation can arise when one of the languages shown on a family tree has incorporated a body of 'impacted' material from a completely alien source. In this case, even though its relationship to the others is beyond dispute, the fact that this particular language has undergone severe distortion is not usually represented in the genealogy.

For the purpose of my basic investigations I did not need to have all these possibilities in mind, since the only thing that has to be postulated to account for the whole range of the sets of cognates is that each item in each individual set is derived from, or is a 'reflex' of a single item somewhere in prehistory, which I shall term a 'root' for the purpose of this paper.

Thus the two sets cited above can each be referred to a hypothetical root, these roots being cited as stems only and distinguished by being spelt in capitals and preceded by an asterisk, i.e. **-DŲ̀NDƐ̀* 'cloud' and **-DĮBÀ* 'pool'. The accents on the vowels represent the fact that in respect to tone also the items in each set correspond in a completely regular way.

Not infrequently different sets of cognates have to be attributed to roots that have the same spelling, as for example the two following sets with the respective meaning 'chief' and 'lion'.

**-KƆ́CĮ̀* 'chief'

Kinga	*ọŋ|kɔsį*	'chief'
Matengo	*lį|kosį*	'chief'
Tswa	*hosi*	'chief'

**-KƆ́CĮ̀* 'lion'

Bali	*ŋ|kwei*	'lion'
Bobangi	*ŋ|kɔsį*	'lion'
Kwanyama	*ohŋosi*	'lion'

It would, however, be unjustified in the initial stages to treat these as other than two distinct sets of reflexes, since they could be regarded as related only if it were to be shown that the two roots of which they are respectively reflexes might have occurred at a similar place and time in prehistory, whereas in fact this is unlikely since the first set occurs only in the east and the second only in the west. In practice it is found that the roots to which the various sets of cognates may be attributed form a wide spectrum in the prehistorical era, both as to their antiquity and as to their location.

An example of this is provided by the geographical distribution of two distinct sets of reflexes, plotted on a chart which is in fact a highly conventionalized version of the map of Bantu Africa: see Diagrams 1 and 2. The first of these is confined to a restricted area in the north-west, while the second covers over a third of the whole field. In view of the disparity between these two patterns of distribution, it cannot be assumed that the two roots should be assigned to the same point in prehistory. The situation is different, however, in respect of the small number of sets of cognates that cover the whole field, since these presumably have to be regarded as reflexes of roots that occurred in an original ancestor language. Such sets are referred to as general, a term that is extended to include also others that cover the greater part of the field, and by determining the extent to which the roots attested by the 500 general sets are reflected in certain selected languages, some provisional conclusions can be reached about the location and characteristics of the postulated ancestor language.

The simplest procedure is to count the number of these reflexes in each language and to plot the percentages on a map of some kind. Nevertheless, the probability that the root attested by a general set of cognates did occur in the original ancestor language is to some extent proportionate to the area of distribution of its reflexes. For this reason it is useful to allot to each set of cognates a figure to express the proportion of the field it covers, and to use these weighted figures in counting the reflexes of the general roots in the selected languages.

Diagrams 3, 4 and 5 illustrate the way in which some of this information has been plotted, the only features being the relative location of each of the twenty-eight languages chosen for this purpose, each denoted by its classificatory code instead of by its name.

Diagram 3 shows what I term the central nucleus area, which is where the weighted count of general reflexes occurring in each language is over 50 per cent of the total for Common Bantu, the three languages involved being Luba-Lulua (L.31), Luba-Katanga (L.33) and Bemba (M.42). Diagram 4 shows the extended nucleus, which is where the weighted count of general reflexes exceeds 45 per cent.

The additional languages involved here are Kongo (H.16) in the west and Ila (M.63) to the south, with Rundi (D.62) and Sukuma (F.21) to the north-east of the central nucleus. The detached part on the east represents Swahili (G.42), and the broken line linking this with the rest of the nucleus serves to emphasize that there do not seem to be languages with equally high scores in the intervening area.

It is from this particular type of evidence that it can be inferred that the original ancestor language may have been located somewhere in the central nucleus area, subsequently spreading westwards to the coast as well as a certain distance to the south-west and the north-east. The presence of the detached part of the nucleus over on the east could be interpreted as meaning that the ancestor of

Swahili may have reached the coast in a sudden jump rather than by a slow spreading from the nucleus.

A further development in the use of experimental statistical methods produces some indications of the probable genealogical relationships of the remainder of the languages chosen for the purpose. It is very difficult to devise a method of displaying this information that is not at the same time misleading, but I have attempted to do so in Diagram 5.

Although this may have some resemblance to a representation of supposed migrations, that is not the intention of the diagram, which is simply a multi-directional genealogical tree that tries to show up the relationship of two different things, (*a*) the relative closeness of languages in respect to their probable prehistory and (*b*) their approximate positions in the Bantu field. I must also refer to the thick bent line down the middle of the diagram, which represents an important feature shown up in the analysis of the sets of cognates.

In addition to the general sets, there are two other important sections of the total collection, one of which contains items found in the western part of the field and the other items found in the eastern part. These two sections contain over 60 per cent of all the non-general sets of cognates and presumably reflect some kind of dialectal separation at an early stage in the development of the ancestor language.

On the basis of the various analyses of the data that have been conflated to produce this diagram, a synthetic picture in prehistory can be built up. This has at its centre the original ancestor language, to which the name Proto-Bantu may suitably be applied, spoken somewhere in the neighbourhood of the central nucleus. At some time this ancestor seems to have split into two dialects, probably while diffusing slowly westwards to the coast and northwards on the eastern side of Lake Tanganyika, but with a jump to the east coast. It then appears at least possible that further expansion to the areas outside the nucleus may have been accompanied by a more rapid spread.

There is evidence in the interrelationships of various sets of cognates that there was a critical point in prehistory, that I designate 'the Bantu threshold'. This was when the two dialects of Proto-Bantu appear to have suddenly begun to fragment into a number of rapidly differentiating languages that were probably the intermediate ancestors of the present-day groups of languages. The main difference in the inferred linguistic development on the two sides of the Bantu threshold is that all the different sound-shifts reflected in the sets of cognates must be assumed to have taken place after the threshold. In other words, the differentiation of Proto-Bantu into its two dialects consisted mainly in the emergence of new words to replace others that disappeared, thereby giving rise to the roots reflected respectively in the western and eastern sets of cognates.

What cannot be determined with any useful measure of probability is how large the extended nucleus may have been at the time of the Bantu threshold. The representation of the nucleus on this diagram has been arrived at by taking a large number of different factors into account, and although it is conceivable that it might indicate the shape of the nucleus at the Bantu threshold, the probability that it may have been like this cannot easily be determined.

Against the background of these rather general conclusions I want to turn to a few of the pieces of evidence contained in the material I have collected that seem to provide clues as to the characteristics of Proto-Bantu. In an earlier article (Guthrie, 1962) I mentioned some of the things for which there seemed to have been terms in Proto-Bantu without discussing any of the evidence for this. In the remainder of this paper I should like to deal with a few interesting cases in order to explain how linguistic evidence can be used to throw some light on the circumstances in which Proto-Bantu was probably spoken.

The first set of cognates I want to mention has the meaning 'to fish with a line', and the shaded area on Diagram 6 represents the geographical distribution of these cognates. As can be seen, the greater part of the field is covered with the exception of the southern and eastern flanks, although reflexes are found in Zulu and Xhosa in the south-east. There is also a reflex in Ngazidya in the Comoro Islands, which is not shown on the diagram.

In view of this distribution it seems reasonable to infer that the root to which these cognates may be attributed was in the original ancestor language, and that during the Bantu dispersion southwards and eastwards the word was lost, probably due to a decreased importance of fishing in the more arid parts both of the southern tropical belt and of the country to the east of Lakes Tanganyika and Nyasa. The distribution of a related set of cognates with the meaning 'fish-hook' is shown in the shaded area on Diagram 7, the value of this evidence being less clear than that on the previous diagram for three reasons. Firstly, we cannot be sure that the source of all of these items goes back to Proto-Bantu, since there is always the possibility that derivation of the stem of a word for 'fish-hook' from a verbal radical meaning 'to fish with a line' took place independently in a number of places. The second thing that points in the same direction is that not all these cognates are in the same classes. An important feature of the Bantu languages is the presence of up to ten different classes in which a singular nominal word can occur, and in this case no fewer than eight classes are represented among the cognates, a fact which in itself could throw some doubt on the validity of attributing all of them directly to a root meaning 'fish-hook' in the ancestor language. Finally, there are several languages in various parts of the field, not included in those marked on this diagram, in which there is a word that cannot be treated as a direct cognate of those plotted on the chart because of some irregularity, a state of affairs that could be due to borrowing at some time or other. The net result of these facts is that whereas it can be asserted with some confidence that Proto-Bantu had a word for 'to fish with a line' it is far from certain that it also had a word for 'fish-hook', which conceivably might mean that originally thorns were used as fish-hooks, being later superseded by hooks made of wire.

The next group of cognates I would like to discuss are concerned with riverine activities, and Diagram 8 plots the distribution of the only set of cognates meaning 'canoe'. It will be seen that the only area where no reflexes of this root are known to occur is all down the eastern seaboard, and a fact that may have some relevance in this connection is the presence in a number of languages of a word for 'canoe' that resembles the Swahili *ngalawa* 'a dug-out canoe with outriggers', represented on the chart by the stippled areas. It proves impossible to establish these various words as direct cognates, and indeed the most that can be said is that they are probably loans from an unknown source, since even the Swahili word itself could not be a direct cognate of a word in any other Bantu language. It therefore seems likely that the term **BỌ|ÁTƆ̀* was lost in the eastward spread of Bantu speakers, but that on the coast a new term for a sea-going canoe emerged.

If we turn now to the widespread set of cognates meaning 'paddle', Diagram 9 shows that these do not extend to the southern part of the field, suggesting that although this root for 'paddle' was probably in Proto-Bantu it did not persist during the southward movement after the Bantu threshold. It is interesting to compare the areas covered by the reflexes of the Proto-Bantu roots for 'canoe' and 'paddle', and this is done in Diagram 10, in which the horizontal shading shows where reflexes of **BỌ|ÁTƆ̀* 'canoe' are missing and the vertical where those of **Ị̄|KÁPỊ̄* 'paddle' do not occur. From this evidence it seems reasonable to infer that the speakers of the proto-language used canoes and paddles, but that these objects became less important as movement southwards and eastwards took place.

For the purpose of building up a picture of the probable prehistory of the part of Africa occupied by speakers of Bantu languages, the terms connected with iron-working are plainly important. Space does not allow an exposition of all the detailed features displayed by the various sets of cognates, but the next two diagrams are designed to demonstrate some of the results that have been obtained by studying them. Diagram 11 shows the distribution of the more important sets of cognates with the meaning of 'metallic iron'. The original root for iron seems most likely to be reflected in the set in the areas with diagonal hatching, and the fact that these are scattered about probably means that this root was present in the ancestor language. Other evidence suggests that the set of cognates that occur in the north-eastern area with horizontal hatching are probably due to a transfer of meaning from a root meaning 'something valuable', while the cognates found in the area with vertical hatching are apparently related to other similar sets meaning 'ironstone'. By taking all the evidence into account it seems likely that the original root for 'iron' was displaced in the south and west by a term originally meaning 'iron-ore'. In the north-east on the other hand it seems possible that iron was rare enough to come to be described by a term that emphasized its value.

The practice of smelting iron existed until recently in a number of areas, but there is no set of cognates meaning 'to smelt', although a special term for 'pig-iron' does form such a set in a few languages in the central part of the field. The terms for metal working are however rather interesting, and Diagram 12 shows the distribution of a widespread set of cognates meaning 'to forge'. One thing to note here is that the area with diagonal hatching includes Swahili which has a reflex of the original root. In the parts with vertical hatching there are reflexes of a totally different root, which suggests that the art of forging might have reached the east from another source, bringing with it a fresh term. There is also the evidence of the area with horizontal hatching in the east where there is a third set of cognates meaning 'to forge', which appears to be superimposed on the second area. It would seem possible therefore that this third set reflects a later development, which gives rise to a curious situation, since this particular set of cognates appears to be due to a root with the primary meaning of 'to strike'. In other words it seems that there may be evidence of people moving into the east in whose language there was no special term for 'forging'.

There are also various sets of cognates meaning 'hammer', but the situation is too confused to represent on a diagram, although the evidence suggests that there must have been an original root with this meaning. Similarly there is a complicated state of affairs involving the terms for 'bellows'. There are cognates scattered throughout the eastern region that attest a root meaning 'bellows' in the eastern dialect of Proto-Bantu, whereas another set of cognates meaning 'smithy' can be attributed to a root of the same shape but in a different class in the western dialect. It seems possible therefore that there may have been a term in Proto-Bantu referring to 'bellows' and 'smithy', which underwent some differentiation of meaning in the two proto-dialects. The overall picture then is that the speakers of the proto-language probably knew how to forge iron before the Bantu dispersion began, but there is no evidence to suggest when the art of smelting was acquired. In addition it is possible that there may have been a later and distinct introduction of iron-working to the east coast, which could mean either that the art had been lost or that a new technique of forging was introduced and with it a term that displaced the earlier one.

At this point we may consider some of the linguistic evidence that bears on the question of the foodstuffs that were raised in prehistorical times. It is not possible to do more than provide some illustrations of the kind of problems that arise in this connection, so I shall confine myself to three crops: bananas, peanuts and sugar-cane.

Among the words for 'bananas' there are two very closely related sets of cognates that may be attributed to a single root, and the distribution of these is shown on Diagram 13 in the area with upward diagonal hatching, which seems to indicate that the original root for 'bananas' was **MA|KƆ̀NDƐ̀*. It is noteworthy that Swahili alone along the east coast has a reflex of this root, which presumably occurred in Proto-Bantu. The other fairly widespread set of cognates occurs in the part with downward diagonal hatching, which it will be seen is continuous but restricted to an inland area in the east. The only other known case of a set of cognates with this meaning is shown in the area with vertical hatching, while in languages in the stippled area there are words that could be indirect reflexes of the same root, a state of affairs that might indicate some kind of loaning. On the linguistic evidence therefore it seems that bananas were probably known to the speakers of Proto-Bantu, but that in the east different terms subsequently emerged, which could have been correlated with the cultivation of a different species of banana.

In the case of the other two crops that may be considered the evidence is less conclusive, and I have chosen these deliberately as examples of the fact that it cannot be assumed that linguistic evidence will necessarily provide clear indications for prehistory. On Diagram 14 is plotted some of the information that bears on the prehistory of the terms for 'peanuts'. In fact there is only one set of direct cognates with this meaning, and as may be seen from the parts with diagonal cross-hatching the distribution of this set consists of four small separated areas. There are however many instances of irregular words that might conceivably be ultimately due to the same root, but if so they must have undergone some abnormal development of the kind caused by loaning; these are shown in the stippled areas. For the most part the words for 'peanuts' in the rest of the field are a miscellaneous collection, no two of which seem to be related to each other. It seems reasonable to infer that there was a root to which the words in the diagonal cross-hatched and stippled areas are due, but it is by no means certain that it meant 'peanuts'. One reason for the uncertainty is that in Kamba, the language marked with horizontal hatching in the north-east, there is a word with the right shape for a cognate, but this refers to an indigenous tree-pea, whereas the word for 'peanuts' in this language is quite unrelated. Another fact is that the term for 'peanuts' in the area with vertical cross-hatching and the Bemba word for an indigenous ground-bean, represented on the chart by single vertical hatching, have the right shape to be cognates, while one of the Swahili words for 'peanut' could be related to them but for an irregularity in its shape. It thus seems either that peanuts were known in Proto-Bantu by the same name as some other crop, or that they were introduced after the Bantu threshold, being given various names, probably by transfer from the term for some local crop. On the whole the words for 'peanuts' do not seem to provide any conclusive evidence for prehistory.

The remaining crop to be discussed here is sugar-cane, which is actually grown by most groups of speakers of Bantu languages. There are two roots only that appear to be reflected in the various terms used for sugar-cane, and these are plotted on Diagram 15, there being a collection of miscellaneous terms in the rest of the field. The set plotted with cross-hatching, which is confined to a restricted and continuous area, may reflect a relatively recent root in the north-west. The other set, represented by the diagonal hatching, gives rise to a different problem, since it occurs in two separate areas and there is some evidence that sugar-cane was not grown until fairly recently in the unshaded part between these two areas. From this it seems possible that sugar-cane may have been grown in the east during the time that the final dispersion was taking place. It may be concluded therefore that the speakers of Proto-Bantu probably did not have sugar-cane, which might have been introduced fairly early into the east, and independently into the west in more recent times.

A quite different sort of subject about which we may try to get some information is concerned with the topography of the region where Proto-Bantu may have been spoken. There is space to mention two only of the features where the linguistic evidence seems to shed some light on the subject, and these are 'forest' and 'savannah'. On Diagram 16 is plotted the distribution of two sets of cognates that can be attributed to roots with the same shape, that have respectively the meaning 'forest' and 'thicket'. If, as seems probable, they are all ultimately due to a single Proto-Bantu root, this is likely to have referred to a patch of forest as distinct from the great unbroken forest of the equatorial region. If this were so, it would not be difficult to envisage a shift of meaning to 'thicket' in those places where patches of true forest are rare. One fact that is probably significant is the complete absence of any reflexes of this root in the languages spoken in the equatorial forest, the southern and eastern boundary of which is shown approximately by the heavy line in the north-east. It would seem a reasonable inference that the only kind of forest known to the speakers of Proto-Bantu was that found in the mixed forest and savannah country to the south of the great forest, and that when the dispersion spread into the unbroken forest area to the north, new terms emerged for what was regarded as a completely new feature.

The second topographical feature cannot easily be illustrated with diagrams. There is in fact one full set of cognates only with the precise meaning of 'savannah', although there are also four fragmentary sets. The one complete set, which is scattered over the area of the extended nucleus but not in the central nucleus, belongs however to a group of sets of cognates, each member of the group being the reflex of a root with the same shape, the others having the meanings 'sand', 'soil' and 'island'. Since all these four sets present no difficulty with regard to their shapes, they could all be ultimately reflexes of the same original root, if some shift of meaning were also postulated. One further fact to be taken into account is that the items in the sets meaning 'sand' and 'soil' are mainly in the same class and are confined to the eastern region, while the set meaning 'island' is in a different class and is confined to the west. It is not easy to frame a hypothesis to account for this complicated situation, but it seems possible that the original root may have referred indifferently to 'sand' and 'sandbank', in the way that unrelated words do in some present-day languages. This meaning might then have shifted to 'island' in the west, where most islands are in fact permanent sandbanks, while in the east, particularly in the semi-desert areas, a shift of meaning to 'soil' would reflect the fact that much of the soil there contains a very high proportion of sand. Since the items in the set of cognates with the meaning 'savannah' are in various classes, we are left with the impression that these might represent a later development, due to the fact that savannah is normally associated with sandy terrain. If this were so, it may well have happened that the speakers of Proto-Bantu had no specific term to distinguish 'savannah' from 'country in general', as is the case in the Luba languages that are spoken today in the area where Proto-Bantu has been located on the basis of other evidence.

What seems to be the most encouraging aspect of these comparative Bantu studies is that although the conclusions are of necessity tentative they do seem to be coherent. For example, when I inferred from statistical evidence that Proto-Bantu was probably spoken roughly in the region we now know as Katanga, I had no idea that much later I should discover that an investigation of topographical terms would also point to this same area. One of my guiding principles has been that each separate aspect of this vast subject must be studied independently, in such a way that inferences from one set of data are never used in the drawing of conclusions from other data. In this way the validity of each conclusion is independent of the validity of the others, so that if any particular result should require modification in the light of further evidence, this would not have far-reaching consequences for the total picture that has been built up. As a result of their having been based on verifiable data, the conclusions obtained from the comparative study of the Bantu languages are of such a character that they can be synthesized with the conclusions reached by specialists in other fields of knowledge that are equally relevant to the prehistory of Africa.

BIBLIOGRAPHY

Malcolm GUTHRIE, 'Some developments in the prehistory of the Bantu languages', *Journal of African History*, III, 2, 1962, 273–83.

——, *Comparative Bantu: an introduction to the comparative linguistics and prehistory of the Bantu languages*, Farnborough, 1967 ff. (in progress).

DIAGRAM 1

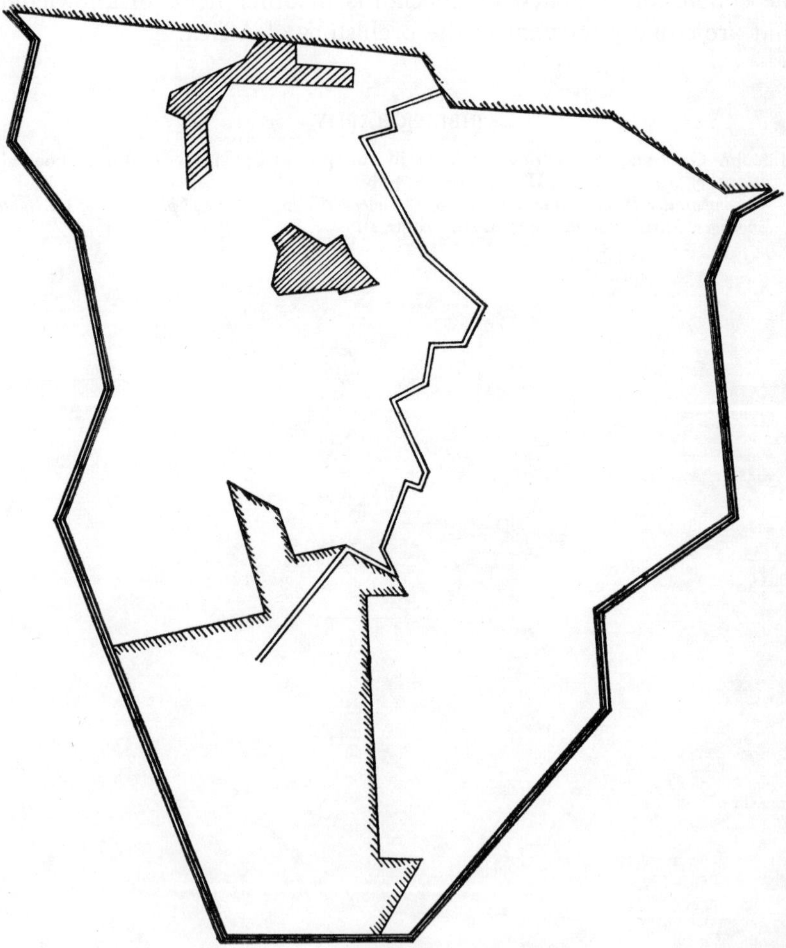

*-*PỌCỌ* 'skin'

DIAGRAM 2

*-*TÓDÒ* 'chest'

DIAGRAM 3

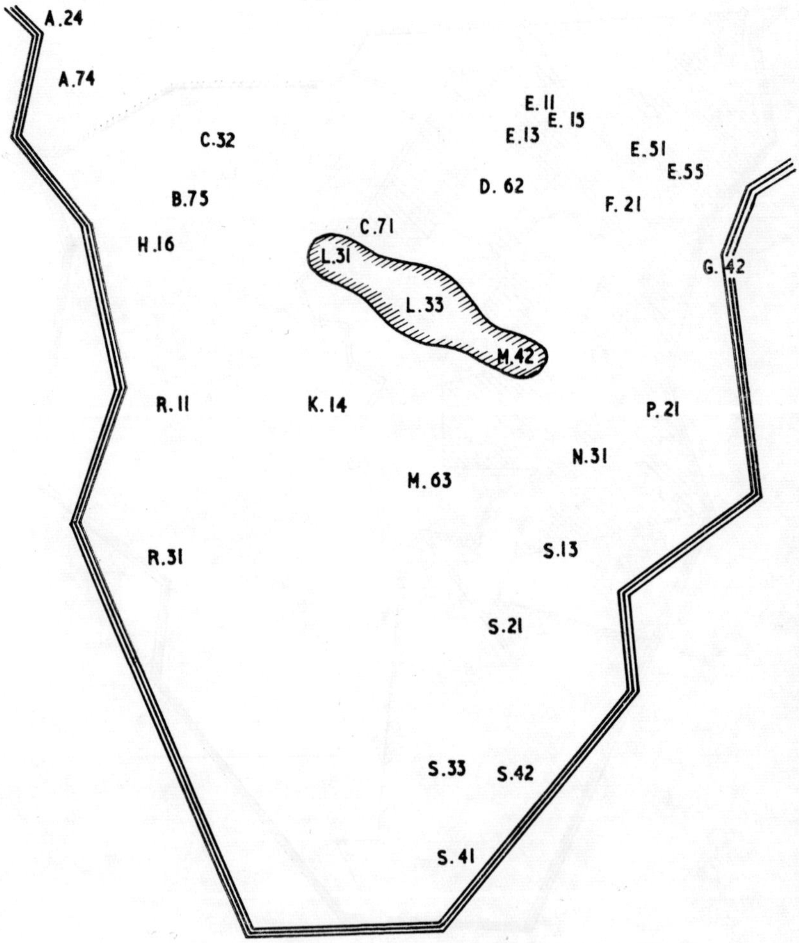

Central Nucleus

DIAGRAM 4

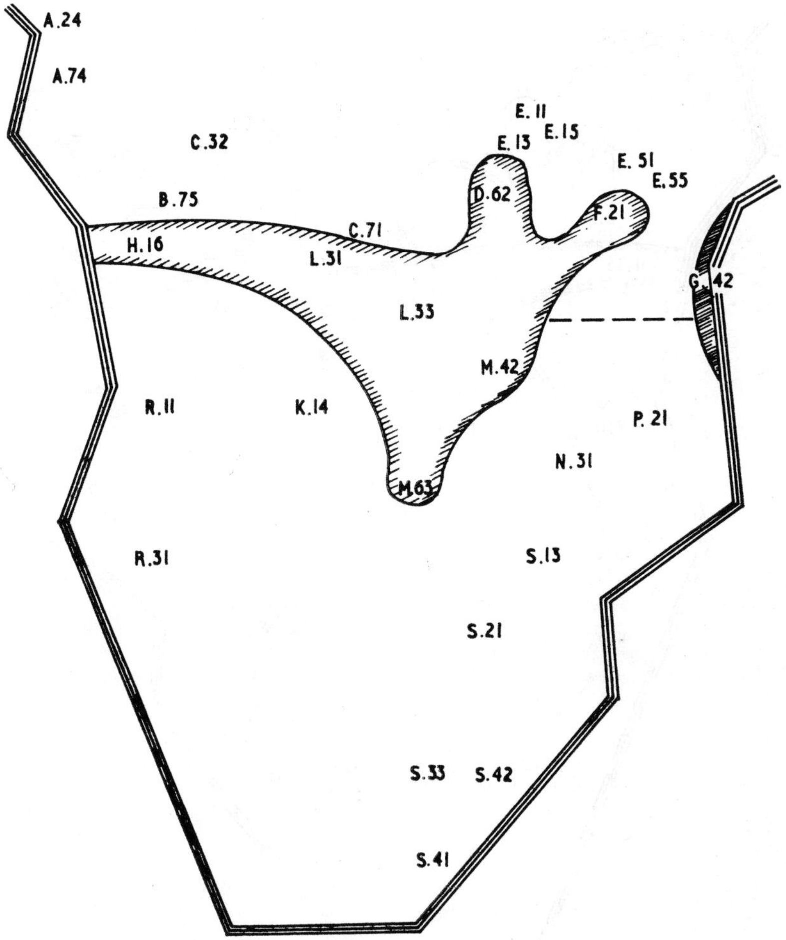

Extended Nucleus

DIAGRAM 5

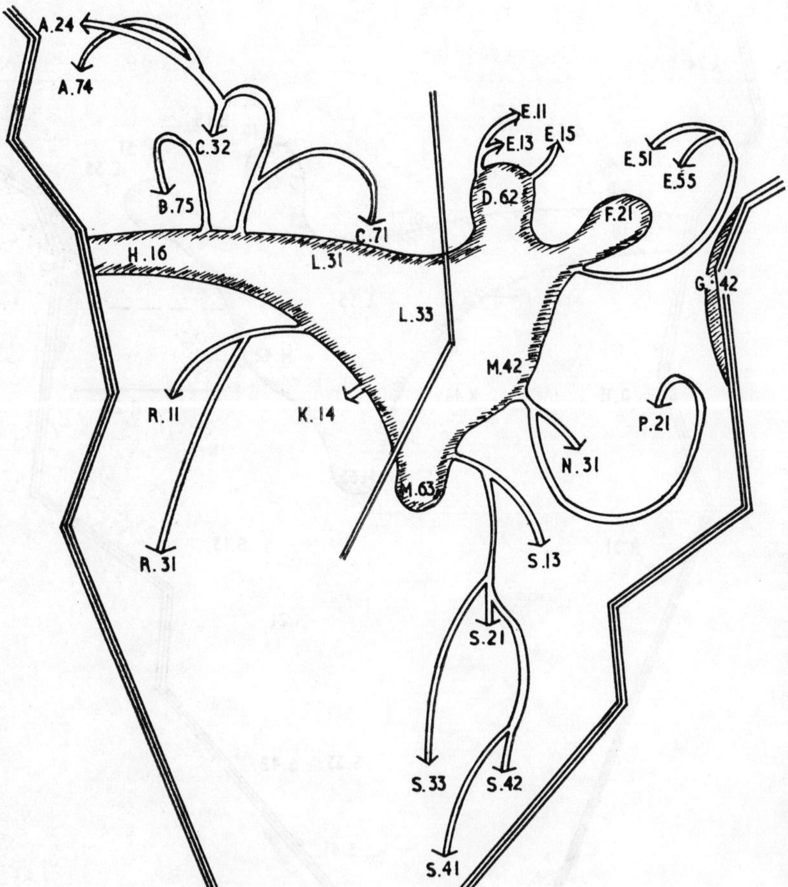

Multi-directional Tree

DIAGRAM 6

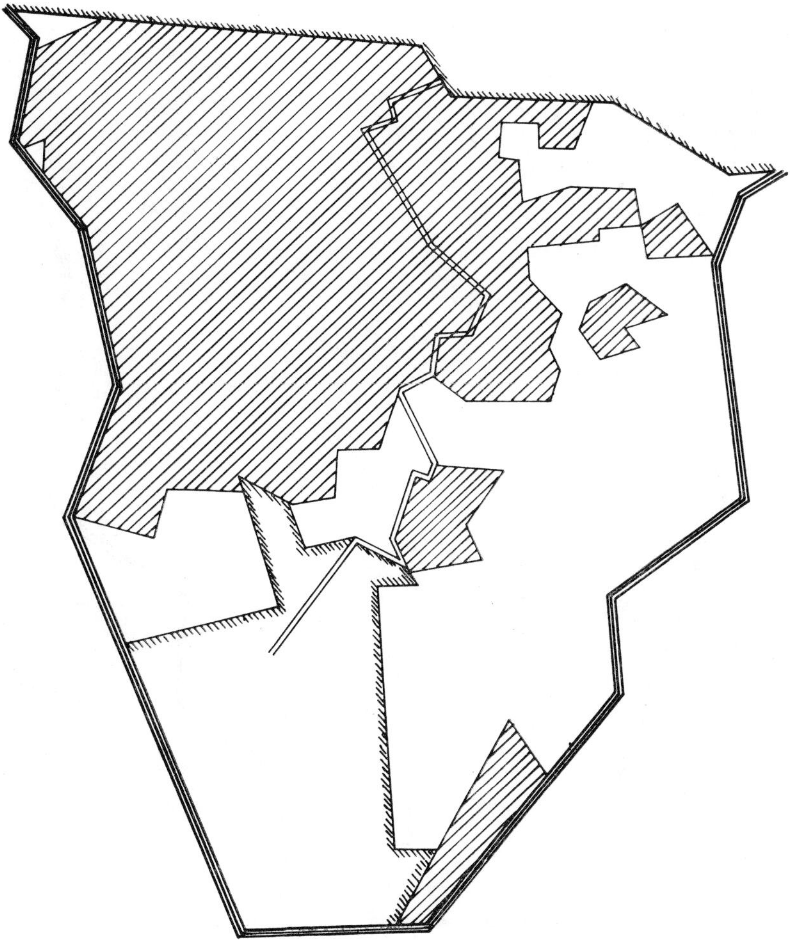

*-*Dɔ́B*- 'to fish with a line'

DIAGRAM 7

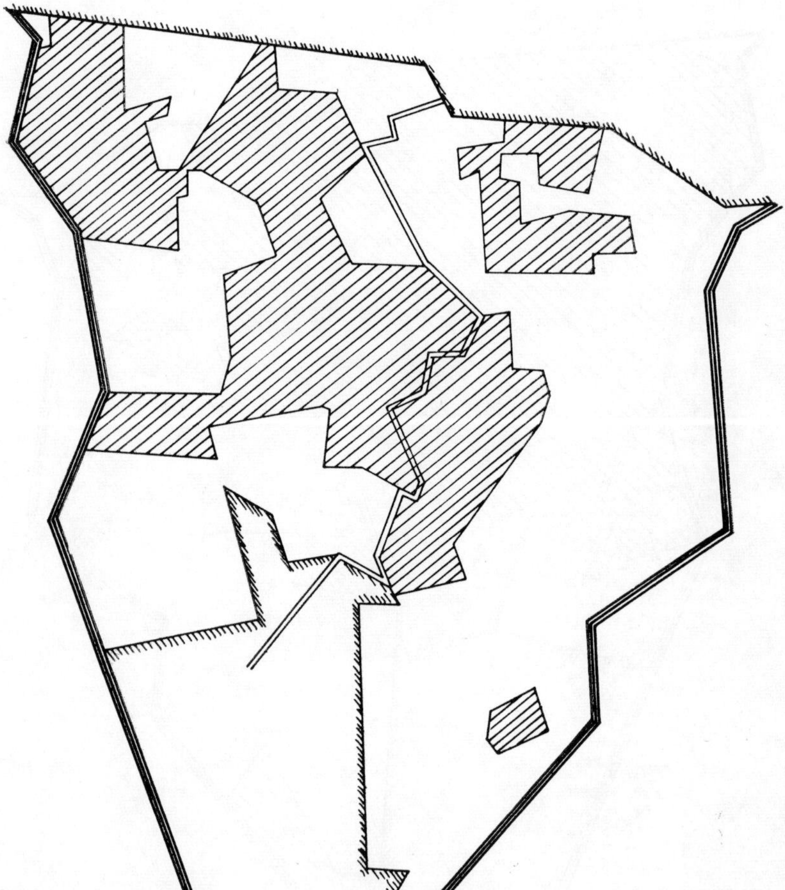

*-*DƆ́BƆ̀* 'fish-hook'

DIAGRAM 8

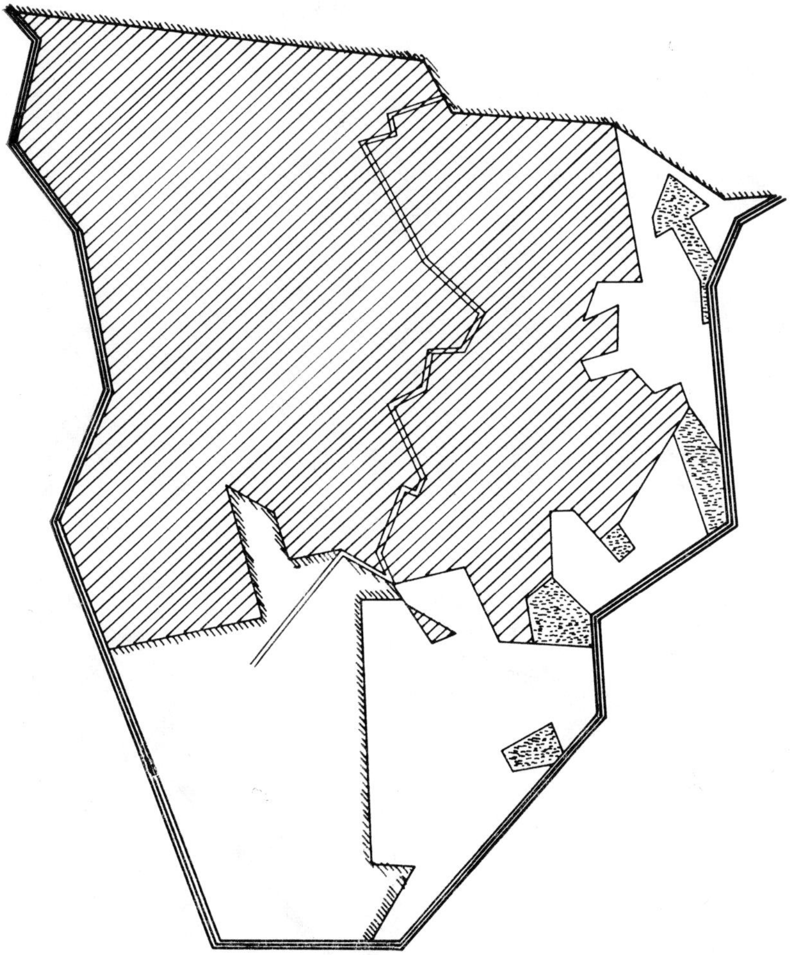

/// **BỌ|ÁTƆ̂* 'canoe'

ngalawa (and similar forms) 'dugout canoe with outriggers'

DIAGRAM 9

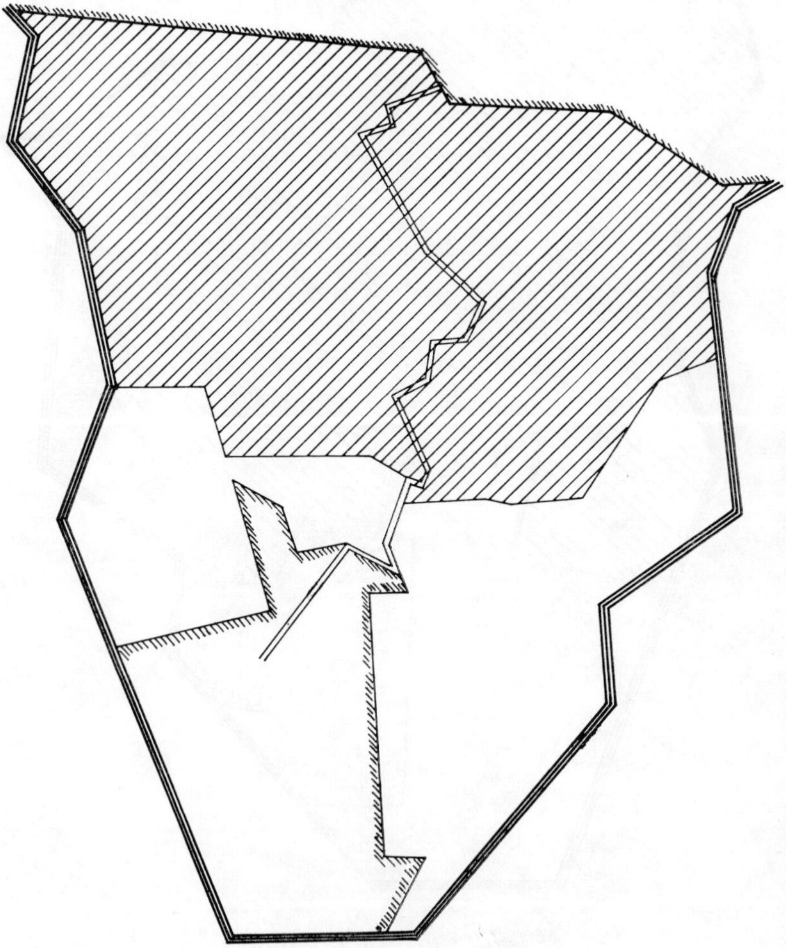

*Ŋ|KÁPĪ 'paddle'

DIAGRAM 10

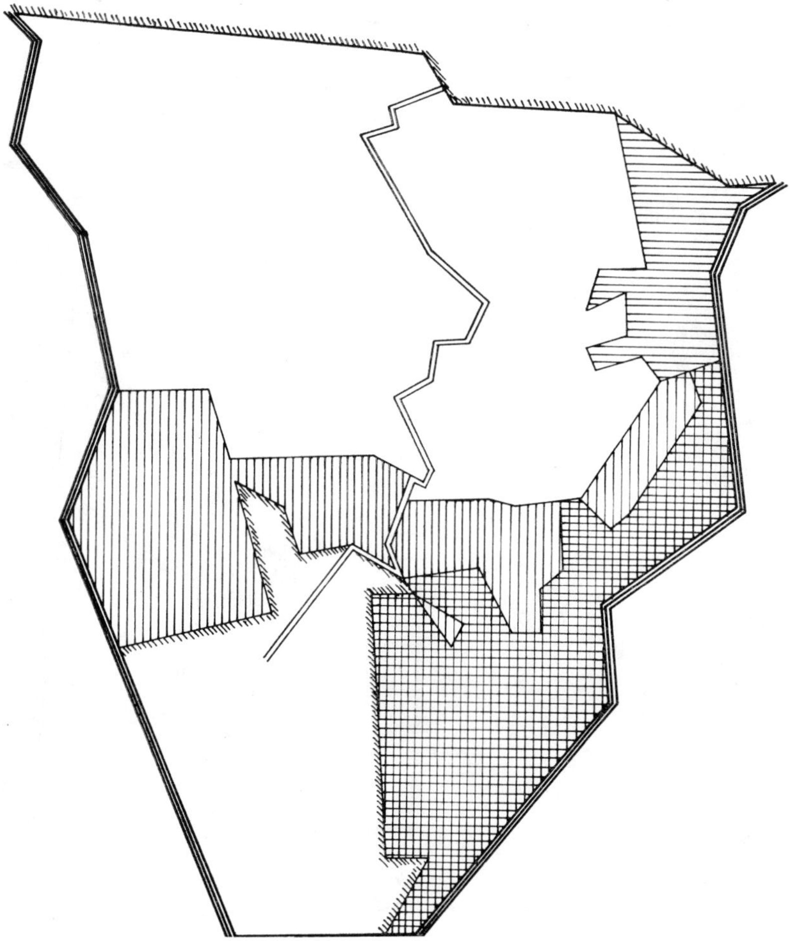

≡ no reflexes of **BỌ|ÁTɔ̀* 'canoe'
||| no reflexes of **Ŋ|KÁPỊ̀* 'paddle'

DIAGRAM 11

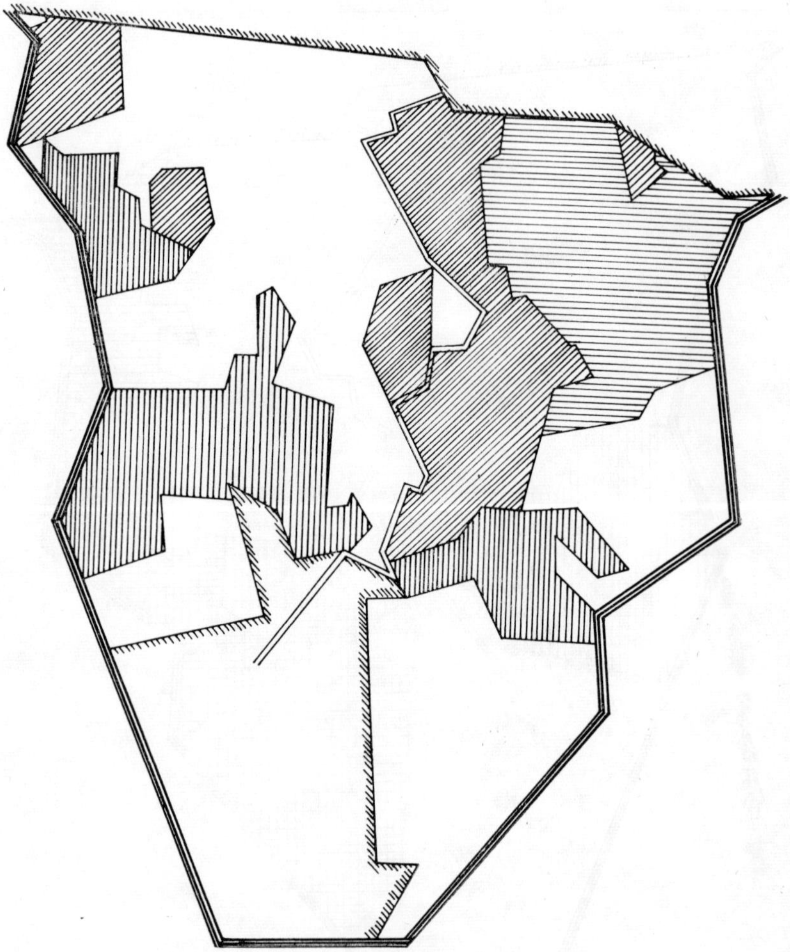

/// *-*GƐ̀DÀ* 'iron'
≡. *-*YỌ́MÀ* 'iron'
|||| *-*TÁDƐ̀* 'iron'

DIAGRAM 12

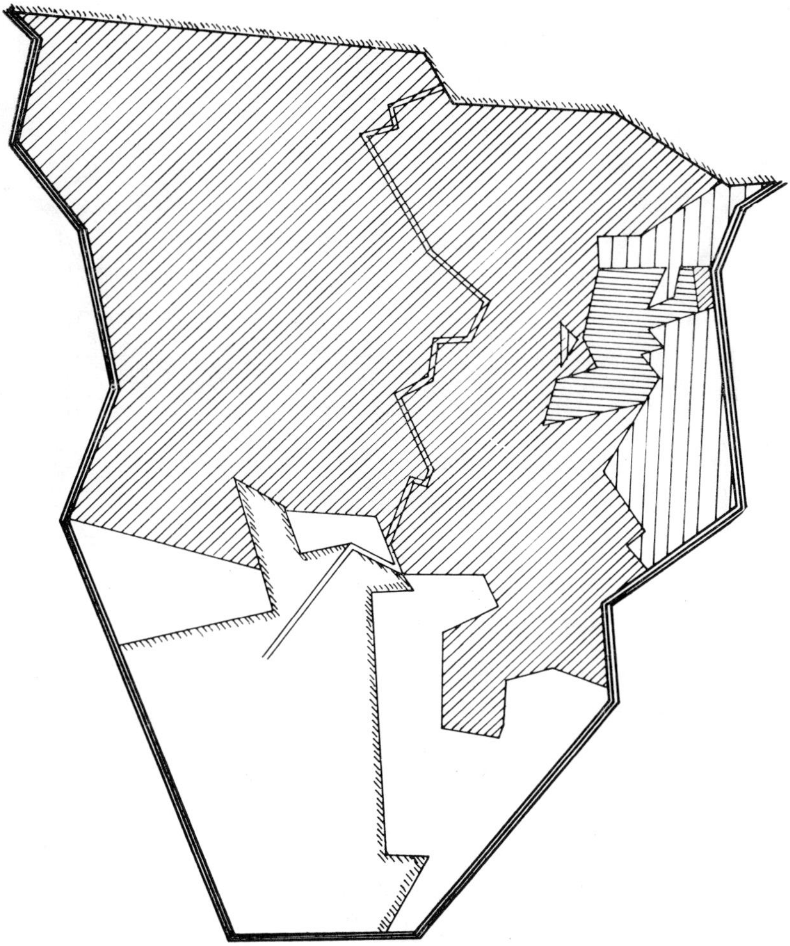

/// *-*TŲ́D*- 'to forge'
||| *-*TĮ́ÁN*- 'to forge'
≡ *-*PƆ́ND*- 'to forge'

DIAGRAM 13

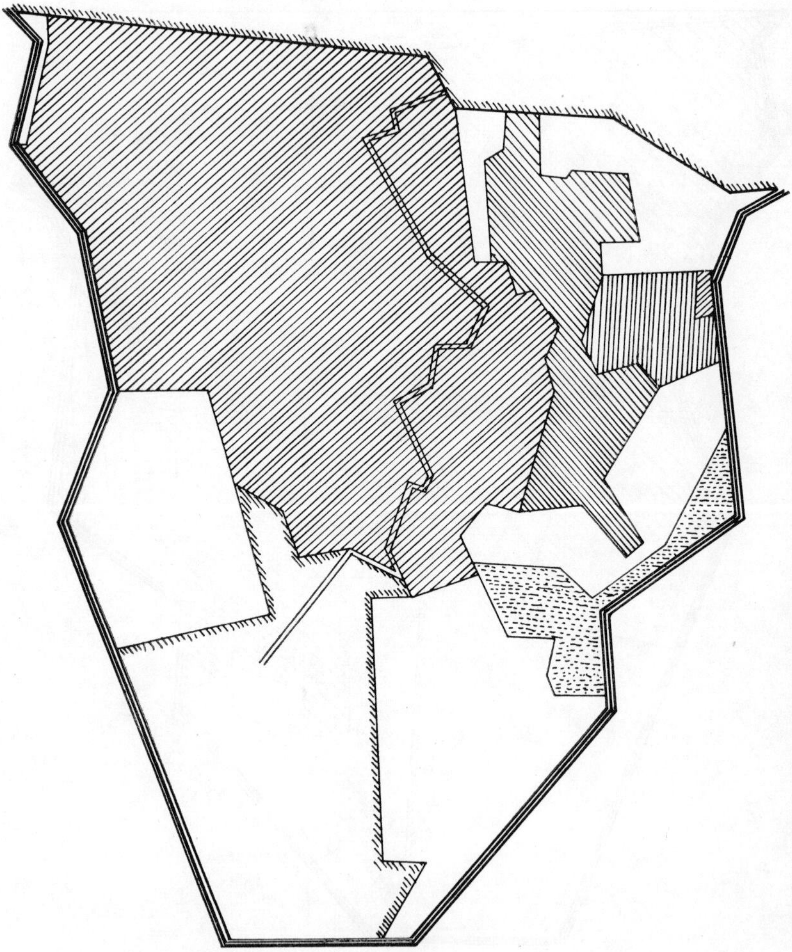

/// *MA|ḲƆ̀NDƐ̀ 'bananas'
\\\\\\ *BI̧|TƆ̀Ɔ̀KȨ́ 'bananas'
|||| *DI̧|ŊGƆ̀BƆ̏ 'bananas' (direct reflexes)
- - - *DI̧|ŊGƆ̀BƆ̀ 'bananas' (indirect reflexes)

DIAGRAM 14

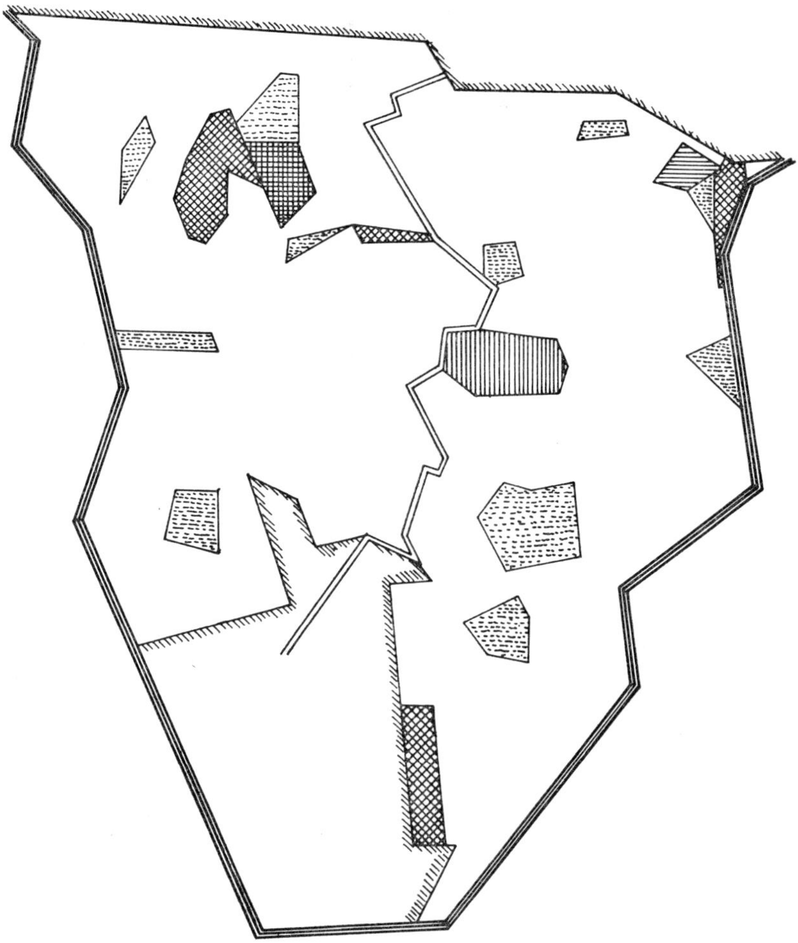

*-JỌ̀GỌ́ 'peanuts' (direct reflexes)
*-JỌ̀GỌ́ 'peanuts' (indirect reflexes)
*-KÀDÀŊGÀ 'peanuts'
*-KÀDÀŊGÀ 'ground-bean'
*-JỌ̀GỌ́ 'treepeas'

DIAGRAM 15

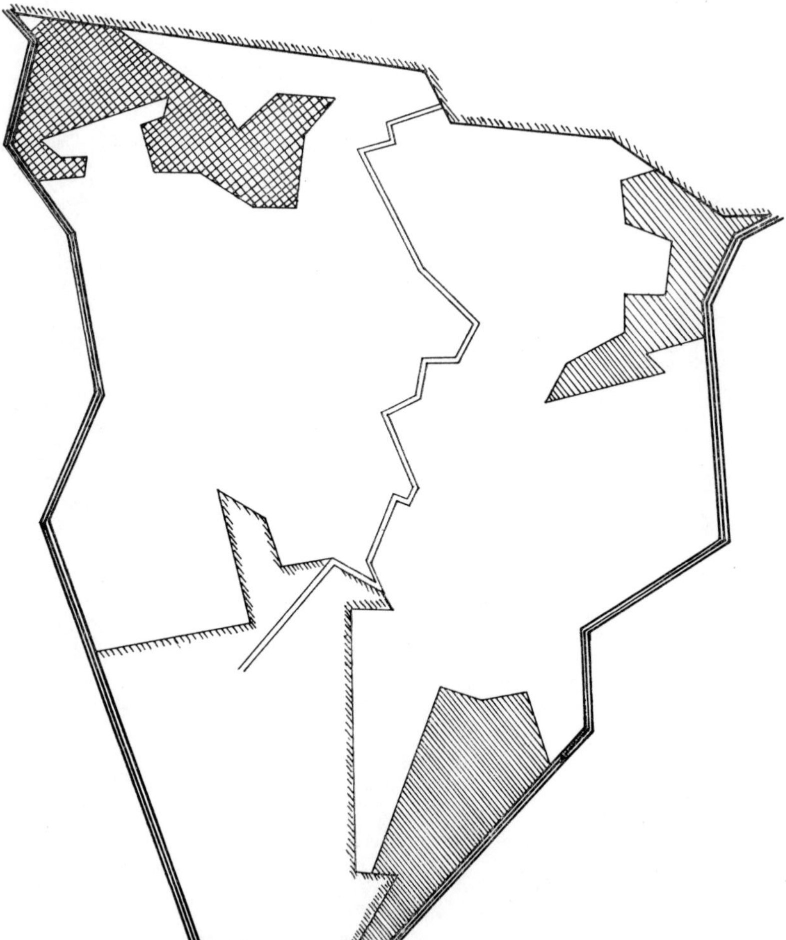

*-*KỌ̀Ọ̀GỌ́* 'sugar-cane'
*-*GỌ̀BÁ* 'sugar-cane'

DIAGRAM 16

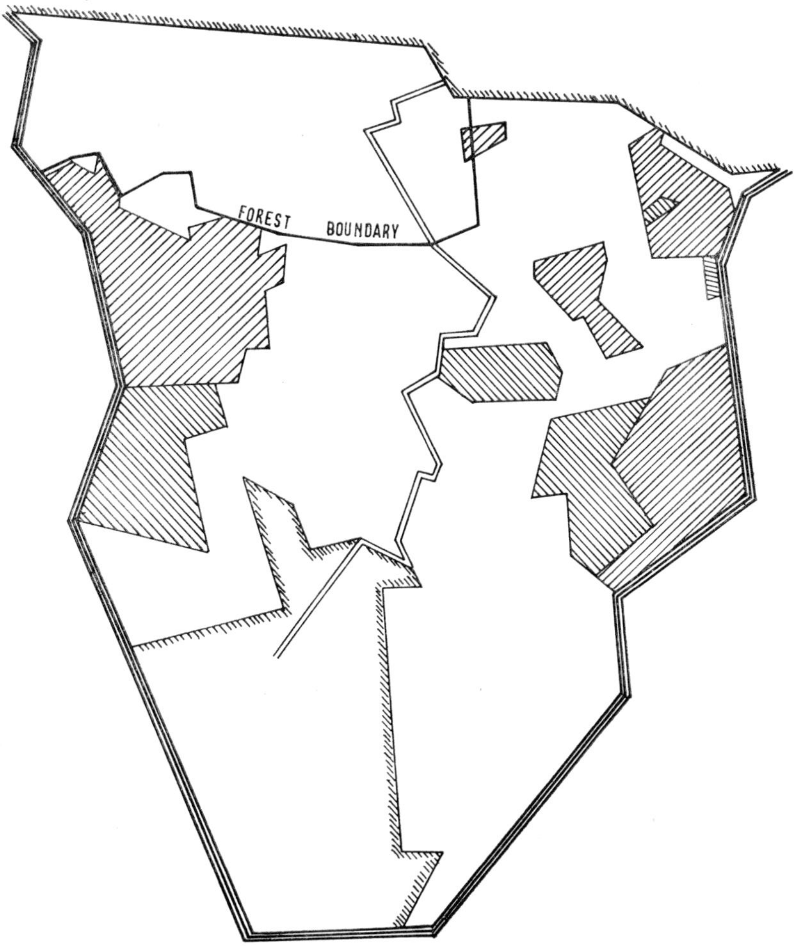

//// *-TÍTỌ 'forest'
\\\\ *-TÍTỌ 'thicket'

The Contribution of Early Linguistic Material to the History of West Africa[1]

P. E. H. HAIR

THE first Africanist to develop a systematic interest in early West African language material was Maurice Delafosse. In the course of editing Arabic texts on the West and Central Sudan, he commented in detail on the material to be found in these texts in the *Soninke*, *Malinke*, *Songhay* and *Fula* languages, and he devoted a paper to this material which was published in 1914.[2] The material is very limited, and the following conclusions by Delafosse appear to be still adequate:

> (*1*) With rare exceptions, all the words cited by Arab authors of the Middle Ages [i.e. between 1100 and 1400] are found in languages spoken today in the Sudan. (*2*) Each of the four languages documented by Arab authors is spoken today in the district where it was spoken earlier. (*3*) Most of the early words are phonetically identical with the modern words—after due allowance has been made for the unsuitability of the Arabic script.

It is curious that this promising start was not followed up by the systematic examination of the much larger amount of West African language material available in European-language texts of between 1450 and 1800—material of course relating mainly to the Guinea coast and hence covering many languages not to be found in the Sudanic material. Such attempts as there were to examine this Guinea coast material were limited in range and application: for instance, René Basset, best known as a Berber scholar, was persuaded (perhaps by Delafosse) to suggest identifications of the terms in a short vocabulary collected on the Gold Coast in 1479–80, but the results were disappointing.[3] In fact, the greater part of the material in European texts has remained unexamined up to the present day: I shall detail below the failure of editors to take African language documentation seriously. Until very recently, there was a marked contrast between the way vernacular material was treated in modern editions of early accounts of America or Asia, and the way similar material was treated in modern editions of early accounts of western Africa. In the former, serious attempts were made to explain vernacular terms and to identify particular languages; in the latter, vernacular terms were regularly passed over without comment or explanation. It was possible by the 1940s for the German scholar Friederici to produce an *Amerikanistisches Wörterbuch*, a handbook of American vernacular terms (the languages ranging from Patagonian to Eskimo) in early printed accounts; while the student of early European contacts with further Asia has had available since 1919 Dalgado's *Glossario Luso-Asiatico*, a handbook of Asian words in early Portuguese sources. Nothing remotely resembling these works exists, as yet, for African studies—one result of which is that the standard dictionaries of European languages, when dealing with words of African origin, have to content themselves with the vaguest ascriptions.[4]

The West African language material in pre-1800 European sources falls into the following formal categories. There are only two full books in and on West African languages, a slight grammatical study of *Fanti* and *Gã* of 1764, in Danish, and a religious text of 1658 in Spanish and *Ewe*.[5] The remainder of the material—and it is this I shall be subsequently discussing—consists of vocabularies, long and short, either in manuscript, or forming a small part of a printed text. One set of vocabularies, that prepared for the Senegal Company probably around 1690, is almost a dictionary, with about two thousand terms in each of seven languages of Senegambia[6] (vocabularies in four further languages, in another manuscript volume, were lost during the French Revolution)—and some of the languages, e.g. *Banyun*, are not particularly well known today. Another set of vocabularies, that published by the missionary Oldendorp in 1777, and collected mainly in the West Indies, had partly a scientific purpose and is a precursor of the *Polyglotta Africana*: here, a brief set of terms is given in each of 24 languages, and this includes a single sentence repeated in each language.[7] All the other vocabularies lack systematic arrangement. Some were collected to serve as conversation-manuals for European sailors and traders, but are poorly organized: the majority were collected perhaps only as curiosities, funny words from a strange land. Finally, a sizeable proportion of the material comes merely in the form of single terms scattered through accounts of exploration or topography or commerce: almost all the very earliest material comes in this form.

A large part of this language material was unlisted and unexamined when Dr. Dalby and I began our research a few years ago: though we have now listed much of it in print, and have examined some of it in varying detail, a great deal still needs attention, and our own researches need checking and elaborating. A brief survey of the sources, categorized by the amount of examination the material has had, will serve to give some idea of the amount of work still to be done. First, there are those early texts in Italian, Portuguese and Dutch, which are available in modern editions, but in which the editing of the language material is inadequate, since African terms are passed over without examination or with only the most casual comment. Three volumes in the Hakluyt

Society series—Crone's edition of Cadamosto and Gomes (*c.* 1460), Kimble's edition of Pacheco Pereira (*c.* 1500), and Blake's extracts from various Portuguese and English sources (to 1560)—fail to do justice to the African language material. In the Dutch equivalent of the Hakluyt series, the volumes of the Linschoten Vereeniging, editors do rather better by West African accounts, but the edition of de Marees (1602), for instance, which contains much *Akan* material, needs further editing.[8] It is pleasant to record, however, that one of the most recent publications of the Hakluyt Society, the facsimile reprint of the original Hakluyt (1589), exhibits a very different approach to African language material: in the lengthy index prepared by Mrs. Alison Quinn, every African term is listed, together with brief suggested identifications for most, Mrs. Quinn having obtained the assistance of Professor J. Berry and Dr. G. Innes of the London School of Oriental and African Studies.

The second category of sources consists of works which have had modern reprints without any detailed editing—the 'editions' by Portuguese scholars of Cadamosto, Almada (1596), de Faro (1654), and Coelho (1669), and of the Jesuit letters (*c.* 1610), like the straight modern English reprints of Jobson (1623), and Bosman (1705), make no attempt to offer explanations of African terms.[9] A third category is more estimable: in these modern editions, the detailed editing has extended to the language material and a serious attempt has been made to examine African terms—the Bissao/Dakar editions of Gomes (1456), Pereira and Fernandes (*c.* 1500), fall within this category. However, their scholarly editors would perhaps be the first to admit that not all terms were examined and that not all the explanations of terms which were examined are adequate. A fourth category would consist of modern editions in which the editing of African terms was comprehensive, detailed, and reasonably definitive—but I cannot think of any work which fulfils these conditions.

So much for modern editions: we now come to early printed sources which have not yet been reprinted, let alone edited. Obvious sources here are—in English, Barbot (the original material written about 1680) and Moore (1738); in Dutch, Dapper (1668); in French, Villault (1669): all are general accounts which contain important vocabularies (for instance, in Wolof, Mandingo, Fula, Vai, Akan and Duala). There is also the more specialized work by Müller on Fetu (or Afutu) in the Gold Coast (1673), which contains a very extensive vocabulary of *Akan*. Lastly, there are the Senegal vocabularies mentioned earlier which were eventually printed in 1845, and Oldendorp's book of 1777: neither source has yet received much attention, and in the hope that this will soon be set right, I have listed the languages represented in these collections in a recent paper.[10]

All the works mentioned so far are probably well known to West Africanists, but I would like to round off this survey of printed sources by drawing attention to the possibility that further material may yet be found in sources not so familiar. A cautionary tale here: the first printed volume in any West African language, the missionary text in 'Arda', i.e. *Ewe*, was lost for nearly three centuries, partly because the surviving copy was catalogued under 'languages of America'. . . In 1966 I discovered an early vocabulary of Cameroons Bantu, not then apparently known to historians of Cameroons, which had been slipped into a Dutch translation of Leo Africanus—a work which normally has nothing to do with the Guinea coast. I have also examined Megiser's universal dictionary of 1603, which certainly includes West African terms in *Wolof*, *Akan* and perhaps other languages, but so far without coming on any original material. While more material may yet be found in even more unlikely sources, it is probable that almost all the early material on West African languages in printed sources is now known, and I hope to add to my published list of material in collections another list of the remaining material, again by the languages represented.

When we come to the manuscript sources, the position is less clear. A manuscript from the Bibliothèque Nationale has provided a *Kra* vocabulary of the 1540s, the earliest substantial West African (and Tropical African) vocabulary—Dr. Dalby and I published our examination of this in 1964.[11] A manuscript in the British Museum has provided a short *Temne* vocabulary of 1582—and also a further cautionary tale. The manuscript was edited in the Hakluyt Society series only a few years ago, but extracts only were printed, and the editor did not see fit to note that among the pages of manuscript omitted from the printed text was a page of African language material.[12] Since other Temne material appears in the printed account of the Jesuit mission to Sierra Leone around 1610, it may be assumed that this much Temne, and perhaps more, is to be found in the original manuscripts in the Jesuit archives in Portugal and Rome.

Naturally, I have searched the catalogues of MSS. in the great libraries for West African language material. I have further studied the recently published guides to West African material in the archives of Holland, Belgium, France, Portugal, Italy and a short while ago I was kindly permitted to inspect the catalogue of Africana in British libraries which is currently being prepared by the Librarian of the School of Oriental and African Studies. The results of this research have been largely negative—I have come across very little listed material. Indeed, so little that a doubt has been raised in my mind—can it be that African language material is often not specifically recorded by those who prepare catalogues and guides? For instance, there is no mention of *Temne* material in the reports on the various Jesuit archives—though I appreciate that these particular reports are guides only, not catalogues, and that the archives have only been sampled.[13] I have not of course seen the instructions given to the compilers of these catalogues and guides, but I suggest that—if in fact this was not done—there is a very strong case for including in future instructions a direction that African language material is to be specifically recorded. It would be sufficient to provide the merest indication, perhaps by a symbol: I am not suggesting that the overtaxed cataloguer need identify the language if no title to the material is supplied in a European language. I am reasonably certain that if this point was made to those who direct library surveys—perhaps as a recommendation of this Seminar—it would be accepted, and thereafter the position would become clearer. Meanwhile, I can only say that some very interesting material has recently been found in manuscript, and that surely more—perhaps a lot more—remains to be discovered.

This concludes my survey of the West African language material in early sources, but before moving on I would like to sum up much of what I have said in a brief comment. Many early texts are currently being edited or re-edited: let us hope that the editors will apply the same resources of scholarship to the elucidation of the African language material as they do to the examination of other matters.

To date, only a small part of the available early language material has been investigated, but already conclusions of interest to the historian or to the linguist, or to both, have emerged. A few examples of lines of research must suffice. In Gomes' account of his 1456 voyage, a single African term is given, which was collected near the end of the voyage: in an attempt to answer the specific historical question—at what point on the Guinea coast did this voyage end? —Dr. Dalby and I have tried to identify the language of this single word.[14] Next, the *Kra* vocabulary of the 1540s from the Paris manuscript, while its range of terms throws light on European trading methods on the Pepper Coast at this period, is perhaps more important because it answers an 'Afrocentric' historical question—what African people then lived on the Pepper Coast? Although the vocabulary does not answer this directly (since the manuscript fails to state where the vocabulary was collected, and the vocabulary is entitled unhelpfully 'the language of Guinea'), we were able to use it to identify other much shorter vocabularies—one in Hakluyt of the 1550s and another in Pacheco Pereira of around 1500—which did state where they were collected. As a result, we can now be certain that at least one part of the Pepper Coast was occupied four centuries ago by a people who spoke a language very close to the *Kra* language today spoken on part of the same coast.

Another example relates to the Sierra Leone region. For some years now, Dr. Dalby and I have been collecting early vocabularies from this region, mainly of *Temne* and *Bullom*, and we hope to publish our material jointly. Now, one of the major events in the pre-colonial history of this region—perhaps the major event for the dating of oral traditions—was the mid-sixteenth century warfare between indigenous peoples described as 'Sapi' in the European sources, and invading armies of a people described as 'Mani' or 'Kquoja' in these sources. None of these three names is a recognized ethnic name in the region today. In 1921, in the course of a long work on the Kpelle people of Liberia, the linguist Westermann inserted a short proof that part of the 'Kquoja' vocabulary given by Dapper in 1668 was similar to the modern *Vai* language: unfortunately, but understandably, this side-comment on Kquoja was missed by historians. In a 1964 paper,[15] I examined the whole of the Kquoja vocabulary and confirmed that Kquoja was indeed *Vai*—a language spoken today in the extreme south of the Sierra Leone region. Meanwhile, among the vocabularies examined by Dr. Dalby and myself were several of 'Sapi', and we have concluded that this language belonged to the *Temne–Baga–Landuma* group of languages, spoken today in Central and Northern Sierra Leone and along the coast of the Republic of Guinea. By identifying the two terms with reference to modern languages, we have come some way to an understanding of the Sapi–Mani/Kquoja clash; and it is of some interest that our conclusions, reached solely from linguistic evidence, fit the non-linguistic evidence as presented and analysed by Dr. Walter Rodney in a recent London thesis.[16]

It will have been detected that the trend of the conclusions above has been to show that a language now spoken at Point A on the Guinea coast was also spoken at Point A on the coast in earlier centuries, as far back as evidence from European sources goes (and one will recollect that Delafosse's conclusion about Sudanic languages in the period since the Arabic sources was similar). I have recently been examining all early coastal vocabularies, and in a series of current papers I claim to show, to a large extent on linguistic evidence, that the geographical distribution of languages along the coast has remained, in the main, unchanged in the documented centuries.[17] If this is correct, then the writing up of moderately recent West African history in terms largely of distant 'tribal origins' and *Völkerwanderung*—an interpretation to which some historians have latterly been much attached—may have to be modified. I suspect that the oral traditions which give this impression of perpetual motion have confused dynastic shuffles with ethnic migrations—rather as if it were held in England that our ancestors crossed the North Sea from Hanover under the first George. And I think that the evidence from the early vocabularies is going to prove, increasingly, a valuable corrective.

What range of purely linguistic conclusions it is possible to draw from the early vocabularies, I am not competent to indicate in detail. I am convinced, however, that there is a prima facie case for the examination of each and every early vocabulary by a linguist expert in the appropriate language—although doubtless in some cases the verdict will be that the vocabulary is too brief, or too peculiar in some respect, for any sound conclusions to be based on it. My conviction is partly the result of witnessing a dramatic growth of interest in the nineteenth century vocabularies of the *Polyglotta Africana*. Until this decade, West African linguists were too few, and too much engaged with synchronic researches, to spare time to hunt out and examine the *Polyglotta*. But since 1963 when it was reprinted, more than a dozen studies of Polyglotta vocabularies of individual languages and groups of languages, by the most distinguished and active African linguists, have appeared in the *Sierra Leone Language Review*, now the *African Language Review*, and at least as many more are due to appear. I, for one, am fascinated by the way in which the studies are becoming more detailed, more elaborate, and more enthusiastic about the evidence of language development to be deduced from the *Polyglotta*. (In parenthesis, I must commend these articles to any historian who has missed them, for though written solely by linguists, often under rather stern titles, they are full of historical comment, sometimes on more general issues: for instance, in the 1966 number, Bowdich's introduction of the English form 'Ashanti' for Asante is discussed and justified; while the legend to the effect that the East Nigerian term for 'white man', *beke*, is derived from the name of the Scottish explorer, is finally exploded.) Though the earlier vocabularies are manifestly less systematic, less detailed and less accurately transcribed than the *Polyglotta* material, the limited amount of research already done on them has shown that Harry Johnston was wrong when he wrote that 'earlier vocabularies . . . are too fragmentary to be worthy of consultation'. A few examples must again suffice. Recent work on *Wolof* of the sixteenth and seventeenth centuries has produced evidence of word-shortening by syllable-loss in modern Wolof—a phenomenon which I am told has been suspected or detected in other West African languages. In the field of the history of orthographies, I have suggested that the use of the two Roman letters *gb* to represent the un-European sound of a labio-velar plosive may have its earliest instance in the Kquoja vocabulary printed in 1668. A third finding relates to the current debate on language classification: in our *Kra* paper, we have suggested, though very tentatively, that initial vowels on nouns in the sixteenth century Kra vocabulary which do not occur in corresponding modern forms, may have been vestiges of a nominal prefix system in the Kru languages. Similarly, our early Sierra Leone material provides several examples of nouns in *Temne* with what appear to be nominal suffixes. These help to confirm the suspicion that Temne has lost a system of nominal suffixes in recent times, as suggested by independent comparative evidence. This is of course a valuable clue in reconstructing the relationship of Temne with other neighbouring class-languages.

I must repeat that very much work remains to be done on the early vocabularies. Those located to date contain, all told, about twenty thousand words—two-thirds of them in the Senegal vocabularies, the remainder scattered through some forty to fifty different sources. The words are drawn from about thirty different languages, a large proportion of the total number of languages spoken along the Guinea coast today. Some of these languages are little known even today, and this is one justification for the papers cited, which must be regarded as forming merely a preliminary investigation of a small part of the field.

This investigation has, however, taught us a few lessons in procedure, which it may be helpful to pass on. Having described the sources and given some idea of what historians and linguists can make of them, I conclude this paper with a series of brief comments on the theory and practice of this line of research. These comments are intended not least as points for further discussion:

1. Early vocabularies purport to record what was said to a non-African in an African language, and the recording is in all cases more or less defective. The non-African experienced difficulty in hearing the strange language and in writing down its unusual sounds: in hearing and in writing, the recorder tended to assimilate the African language to the pattern of sounds and spelling to which he was accustomed. It helps to make allowance for these defects if the recorder's language is also studied. Thus, when investigating the Kquoja vocabulary, I sought advice on early seventeenth century Dutch pronunciation and spelling practice, and in studying vocabularies in Hakluyt and Purchas, it was useful to know something about Elizabethan English. There is much more to be done on these lines, particularly for anyone with a sound knowledge of sixteenth and seventeenth century Portuguese. The Portuguese were particularly fond of discovering Portuguese words in African utterances, so that for instance the *Temne* word *ka-bonklo*, 'bush-cat (with shining eyes)', became equated with the Portuguese *carbunclo*, 'carbuncle, precious stone'.

2. A less obvious point is that the vocabularies have become more defective as they were copied by Europeans. Almost all the sources as we now have them are copies of manuscript originals. The degree of miscopying is likely to be highest in the part of a manuscript which is gibberish to the copier. Hence, it is advisable, when working on an early vocabulary, to check the African terms in the

original manuscript—if this is available. A Mina vocabulary of 1479–80 was printed in 1897 by a French Romance philologist—who of course knew no *Akan*: I am now trying to persuade an Africanist in France to check the manuscript.[18] Again, I have noticed that the African terms in the standard printed edition of Fernandes by a Portuguese scholar do not agree in spelling with the same terms in an earlier edition by a German scholar—one of the editors (if not both) is misreading, but which is difficult to say, for though Fernandes wrote in Portuguese he was a German by birth and may have spelt African terms in the conventions of his mother tongue. Another rudimentary point—but perhaps worth making since it has escaped several historians—is that the African terms should be investigated in the form they bear in the text (whether manuscript or printed) of the language of recording. Dapper's account, for instance, containing African terms collected by Dutch traders, was translated from Dutch into German, French and English: in the two latter translations, the African terms are re-spelt by the translator, to fit, in the orthography of the language translated into, what he imagined was the Dutch pronunciation intended. This may perhaps throw some light on contemporary European pronunciations and orthographies, but only confuses the issue when it comes to investigating the African terms.

3. We cannot expect an early vocabulary to represent the living speech of the period at all exactly. The linguist who is studying language-change finds the evidence of the early vocabularies difficult to assess, since often he cannot be certain whether a difference from the modern form is due to faulty recording or to real change. Sometimes, however, the first possibility can be excluded, if the term is repeated in the same un-modern form in several early vocabularies, independently compiled of course and preferably by speakers of different European languages. Fortunately, there was a tendency for collectors at different periods to collect similar terms. This is undoubtedly an argument in favour of collating the early vocabularies and dealing with them by languages, instead of leaving them to the piecemeal attention of editors of individual texts.

4. Despite these defects of recording, in the papers cited a great many terms in early vocabularies have been compared with terms in modern African languages. To use an expression which I endeavoured to avoid earlier, we have 'identified' the early vocabularies, identified them 'as' vocabularies of particular known African languages. What exactly does this mean?

Here a slight digression is necessary. I believe that many African historians have been misled by the current enthusiastic debate about language classification into supposing that African languages are much more alike in vocabulary than they in fact are. To take an extreme case, a historian in a recent book begins his essay on a West African territory in the nineteenth century with the triumphant observation that all the languages spoken in this territory belong to the 'Niger–Congo' family: he clearly thinks that this revelation strikes a blow for national unity. One might as well, of course, argue for the historical appropriateness of the British Raj on the grounds that Hindi and English are fellow Indo-European languages (and in fact much more closely related than many West African languages). It is, contrariwise, highly relevant to the political and economic analysis of modern Africa that not only does intense linguistic fragmentation still exist but that, in West Africa at least, the languages shown in patchwork on the language map are, with few exceptions, mutually unintelligible. (The quality of published writing on, for instance, contemporary Nigeria, might be distinctly raised if it were compulsory to head each chapter with the observation that a nation–state was being built on a foundation of around 150 mutually unintelligible languages.)

5. I am drawing on a recent article in *African Language Studies* when I point out, that even in the more closely-related language groupings of Africa, it may ultimately be as important to find explanations for the large proportion of vocabulary in each language not common to other members of the group as to find explanations for the normally much smaller proportion of common roots.[19]

6. A related point is that current discussion about common roots gives rise to the misconception—which I have found among students at least—that the *Bantu* languages are over a wide area mutually intelligible. Granted that this is not so, to what extent can any degree of regular understanding be achieved between speakers of different, even near-neighbouring, Bantu languages? I have never lived in Bantu Africa, but some historical works on the area, by their failure to discuss problems of communication, have given me the impression that their authors assume that even a little in any one Bantu language goes a long way in Southern Africa. Is this really so? If it is, then this is another respect in which West Africa and Southern Africa are vastly different, since in the former it is difficult to think of any language which is intelligible to monolingual speakers of neighbouring languages, for any distance outside the homeland (communication being by bilingualism, not by mutual intelligibility). The travels of Livingstone are, for me, still a puzzle on the linguistic side. Reading Professor Omer-Cooper's recent book on *The Zulu Aftermath*, I have been reminded that, for a time at least, Livingstone was catching up with dispersed *Sotho* and *Nguni* speakers, which presumably helped a traveller who himself spoke *Tswana*: but further afield, did the fact that his travels were carried out solely among Bantu speakers, make his problems of

communication any easier than those, for instance, of an explorer on the Niger? And I should like to ask another question relating to language diversity in Southern Africa: around 1500, according to Portuguese sources, a *Kongo*-speaking interpreter claimed to have gained detailed information when put ashore in Pondoland: was he telling the truth or had he perhaps communicated only in signs?

7. But to return to West Africa. There, once we have ascended above the level of alleged 'Niger–Congo' relationships, with their consequent enormous time-depths, we are confronted with a wide diversity of languages, as reflected in the numerous language groupings which have been proposed for this area. Even within these groupings, there is normally very considerable diversity of vocabulary—sometimes sufficient for the unity of an individual grouping to be still in doubt. The so-called 'Kwa languages', for instance, appear to have very little common vocabulary throughout the group. What all this amounts to is that West African languages tend to be lexically discrete to an extent which makes it reasonable to ascribe a vocabulary—even a relatively short one, and even one subject to the defects in recording noted earlier—to a particular language and to none other. Of course, in general, the longer the vocabulary, the more certain the ascription. In one paper, Dr. Dalby and I attempt to find the language of a single word—and I think we very nearly succeed—but we don't intend to make a habit of this extremely hazardous proceeding!

8. So far I have simplified the problem by leaving out the time element. In practice, we compare an old vocabulary with a modern language. It is certain that the living speech of an earlier century was not the same as the living speech of today: even if, therefore, our early vocabulary was accurately transcribed, we would not expect the words to be exactly the same as the words in the modern language. As it happens, our early Guinea coast vocabularies are never more than five centuries old and more often are only four, three or two; we would not expect a great deal of linguistic change in this relatively short period, and it is in fact clear from the work already done that much of the identified vocabulary has changed little. (Delafosse, whose vocabularies were rather older, also thought that there had been little change.) Nevertheless, it is misleading to simplify, as I have done, by saying that an early vocabulary has been 'identified as Vai', since the term Vai refers to the language known today (although the linguists might agree to extend 'today' to cover the period since 1850 during which Vai has been studied). Strictly, when I claim to 'identify a vocabulary as . . .', I mean that the terms in the vocabulary bear a closer phonological resemblance to the corresponding terms in a particular modern language than they do to corresponding terms in any other known language; and that

such differences as appear are reasonably explicable either in terms of language change over the relevant period or in terms of poor recording. Not having discovered a brief way of saying this, I fall back on 'identify as': but I do suggest that, in written work, it would heighten awareness of the problem if language names employed in historical discussion were given a century indicator, thus distinguishing Vai.19 from Vai.17. I could then say that by comparison with Vai.19, the vocabulary appears to be Vai.17.

9. To obtain modern terms for comparison with an early vocabulary, we can employ (*a*) an informant, (*b*) a dictionary. Instinctively, perhaps, the historian reaches for written documentation, the linguist for a living source. Ideally, no doubt, one should use both, but in practice we have found that often one or the other is not available, and this has helped us to appreciate the limitations of each. I need not elaborate on the fact that for some languages there are no dictionaries or even reliable word-lists. For many other languages, the dictionaries are clearly very inadequate, and one's first thought is that any informant would have much higher lexical resources. Nevertheless, when, as not infrequently happens, an informant asserts that a dictionary term is wrong or does not exist, I reserve judgement. One reason for this is that the informant speaks a mid-twentieth century language, while the dictionary is often of much older vintage. (Again of course the informant may employ one dialect, the dictionary another.) I would certainly suggest that in working with early vocabularies, all other early material in the language should be consulted for comparison, and probably this should be done before one's judgement is prejudiced by the modern language of an informant.

10. It has further become clear in the course of our research that a special kind of informant is called for, one who is much more than an unconscious but tappable store-house of lexical and grammatical items. Usually we begin work on an early vocabulary with little idea of the pronunciation of the terms. If the meaning is also vague (e.g. 'a tree with a bushy top and yellow fruit smelling like medlars, the bark used as a purgative'), we cannot feed in to the informant either an immediately recognizable phonological sequence in his own language, or a precise meaning in English. Instead, we have to try out on him a variety of possible pronunciations until he recognizes a meaningful one: with an unimaginative informant, this has to be done very methodically—including if necessary tone-variants—and the procedure can be very wearing for all parties concerned. What is therefore needed is an informant who has imagination and some interest in what is being attempted. We can give him guidance on possible errors of recording, and then leave him to run over in his mind all the phonological and semantic possibilities which approxi-

mate to the written term. To the unreflecting speaker of any language there are of course no phonological resemblances—a word is a word is a word—and we need therefore an intelligent and preferably highly educated informant. It follows that the ideal student of early vocabularies is the linguistically trained native speaker, who can be investigator and informant combined.

11. My last point is about the presentation of 'identifications'. If I identify an early vocabulary by using a nineteenth century dictionary, I have identified it in terms of the nineteenth century language, not of the present-day living speech. This is a perfectly legitimate procedure, provided that I make it absolutely clear on the printed page what I have done—that is, with what source of information I have compared the early vocabulary. The standard rule of history applies: references must be given for each piece of evidence, in this case, for each word cited. If a dictionary has been used, its name and date should be stated and the terms found in it fully quoted. Similarly, if an informant has been used, particulars about him which will throw light on his form of speech, such as home-district and clan-affiliation, his education and occupation, etc., should be stated. In this way, it becomes possible for the next worker, perhaps a linguist who is delving more deeply into the language, to assess the value of our identifications, to test them, to correct, modify or elaborate on our results. May I go on to suggest that the same rule applies in a wider context. Writing on matters other than early vocabularies, some African historians are inclined to offer footnote explanations of African terms they mention in their texts, without supplying any indication of how they acquired this knowledge. My suspicion that they asked a man at the club, or their cook, may be unfair: perhaps they do possess a scholarly knowledge of the language in question—but if so, they should state this somewhere. And, if not, they should provide a reference, to a written work or to an informant, for *each word* explained. Here again, I think we African historians owe it to the devoted labours of several generations of African linguists to take African languages absolutely seriously—to make full and obvious use of the resources of scholarship—and to treat African language material as we would treat language material in all other closely-studied tongues of the world.

NOTES

1. This paper was read to the Seminar in January 1967, opening the series. Although the notes have been up-dated, the text is substantially as delivered, and does not therefore take account of reprints and re-editions appearing since the earlier date.
2. M. Delafosse, 'Mots soudanais du moyen âge', *Mémoires de la Société Linguistique de Paris*, 18, 1914, 281–8.
3. R. Basset, 'Notes sur la langue de la Guinée au XVe siècle', *Boletim da segunda classe, Academia das Sciencias de Lisboa*, 5, 1911, 417–22; cf. P. E. H. Hair, 'A note on de la Fosse's "Mina" vocabulary of 1479–80', *Journal of West African Languages*, 3, 1966

55–7, and David DALBY and P. E. H. HAIR, 'A further note on the Mina vocabulary of 1479–80', *ibid.*, 5, 2, 1968, 129–33.

4. For instance, in the *Oxford dictionary of English etymology* (1966), *zebra* 'of Congolese origin', *chimpanzee* 'native name in Angola', *dash* 'native word of Guinea'; and, in the *Oxford English dictionary*, *cola* 'Negro language of West Africa'.

5. C. PROTTEN, *En nyttig Grammaticalsk Indledelse til tvende hidindtil gandske ubekiendte Sprog, Fanteisk og Acraisk*, Kiöbenhavn, 1764 (to be republished by Frank Cass, with a new introduction by M. E. KROPP); *Doctrina Christiana . . . en nuestra idioma Español, y en la lengua Arda*, Madrid, 1658, reprinted in H. LABOURET and P. RIVET, *Le royaume d'Arda et son évangélisation au XVIIe siécle*, Paris, 1929.

6. D'AVEZAC, 'Vocabulaires guiolof, mandingue, foule, saracole, séraire, bagnon et floupe receuillis à la Côte d'Afrique pour le service de l'ancienne Compagnie royale du Sénégal . . .', *Mémoires de la Société Ethnologique*, 2, 1845, 207–67.

7. G. C. A. OLDENDORP, *Geschichte der Mission der Evangelischen Brüder auf den Caraibischen Inseln . . .*, Barby, 1777; cf. P. E. H. HAIR, 'The languages of Western Africa c. 1770: a note and a query', *Bulletin of the Society for African Church History*, 1, 1, 1963, 17–20.

8. This Akan material has in fact already received a preliminary examination in I. WILKS, 'An early Twi word-list: a lexico-statistical analysis', a paper read at the Third Conference on African History and Archaeology, at the School of Oriental and African Studies, London, 1961.

9. Since this paper was presented, I have learnt that new editions of these Portuguese works, comprehensively edited with regard to the African language material, are being prepared by the Agrupamento de Estudos de Cartografia Antiga of Lisbon, and should begin to appear in 1970 (personal communication from Dr. A. Teixeira da Mota, one of the editors). A new edition of Bosman has already appeared.

10. P. E. H. HAIR, 'Collections of vocabularies of Western Africa before the Polyglotta: a key', *Journal of African Languages*, 5, 1966, 208–17.

11. David DALBY and P. E. H. HAIR, ' "Le langaige de Guynee": a sixteenth century vocabulary from the Pepper Coast', *African Language Studies*, 5, 1964, 174–91. The same source included an early Amerindian vocabulary, studied in David DALBY and P. E. H. HAIR, ' "Le langaige du Bresil": a Tupi vocabulary of the 1540s', *Transactions of the Philological Society*, 1966, 44–66: the latter study provides a significant parallel with that of the African language.

12. E. G. R. TAYLOR, *The troublesome voyage of Captain Edward Fenton 1582–3*, 1957, 178 ff.; the entire manuscript is now being re-edited by Dr. Elizabeth Story Donno of Columbia University.

13. More disturbingly, in P. CARSON, *Materials for West African history in French archives*, 1967, the de la Fosse material at Valenciennes (see note 3) and the Senegal vocabularies in the Bibliothèque Nationale (see note 6) are not noted.

14. David DALBY and P. E. H. HAIR, 'A West African word of 1456', *Journal of West African Languages*, 4, 1967, 13–14.

15. P. E. H. HAIR, 'An early seventeenth century vocabulary of Vai', *African Studies*, 23, 1964, 129–39.

16. The relevant section has been published in W. RODNEY, 'A reconsideration of the Mane invasions of Sierra Leone', *Journal of African History*, VIII, 1967, 219–46.

17. P. E. H. HAIR, 'Ethnolinguistic continuity on the Guinea coast', *Journal of African History*, VIII, 1967, 247–68; P. E. H. HAIR, 'An ethnolinguistic inventory of the Upper Guinea coast before 1700', *African Language Review*, 6, 1967, 32–70; P. E. H. HAIR, 'An ethnolinguistic inventory of the Lower Guinea coast before 1700', *African Language Review*, (Part I) 7, 1968, 47–73; (Part II) 8, 1969, in press.

18. Cf. the article by DALBY and HAIR cited in note 3.

19. David DALBY, 'Levels of relationship in the comparative study of African languages', *African Language Studies*, 7, 1966, 171–9, on p. 174. It may be questioned for example, whether there is much African history to be deduced from study of the comparative 'Bantu-ness' of the Bantu languages until their comparative 'non-Bantu-ness' has also been studied.

The Contribution of Linguistics to History in the Field of Berber Studies

J. BYNON

I. Aims

In the following attempt to outline the actual and potential contribution of Berber linguistic studies to historical research I have treated this latter term as including what is perhaps more properly the domain of the prehistorian, whereas I have expressly excluded from under the heading 'linguistic' the oral traditions and literary productions of the language as well as its practical employment by researchers in the field, although these obviously have a rôle to play in the historical investigation of the regions concerned.

Attention was drawn at an early meeting of this Seminar to one of the dangers inherent in operations of an interdisciplinary nature, namely the habit, sometimes indulged in, of 'worming one's way along the No-man's-land which separates two disciplines, thus escaping the full weight of fire from either side'. The only means of avoiding this criticism, I think, is to make it explicitly clear at every point in the argument from which of the two disciplines one is drawing one's data and methods. In the present paper it was decided to employ as a framework the actual subdivisions of the methodological approach adopted, after describing this in outline. If the linguistic material is approached in this way from the point of view of the methodology we may hope to exclude a number of what profess to be historical 'conclusions' based upon linguistic evidence which are, in fact, no more than plausible historical 'explanations' of the linguistic phenomena.

II. Methodological approach

No valid conclusions can be drawn from data unless they are obtained by the application of a systematic methodology which has been explicitly stated, adequately tested, and rigorously applied. The methodological approach adopted in the present outline is contained in the so-called Comparative Method which was developed and proven in the field of Indo-European studies.[1] The available linguistic material in the Berber and Hamito–Semitic fields does not, in my opinion, differ in any fundamental respect from that of the Indo-European, the documents are comparable and in many cases superior from the points of view of quantity and age, and there is, therefore, no *a priori* reason why the same methods should not be applicable.

This certainly does not mean that the method as developed so far for the Indo-European sphere is incapable of improvement or supplementation, nor that it is necessarily equally applicable in the case of certain other language groups where historical documentation is entirely lacking. But I think that it may be safely assumed that if new methods are to be introduced to meet special cases these too will have to be explicitly stated, adequately tested against control material, and systematically applied if they are to give acceptable results.

It is not the primary concern of the Comparative Method to provide data for historians and I would suggest that much remains to be done with regard to the development and testing of an effective methodology specifically designed for this purpose. The 'historical' information obtained as one of its by-products is for the most part of a cultural or social character and developments in the relatively new field of Sociolinguistics may be expected to prove of value in the interpretation of material.

Attempts have also recently been made to develop new methods depending upon the quantitative analysis of lexical material. Although at present to some extent discredited because of exaggerated claims and inadequate testing, it is likely that the quantitative study of diachronic phenomena is with us to stay and it is a reasonable hope that it may eventually provide reliable evidence regarding the relative if not the absolute chronology of linguistic change.

It also appears probable that progress in the field of typological comparison will, by the clarification of linguistic processes at the universal level, effect the interpretation of structural, as opposed to lexical, similarities between languages.

As matters stand at present, it may be fairly stated that information of positive significance to the historian can only be obtained from linguistic material as the result of one of the following five operations:

(*a*) the establishment of genealogical relationship between languages,
(*b*) the examination of the content of the proto-lexicon of a reconstructed language,
(*c*) the study of elements borrowed by a language and of those loaned from it into other languages during the course of its history,
(*d*) the isolation of substratum phenomena in a language,
(*e*) the study of the current geographical distribution of a language and the evidence obtainable from toponymy, etc. as to its former extension.

By far the most significant of these operations from the view point of the historian is the establishment of genealogical relationship. The diversification of a parent language to the point that it results in the development of discrete new languages implies a loss of contact which is normally the result of a physical expansion due to the political, economic or military success of its speakers. At the same time, previous to the introduction of modern media of mass communication, the taking over of a region by a new language can hardly be explained otherwise than as the result of peaceful colonization or military conquest. The historian will therefore be particularly interested in the establishment of genealogical relationships between languages, and this demands historical reconstruction. For, although superficial comparison of an unsystematic nature may make kinship extremely probable and show in what areas systematic comparison is most likely to be profitable, it is only by the process of reconstruction that genealogical relationship can be established beyond all doubt. It should be given absolute priority in the present methodology not only because of the importance of the direct historical implications of genealogical relationship but because all the other operations are dependent upon its having been previously carried out.

An immediate result of reconstruction is the establishment of a proto-lexicon of starred forms for the parent language. Provided that arguments *ex silentio* are avoided, the study of this can provide positive information regarding the culture of the speakers of the proto-language, their economic and social organization, etc. Attempts at obtaining an indication of their place of origin (*Urheimat*) by this method have so far met with less success.

It is also only after reconstruction has been carried out that we can identify with certainty at least many of the older loan words. The establishment of soundshifts may also permit the relative dating of entry of many of the loans. By their direction, their density, and the sectors of vocabulary occupied loans can, when studied as systems and not as individual items, give useful indications as to the extent and nature of contacts with other speech communities. It is likely that some idea will be obtained of the relative cultural or technological status of the two communities, either as a whole or at least in respect of the particular sectors where loaning is densest.

The detection of a linguistic substratum is also dependent upon the reconstruction of the parent language. If such a substratum can be related to a known language family or to a substratum identified in another region, it will provide information regarding the nature and extent of the language community which occupied the area previous to the arrival of the speakers of the proto-language. Such relicts are likely to be found in greatest quantity, if not exclusively, among toponyms.

Finally, although relatively unexploited so far, certain aspects of dialect geography can have historical implications, such as characteristic patternings indicative of retreat areas, the fringe distribution of archaisms around centres of innovation, etc.

III. Application to Berber Studies

With the above aims and choice of methodological principles in mind we will now attempt to outline what has been accomplished to date in the field of Berber studies constituting reliable data for the historian.

(A) *The genealogical relationships of Berber*

(i) *The unity of the Berber group of languages*

Berber is spoken today in a series of discrete patches, some twenty or more in number, which are scattered across the north-western third of Africa from Siwa in Egypt to the Atlantic coast of Morocco in the north, from the Senegal river to Zinder near the Nigerian border in the south.

The individual constituent languages of the group began to become known through the publication of vocabularies during the course of the eighteenth century[2] and, the degree of differentiation of the members being no greater than that of, for instance, the Semitic, Romance or Germanic languages, their relationship to one another was clearly recognized by the beginning of the nineteenth century.[3] Guanche on the other hand, although it was grouped with Berber as early as 1812 and a close connection has been more or less tacitly accepted ever since, has never in fact been satisfactorily demonstrated to be related to Berber. No comparative study of the members of the Berber group has yet been made and no reconstruction of the proto-language nor sub-grouping of its members has been carried out.[4] Although this would hardly seem necessary as a proof of the genealogical relationship of the constituent languages it will be an essential preliminary to comparison with a view to establishing relationships at a higher level, as well as for the purpose of isolating loanwords and substrata.

(ii) *The relationship of Berber to Old Libyan*[5]

Almost from the moment that observers became aware of the co-existence of Berber and of Ancient Libyan inscriptions in North Africa, it was being taken for granted that modern Berber is the direct continuation of Old Libyan. This assumption was presumably based upon observations of an historical and geographical nature, namely the absence of any oral tradition or any historical record, either from Egyptian or Classical sources, concerning any other indigenous language than Libyan being spoken in the region, or of the entry into North Africa of a people that could have been the bearers of the Berber language subsequent to the period of the Libyan inscriptions. The obvious similarities between the script of the Libyan inscriptions and the *tifinagh* alphabet still employed by the Twareg must also have favoured such an assumption.

Positive evidence of a purely linguistic nature, however, is extremely meagre and one cannot claim that even today the direct descent of the modern Berber languages from Old Libyan has been established beyond all doubt. This is probably in part due to the nature of the documents that we have at our disposal, for these, with one or two notable exceptions, are all gravestones bearing little else than personal names. But the tradition of personal names has been extinguished for Berber due to the process of islamization and very little work has so far been done on the onomastic material preserved in the historical records. However:

(*a*) Bilingual inscriptions have given a small number of certain or highly probable lexical correspondences with Berber (*GLD* = Berber *agllid*, 'king'; *W-* = Berber *u-*, 'son (of)'; *WLT* = Berber *ult-*, 'daughter (of)'; *MT* = Berber *m*(*m*)*a*(*t*), 'mother'; and perhaps *D* = Berber *d-*, 'and', etc.).

(*b*) It is likely that neither the texts already studied nor the toponymic material have yet given all of which they are potentially capable.

(*c*) At the rate at which inscriptions are continuing to be discovered the corpus upon which we have to draw, already well into the second thousand texts, will eventually be very much greater than it is today.

It is therefore not unreasonable to hope that we may one day have a satisfactory description of Old Libyan and that its relationship to Berber will be put on a solid footing. In the meantime the assumption that modern Berber is the direct continuation of Old Libyan rests more upon non-linguistic than upon linguistic evidence.

(iii) *The relationship of Berber to Hamito–Semitic*[6]

From its inception, Berber has been a 'founder-member' of the Hamito–Semitic language family. Although this has undergone contraction and expansion, internal rearrangement of its members and changes of name, a nucleus of Semitic, Ancient Egyptian and Berber, and somewhat more hesitantly the Chadic and Cushitic languages, are probably by now accepted as constituting a related group by the majority of linguists. While personally convinced of its reality, I would none-the-less resist the claim that the existence of a Hamito–Semitic language family based upon genealogical relationship has yet been objectively established beyond all doubt nor, in fact, do I think that this is likely to become a practical possibility until the proto-forms of its component languages have first been set up.

Present comparisons are based upon similarities of lexicon, grammatical morphemes, and structure. For Berber these are often impressive, but we must recognize that there is no reliable way of distinguishing between older loans, cognates, and relicts of a substratum until reconstruction has been carried out, while purely structural similarities can be explained areally or as chance typological resemblances. In the case of grammar, as for lexicon, the reconstruction of actual morphemes is the only real proof of inheritance.

(iv) *Other proposed relationships of Berber*

An attempt has recently been made to situate Berber within an *enlarged Semitic group* as the member which comes closest to Proto-Semitic.[7] The arguments employed are of a very general nature and, in any case, until the parent language has been set up the sub-grouping of its members would appear to be premature.

Almost from its discovery *Guanche*, the now extinct language of the Canary Islands, has been compared to Berber and has been repeatedly grouped with it in, or in association with, a Libyco–Berber branch of Hamito–Semitic. As in the case of Libyan, historical and geographical factors have probably weighed heavily in favour of such an idea. A small number of words are certainly closely connected with Berber (*azuquahe* = Berber *azggʷaγ*, 'red'; *aemon* = Berber *aman*, 'water'; *tamozen* = Berber *timẓin*, 'barley'; *ilfe* = Berber *ilf*, 'pig'; *irichen* = Berber *irdn*, 'wheat'; *chamato* = Berber *tamṭṭutt*, 'woman'; *oche* = Berber *udi*, 'butter'; *tazufre* = Berber *tasufra*, 'water-skin', are among the best examples) but they could perfectly well be recent loans from the mainland. Largely on the basis of such examples Wölfel[8] has attempted to establish the concept of a Megalithic language which would have been preserved as a substratum in a number of Western European and African languages, in particular in Guanche, Berber, Basque and Hausa, to a lesser extent in Ancient Egyptian, Latin, Greek, Celtic and Germanic. His total rejection of the Comparative Method in favour of a Marrist approach, however, places his conclusions outside the scope of the present survey.

Berber also occupies an important place in the theories of Mukarovsky[9] who believes it to be closely related to *Basque* and proposes the creation of two new extinct language families (*Eurafrican, *Eurosaharan) and an extinct language (*Mauritanian). *Eurafrican would have given rise to Hamito–Semitic (parent of Berber) and *Eurosaharan, this latter giving rise in turn to Basque, *Mauritanian (surviving as a substratum in Fulani) and a substratum in Sardinian, etc. Of the equations proposed between

Basque and Berber, those which concern the Basque case-suffixes and the Berber prepositions are the only ones which appear to me to be in any way suggestive. For the rest I think that an abusive use is being made of the concept of substratum. Comparisons between Berber and Basque have been made by a number of writers in the past,[10] none very convincingly.

Berber is currently being enlisted in efforts to define a *Mediterranean substratum*[11] and it is to be hoped that the Thesaurus Praeromanicus being produced by Hubschmid will give us some positive data to work with. It seems unlikely however that anything of a dramatic enough nature to warrant the attention of the historian will emerge in this sphere in the very near future.

Several attempts have been made at grouping Indo-European and Hamito–Semitic into a larger genealogical unit, termed *Nostratic* in its most recent presentation.[12] That the efforts so-far deployed in this field have failed to produce any generally acceptable results is hardly surprising in view of the fact that we have no reconstructed Hamito–Semitic forms to relate to the starred forms of Indo–European. In my view the drawing of conclusions from work in this field would at present be premature but there is no *a priori* reason why such a comparison should not be attempted in due course, nor why, apart from the difficulties that we may expect to encounter as a result of the considerable time-depths involved, a genealogical relationship should not eventually be established. It is likely, however, that the differentiation between loan, cognate and relict will prove to be extremely difficult, if not impossible, when operating at such depth.

(B) *The lexical content of proto-Berber*

The proto-lexicon of Berber has not been systematically isolated and the only observations that have been made so far in this field are of a disconnected and casual character. A few attempts have been made at examining individual items or sectors of the vocabulary, such as the name of the camel[13] or the names of metals.[14] In the sphere of crops and domestic animals interesting results might be expected. What is perhaps the most significant study under this heading is one by Marcy[15] in which he draws attention to the fact that the terms for brother and sister in Berber are, etymologically, 'son of my mother' and 'daughter of my mother' respectively and puts this forward as evidence of a matriarchal state in primitive Berber society.

(C) *Loans*

Borrowing both into and from Berber has been studied principally at the level of lexicon. As has already been remarked this has nearly always been done on a basis of superficial resemblance and very few attempts have been made at setting up regular series of correspondences. Except for the more recent loans from Arabic and the European languages, therefore, the findings are nearly always open to alternative interpretation. In the absence of reconstruction some of the possible older loans become the subject of potential dispute (Berber *mmt*, 'to die', for instance, is clearly connected with Arabic *māta*, but is it a loan or are they cognates through Hamito–Semitic? The same doubt surrounds such pairs as Berber *idammn*/Arabic *dam*, 'blood'; Berber *aman*/Arabic *mā'*, 'water', etc.).

Borrowing into Berber

(i) *from Arabic:* Loans from Arabic constitute by far the largest section of the lexical borrowings in any Berber dialect and the more recent Arabic loans at least are very easily recognized. In spite of this little has been done, perhaps because the scale of the operation has tended to frighten off workers from such a study. Yet the very quantity of the material and the excellent state of documentation of the donor language should make it attractive and ensure significant results. If, as René Basset has suggested,[16] the periods of borrowing can be isolated on phonetic and morphological grounds, information regarding the impact of Islamic culture on the native Berber culture at different periods might be obtained.

Pellat has studied the Arabic loan words in Foucauld's four-volume dictionary of the Ahaggar dialect of Twareg.[17] He has not, however, devoted much space to the significance of the semantic categories that have received the greatest number of loans.

At the grammatical level Arabic seems to have had very little impact upon Berber, even in those dialects that have been most heavily attacked lexically.

(ii) *from Latin:* Latin loans into Berber have been cited by numerous authors[18] and such pairs as the following turn up repeatedly in articles and manuals:
asnus, 'young donkey' (Lat. *asinus*); *tifirst*, 'pear-tree' (Lat. *pirus*); *anʒlus*, 'child' (Lat. *angelus*, or Gk. ἄγγελος); *afiθal*, 'guest room' (Lat. *hospitale*); *afullus*, 'chicken' (Lat. *pullus*); *igr*, 'field' (Lat. *ager*); *targa*, 'irrigation ditch' (Lat. **riga*); *ifilu*, 'thread, cord' (Lat. *filum*); *taγawsa*, 'thing' (Lat. *causa*); etc.

Since the equations have been established on a purely impressionistic basis there is, here too, a large area of disputable territory and many terms to which a Latin origin has been attributed could equally well be claimed by the exponents of a Mediterranean substratum, e.g. *alili*, 'oleander' (cf. Lat. *lilius*);[19] *balfʃ/balk^{w}ʃ*, 'mallow' (cf. Lat. *malvas/malvax*). Even such generally acclaimed Latin loans as the names of the months in the Julian calendar . . . in Chleuh, for instance, *innayr* (Lat. *januarius*), *xubrayr* (Lat. *februarius*), *maṛṣ* (Lat. *mars*), *ibrir* (Lat. *aprilis*), *mayyuh* (Lat. *maius*), *yunyu* (Lat.

junius), *yulyuz* (Lat. *julius*), *yuʃt* (Lat. *augustus*), *ʃuṭambir* (Lat. *september*), *kṭubṛ* (Lat. *october*), *nuwambir* (Lat. *november*), *dujanbir* (Lat. *december*) . . . have been claimed by one recent writer to be 'obviously borrowed from Spanish'. In spite of the extreme unlikelihood of this on distributional and historical grounds a mere confrontation of the forms (Spanish *enero*, *febrero*, *marzo*, *abril*, *mayo*, *junio*, *julio*, *agosto*, *setiembre*, *octubre*, *noviembre*, *diciembre*) without reconstruction is not sufficient in itself to allow a decision based upon purely linguistic criteria.

(iii) *from Phoenician:* The Phoenicians were present in North Africa from the foundation of Carthage around 800 B.C. until its destruction in 149 B.C., and one might therefore reasonably expect to find some trace of their former presence in Berber. A number of loans have in fact been proposed,[20] Hebrew forms being normally used for comparative purposes in the absence of Punic equivalents. The following is a selection:

agusim, 'nut' (Heb. *ĕgōzīm*); *aẓalim/tibĕslim*, 'onion' (Heb. *bĕṣālīm*); *agadir*, 'wall' (Heb. *gādēr*); *ĕlmĕd*, 'to learn' (Heb. *lāmad̲*, *yilmad̲*); *aglzim*, 'axe, adze, pickaxe' (Heb. *garzen*); *aγanim*, 'reed' (Heb. *qānīm*); *aγṛum*, 'bread' (Heb. *qĕrūm*, 'crust'); *tĕγurmit*, 'crust of dirt on a wound' (Heb. *qĕrōmīt*, 'peel, rind, shell'/*qāram*, *yiqrōm*, 'to form a crust, cover with skin'); *armun*, 'pomegranate' (Heb. *rimmōn*, cf. Ar. *rummāna*); *dffu*, 'apple' (Heb. *tappūḥ*); *ahatim*, 'olive oil, fruit of wild olive tree' (Heb. *zētīm*); etc.

However, except in those cases in which the Berber word ends in *-im* and this is interpreted as coming from a plural suffix *-īm* in Punic, some at least of these might equally well be claimed (as things stand at present) for Hamito–Semitic.

Another vestige of the Phoenician presence in North Africa has survived in the term which designates 'a written character in the Twareg script', *tafineq*, which is clearly a derivative of Latin *punica* or its equivalent in another language, as A. Basset points out. Naturally, this is no indication that the script itself had a Punic origin.

(iv) *from other sources:* Although several studies have been made of the European (in practice, Romance) loan words in Maghribi Arabic, none have been carried out for Berber. In practice, however, most European loans have entered Berber through Arabic or at any rate have been treated as if they had done so, the confusion being facilitated in the case of nouns by the resemblance between the French and Arabic definite articles. The more recent European loans are unlikely to provide the historian with information that he could not obtain more satisfactorily by other means, but some of the older ones might provide useful indications regarding trade. A case in point is the word employed throughout North Africa to designate 'green tea', *atay*, because it has entered Arabic not directly from English or Dutch but via Berber. Many of the names indicating types of imported cloth can also be traced to European originals and their systematic study might supplement the written sources.

Borrowing from Berber

(i) *into Arabic:* Words of Berber origin occur in small numbers in Maghribi Arabic. Since however the great mass of the population of North Africa is of indigenous stock and therefore originally Berber-speaking, these should more correctly be treated under the heading of relicts (see D below). There is no overall study of the subject, the information being scattered throughout dictionaries, grammars, etc. The works of Philippe Marçais, William Marçais, G. S. Colin, and the *Supplément* of Dozy contain numerous examples.[21]

(ii) *into other languages:* For the period of antiquity, Latin *birrus/burrhus*, 'cloak', may have a Berber origin.

According to the zoologists the domestic cat is of North African origin and a Berber origin for *cattus* has been suggested.[22] At any rate the Berber term *mušš̤* (cf. English *puss*), itself perhaps a loan from Ancient Egyptian (*Paʃt*, *Bastet*), may have entered Hausa (*mùzūrū*, *mussā̀*), Fulani (*mūs!*, 'call to make a cat come'), etc., although no linguistic study has been carried out to determine the direction of the borrowing.

Berber *alγʷm*, 'camel' resembles Hausa *rakumi*, Wandala *algôme*, and borrowing again seems likely.

(D) *Substratum effects*

(i) *Berber substratum in Maghribi Arabic:* If we did not have the evidence of historical documentation as to the indigenous origin of the mass of the North African population, it is doubtful whether we would ever suspect it from the small number of relict features detectable in the Arabic dialects. In the Arabic dialect of Djidjelli for instance, spoken by a population which must be as nearly pure Berber in origin as any in North Africa, Philippe Marçais counted only some 150 Berber words and less than 100 words of Arabic origin that had been Berberized in form.[23] In the speech of the towns the proportion is less, often amounting to little more than a few words for utensils, garments and foodstuffs (such as the name of the national dish, couscous) and one or two traces in the grammar which could probably be just as well accounted for by the natural process of divergence. The Berber–Arabic situation in North Africa is, in fact, a perfectly typical example of the principle expressed by Windisch at the end of the last century,[24] that when a people adopts a foreign language it does not carry over into it many words from its own language but strives rather to speak it as purely as possible, whereas it is its own native language which becomes mixed under the influence of the foreign language.

If however one turns to those sectors of the vocabulary which have strong local attachments, such as that of plant names, the proportion becomes more important and it is finally in the domain of toponymy that we find the true Berber substratum everywhere underlying the Arabic and of course quite unsuspected by the modern speakers.

The study of toponyms has so far been undertaken only sporadically for North Africa, usually with reference to individual names, and it really only begins to give significant results when carried out exhaustively for entire districts. It would be wrong to suggest however that nothing has been done,[25] and the mapping of the entire area by the French has put an immense quantity of data at the disposal of the would-be investigator. A study of place-names in the Arabic speaking areas might give valuable information regarding the dialects of Berber previously spoken there. So far, to the best of my knowledge, the question has only been briefly touched upon for Mauretania.[26]

(ii) *pre-Berber substrata in North Africa:* Until starred Proto-Berber and Hamito–Semitic forms have been set up a pre-Berber substratum is unlikely to be identifiable. At any rate it is only in the field of toponymy that such a substratum is likely to be detectable.

(iii) *other substrata involving Berber:* Wölfel's 'Megalithic', Mukarovsky's 'Mauritanien', and Hubschmid's 'Mediterranean' substrata have already been mentioned. In addition to the above, traces of a substratum involving Berber are sometimes claimed for the Celtic of Ireland.[27] Although there is again no *a priori* historical reason why the Neolithic population which spread up the Atlantic sea-board from the Mediterranean region should not have been speakers of some pre-Libyan or related language, the linguistic evidence so far presented appears to be very flimsy.

(E) *Dialect Geography and Toponymy*

The breaking up of the Berber language area into over a score of discrete islands embedded in an Arabic-speaking continuum can be most economically explained by the assumption that it is the Arabic-speaking area which has expanded at the expense of the Berber-speaking one (the opposite hypothesis would require the unlikely assumption of multiple points of implantation for Berber). If we add to this the nature of the terrains occupied (open plains and lines of communication for Arabic, mountainous and desert retreat areas for Berber) it is obvious that, even if we lacked the evidence of historical record, we could predict that it must have been Berber which preceded Arabic in the area and not the other way round (cf. the present distribution of Celtic). In view of our other sources of information, this is, of course, of merely methodological interest.

The present distribution pattern of Berber also suggests that, immediately prior to the arrival of the Arabs, the whole of North Africa was peopled by Berber speakers. This conclusion would have to be confirmed of course by the evidence of toponymy. It does not follow, however, that the direct ancestor of Berber necessarily occupied the same area to the exclusion of possible other more or less closely related languages or even entirely unrelated ones. Thus, even if the ancestor of modern Berber were demonstrated to be Libyan (as recorded in Numidian inscriptions) its pre-Arabic distribution might have been the result of an extension at the expense of other languages. Conversely, Numidian may not have been in the direct line of ancestry of Berber but have been a cognate language eliminated by an expanding proto-Berber population. Problems such as these may hope to receive an answer when more is known of the relationship of Libyan to Berber and more has been done in the field of North African toponymy.

IV. Conclusions

It is clear that Berber studies have reached a point where little further progress can be made in the diachronic field until systematic reconstruction of the proto-language has been carried out (this was already being urged by Cust[28] in 1883 as a pressing necessity!). A somewhat similar situation would appear to exist in the wider field of Hamito–Semitic studies.

Until this has been done, with the possible exception of studies restricted to more recent events, it seems unlikely that the evidence produced by purely linguistic means will be of a reliable enough character to be of much real assistance to the historian.

On the other hand, there is probably a large amount of potential information, especially for the earlier periods, preserved in the linguistic material which the historian could not obtain by any other means.

BIBLIOGRAPHY

1. On the comparative method consult, for instance:
A. Meillet, *La méthode comparative en linguistique historique*, Oslo, 1925 (Engl. trans. *The Comparative Method in Historical Linguistics*, Paris, 1967).
K. L. Pike, *Axioms and Procedures for Reconstructions in Comparative Linguistics: An Experimental Syllabus*, Santa Ana, 1957.
H. Hoenigswald, *Language Change and Linguistic Reconstruction*, Chicago, 1960.
P. Thieme, 'The Comparative Method for Reconstruction in Linguistics', *in* D. Hymes, (ed.) *Language in Culture and Society*, New York, 1964.

2. Jezreel Jones, 'Dissertatio de Lingua Shilhensi', *in* Chamberlayne, *Oratio dominica in diversas omnium fere gentium linguas versa*, Amsterdam, 1715, 150–6.
Thomas Shaw, *Travels into several parts of Barbary and the Levant*, Oxford, 1738.
George Höst, *Efterretninger om Marókos og Fes*, Kiöbenhavn, 1779.
De Chenier, *Recherches historiques sur les Maures*, Paris, 1787.

3. L. Hervas, *Catalogo delle lingue conosciute*, Madrid, 1784.
W. Marsden, 'Observations sur la langue de Syouah', *in* F. Hornemann, *Voyage dans l'Afrique septentrionale*, Paris, 1803, II, 405–11.
J. Adelung and J. Vater, *Mithridates*, III, Berlin, 1812.

4. The only attempts at synthesis are:
R. Basset, *Etudes sur les dialectes berbères*, Paris, 1894.
A. Basset, *La langue berbère: morphologie: le verbe*, Paris, 1929.
——, *La langue berbère*, Oxford, 1952.
L. Galand, article 'Berbères' (V—Langue), *Encyclopédie de l'Islam*, 2nd ed. (the best overall description).

5. On Libyan see:
J. Chabot, *Recueil des inscriptions libyques*, Paris, 1940.
J. Fevrier, 'Que savons-nous du libyque?', *Revue Africaine*, C, 1956, 263–73.
O. Rössler, 'Die Sprache Numidiens', *Sybaris, Festschrift Hans Krahe*, Wiesbaden, 1958.

6. See bibliographies in:
M. Cohen, *Essai comparatif sur le vocabulaire et la phonétique du Chamito-Sémitique*, Paris, 1947.
S. Moscati, etc., *An introduction to the comparative grammar of the Semitic languages*, Wiesbaden, 1964.

7. O. Rössler, 'Libysch—Hamitisch—Semitisch', *Oriens*, 1964, 17, 199–216.

8. D. Wölfel, *Monumenta Linguae Canariae*, Graz, 1965.

9. H. Mukarovsky, *Die Grundlagen des Ful und das Mauretanische*, Vienna, 1963.
——, 'Baskisch und Berberisch', *Wiener Z.f.d. Kunde d. Morgenlandes*, 59/60, 1963/4.
——, 'Les rapports du basque et du berbère', *GLECS*, mai 1966.

10. From among many can be mentioned:
G. Gabelentz, *Die Verwandtschaft des Baskischen mit den Berbersprachen Nordafrikas*, Brunswick, 1894.
H. Schuchardt, 'Baskisch-Hamitische Wortvergleichungen', *Revue Internationale des Etudes Basques*, 7, Paris, 1913.
E. Zyhlarz, 'Zur angeblichen Verwandtschaft des Baskischen mit afrikanischen Sprachen', *Zeitschrift für Prähistorie*, Vienna, 1932, 69–77.

11. J. Hubschmid, *Sardische Studien: das mediterrane Substrat des Sardischen, seine Beziehungen zum Berberischen und Baskischen sowie zum eurafrikanischen und hispanokaukasischen Substrat der romanischen Sprachen*, Bern, 1953.
——, *Mediterrane Substrate, mit besonderer Berücksichtigung des Baskischen und der west-östlichen Sprachbeziehungen*, Bern, 1960.
G. Serra, 'Appunti su l'elemento punico e libico nell' onomastica sarda', *Vox Romanica* 13, 1963, 51–65.
——, 'L'action du substrat libyque sur la structure des mots de la langue sarde', *Orbis* 9, 1960, 404–18.
D. Wölfel, *Eurafrikanische Wortschichten als Kulturschichten*, Salamanca, 1955.
R. Ricard, 'Latin "olea", touareg et portugais "aleo". Hypothèses et rapprochements', *Bull. hispanique* 63, 1961, 179–85.
A. Tabachovitz, 'Vivre-coeur. Etude d'étymologie comparative', *Vox Romanica* 18, 1959, 49–93.
——, 'Homme-femme. Seconde étude d'étymologie et de morphologie comparatives', *Vox Romanica* 19, 1960, 341–85.

12. H. Möller, *Vergleichendes indogermanisches semitisches Wörterbuch*, 1911.
A. Cuny, *Etudes prégrammaticales sur le domaine des langues indo-européennes et chamito-sémitiques*, Paris, 1924.
——, 'Contribution à la phonétique comparée de l'indo-européen et du chamito-sémitique', *Bull. Soc. Ling.* 32, 1931, 29–53.
——, *Recherches sur le vocalisme, le consonantisme et la formation des racines en 'nostratique', ancêtre de l'indo-européen et du chamito-sémitique*, Paris, 1943.
——, *Invitation à l'étude comparative des langues indo-européennes et des langues chamito-sémitiques*, Bordeaux, 1946.

13. R. Basset, 'Le nom du chameau chez les Berbères', *Actes du 14ème Congrès International des Orientalistes*, II, Paris, 1906.

14. R. Basset, 'Les noms de métaux et de couleur en berbère', *Mem. Soc. Ling. Paris*, 9, 1895, 58–92.
A. Cuny, 'Linguistique et préhistoire, noms de métaux en chamito-sémitique et en indo-européen', *Scritti in onore di Alfredo Trombetti*, Milan, 1936.

15. G. Marcy, 'Les survivances juridiques de la parenté maternelle dans la coutume du Maroc Central', *Actes du 9ème Congrès de l'institut des Hautes Etudes Marocaines*, Rabat, 1937, p. 33.
——, 'Les vestiges de la parenté maternelle en droit coutumier berbère et le régime des successions touarègues', *Revue Africaine*, 1941, pp. 187–211.

16. R. Basset, 'Les mots arabes passés en Berbère', *Orientalische Studien Theodor Nöldeke . . . gewidmet*, Gieszen, 1906, 439–43.

17. Ch. Pellat, 'Les emprunts arabes dans le parler ahaggar', *Etudes d'orientalisme dédiées à la mémoire de Lévi-Provençal*, Paris, 1962, 239–59.

18. Among the more important are:
H. Schuchardt, 'Die romanischen Lehnwörter im Berberischen', *Kais. Akademie der Wissenschaften in Wien*, phil.-hist. Klasse, Sitzungsb. 188, 4, 1918.
G. S. Colin, 'Etymologies maġribines', *Hespéris*, 1926, 55–82 and 1927, 85–102.

19. M. Cohen, 'Quelques mots périméditerranéens', *Bull. Soc. Ling.* 31, 37–41.

20. H. Stumme, 'Gedanken über libysch-phönizische Anklänge', *Zeitschrift für Assyriologie* 27, 1912, 121–8.
H. Basset, 'Les influences puniques chez les Berbères', *Revue Africaine*, 62, 1921, 340–74.
W. Green, 'Augustine's use of Punic', *Univ. of California Public. in Semitic and Oriental Studies: a volume presented to William Popper*, University of California Press, Berkeley and Los Angeles, 1951, 179–90.
W. Vycichl, 'Punischer Spracheinfluss im Berberischen', *Journal of Near Eastern Studies*, 11, 1952, 198–204.

21. W. Marçais and A. Guîga, *Textes arabes de Takroûna II, Glossaire*, Paris, 1959.
R. Dozy, *Supplément aux dictionnaires arabes*, 2nd ed., Paris, 1927.

22. F. Zeuner, *A History of Domesticated Animals*, London, 1963, p. 390.

23. Philippe Marçais, *Le parler arabe de Djidjelli*, Paris, n.d.; esp. 608–11.

24. E. Windisch, 'Zur Theorie der Mischsprachen und Lehnwörter', *Verh. d. sächsischen Gesellsch. d. Wissensch.*, 49, 107.

25. L. Galand, 'Afrique du Nord', *Revue internationale d'onomastique*, Paris, 1954, 72–9; 1958, 221–31; 1960, 293–308; 1965, 127–45.
L. Galand and E. Meeussen, 'Afrique—Africa', *Onoma*, Louvain, 1953, 231–3; 1954, 261–3; 1955–56, 281–2; 1956–57, 119–20; 1958–59, 192–6; 1960–61, 231–5; 1962–63, 167–70.

26. Vincent Monteil, 'La part du Berbère dans la toponymie du Sahara maure', *Proceed. 3rd Int. Congr. Topon. and Anthropon. Brux. 1949*, Louvain, 1951, 478–9.
Gustave Mercier, 'La langue libyenne et la toponymie antique de l'Afrique du Nord', *Journal Asiatique*, 105, 1924; 189–320.

27. J. Pokorny, 'Origin of the Celts', *Nature*, 132, 1933, 648.
J. Byrne, *General principles of the structure of language*, London, 1885.
J. Morris Jones, 'The pre-Aryan syntax in insular Celtic': Appendix B of J. Rhys and D. Brynmor Jones, *The Welsh People*, London, 1900.
J. Pokorny, 'Das nicht-indogermanische Substrat im Irischen', *Zeitschrift f. Celt. Philologie*, 16, 1926, 95–144, 231–66, 363–94; 17, 1928, 373–88; 18, 1929, 233–48.
A. Mourant and I. Morgan Watkin, 'Blood Groups, Anthropology and Language in Wales and the Western Countries', *Heredity*, 6, 1952, 13–36.
H. Wagner, *Das Verbum in den Sprachen der Britischen Inseln*, Tübingen, 1959.

28. R. Cust, *A Sketch of the Modern Languages of Africa*, London, 1883; Chap. 9, p. 104.

Contribution from the Study of Loanwords to the Cultural History of Africa

JAN KNAPPERT

THE term *loanword* is not a satisfactory one. Obviously a word that people have 'borrowed' cannot be returned after use. The German *Fremdwort* (lit. 'alien word') seems more appropriate since our first task will be to note the foreign quality of certain words in the languages we are studying. But for how long may such a word be regarded as foreign? Are the English words *chair* and *school* still to be regarded as Greek words? If not, at what date in history did they become English words? These two words do not *sound* foreign to the English speaker but many other borrowed words do, such as *cocoa, banana, pawpaw*. These words denote products that will not grow in the British Isles and therefore do not form part of the original Anglo-Saxon culture and language. But there is another criterion by which we can recognize these words as of foreign origin —their shape. In English the reduplication of syllables has a foreign ring about it and this unusual morphophonemic form is the symptom of an overseas origin. In nine cases out of ten, the exceptional shape of a word gives it away as a *Fremdwort*. In African languages it is often an unusual tone pattern that leads the searcher for loanwords on the right track: in Alur, for example, one of the Nilotic languages, a final High–Low tone pattern is exceptional, and the great majority of words with that pattern are borrowed from Swahili. Yet, for a more profound study, especially of the older and therefore more interesting loanwords, the criterion of structure is too narrow because the oldest loanwords are no longer recognizable from their form (as we have seen from the first two English examples).

A second method for the detection of loanwords is the following. If we suspect that a given word in *Language A* is of foreign origin (on the grounds either of its shape or of its meaning), we can look for a similar word with a similar meaning in *Language B* (spoken in a territory adjacent to that of *Language A*). If we find it, then we can look for it in *Language C* (a neighbour of *B*, although already some distance away from *A*). If the word *is* a loan, then there is a good chance that we shall find it not only in *Language C* but in *D*, *E* and possibly in a whole chain of languages across part of the African continent. We shall see how the word may gradually change in shape and sometimes also in meaning, and these changes must always be accounted for. In this way we shall see that not just one word but whole clusters of words—belonging to some well definable provinces of meaning—travel a long way over the surface of the continent of Africa, gradually changing in form. It is for such words that I would propose the term *travel-word.* Once a word has left its homeland—because the speakers of a neighbouring language found it a useful term—it may start on a journey of a thousand miles or more, not without damage both to its shape and meaning and often to the extent that it becomes unrecognizable. For instance, if someone were tempted to compare the Rwanda word *zuzi* with Kikuyu *njanji* (of the same meaning), he might be surprised to find that their origin is ultimately the Latin word *iudex* (a judge), one word having been introduced via the East Coast from English and the other word via the West Coast from French. The Lingala word *yema* (tent) and the Hausa word *alaima* (tent) are both from Arabic *khayma* (tent), the Hausa word having preserved the Arabic article *al-*. The Lingala word arrived in Congo via Swahili, travelling up-country from the East Coast; the Hausa word was carried across the Sahara, possibly via Twareg. Hence my term *travel-word.*

An example of a more sophisticated change in shape is the following. The Luba word for 'box' or 'chest' is *mushete.* Its meaning aroused my suspicion from the start, but I was unable to pin down its origin. When I found it in Kimbundu as well, I was certain it must be a loanword and that its origin must be Portuguese. The Portuguese word for this article is *caixete* and this would become something like **kashete* in a Bantu language. But the Bantu speakers seem to have rejected this form of the word since the first syllable *ka-* has the shape of the prefix of class 12, which denotes only small things; for big things and for things made of wood, the *mu-* prefix is used and has therefore been substituted. Cf. Shona *mufarinya* (cassava) from Portuguese *farinha.*

The following may be cited as examples of changes of meanings in loanwords: The Swahili word for 'lamp' (*taa*) has come to mean 'brass' in some of the languages of Eastern Congo (probably because lamps were the only things of brass the upcountry people ever saw). Similarly the Swahili word for 'thread' (*uzi*) has become the word for 'cotton' in Eastern Congo languages. It is interesting to note in this connection that the English word 'silk' is derived from Arabic *silka* (thread). The Luganda word *eppeesà* (button) is derived from Swahili *pesa* (coin, money) via Hindustani from Portuguese *pesa.* The ultimate origin of the word is again Latin, i.e. *pensa* (weight) from *pendere* (to hang). That the word has travelled to East Africa via India is confirmed by its shape: if it had come direct from Portuguese, it would have been pronounced with *z* instead of *s*—compare Swahili *meza* (table) via Portuguese *mesa* from Latin *mensa.* In Hindustani, this type of *z* coalesces with the *s*-phoneme. The Swahili word *unga* (flour) comes to mean 'gunpowder' in Tswa,

Lala and some other East African languages because, having a word for 'flour' in their own languages, these peoples adopted the Swahili word for 'flour' or 'powder' in the special sense of 'gunpowder', possibly for euphemistic reasons. It shows that the peoples of the Northern half of Moçambique learned the art of shooting with guns from the Swahili and so learned it probably before the Portuguese arrived. This is confirmed by other words in the same cultural context, such as *muzinga* (gun). Both words have penetrated into Shona.

A third method of identifying loanwords is to make classified lists of words within certain categories of meaning—such as tools, clothes, fruits, spices, weapons, furniture, parts of the house, metals, cereals—and to study these words in all the languages of a given area. Loanwords will be found in these categories in almost all African languages.

Two interesting historical conclusions can be drawn from a collection of loanwords, provided one has assembled a large number of them in a variety of languages spoken over a wide area. The first conclusion is about the route and the direction which a word or a group of words has followed. Normally it will be found that such words have travelled inland from the coasts of Africa, up-river along the Nile, the Congo, the Zambezi and the Senegal, and finally from the riverbanks into the interior. In parts of West Africa, however, we find that loanwords (mostly Arabic) have penetrated as far as the coast from the northern inland regions. As we have seen, the shapes and the meanings of these words may change *en route*, but something else changes as well—their quantity—and this factor is highly indicative not only of the direction in which a group of words has travelled, but also of the extent to which the speakers of that language have become accessible to the influence of foreign culture, and of the identity of the culture which brought them these particular articles. I shall return to this point below.

Another important guide for establishing the route of a group of loanwords is their phonetic form. On purely linguistic grounds we can determine the direction of loaning, if we know the phonemic systems of the languages concerned. We can thus indicate the *giver*-language and the *receiver*-language and observe how a group of words with meanings which describe a particular aspect of life (e.g. horse-riding or the money-economy) have been adopted *en bloc* from one *giver*-language. In Bantu Africa the principal giver-languages are all spoken along the coast: Nguni (Zulu–Xhosa), Swahili, Kongo and Kimbundu (Ngola). Trade languages such as Hausa, migrant-labour languages such as Nyanja, and administrative languages such as Lingala and Luganda also function as giver-languages in the area where they are employed outside their home territory. All the languages mentioned have acted in fact as mediators, their speakers having handed on European and Oriental culture to other Africans. Thus the Arabic word *fitila* (lamp) was brought to Yorubaland by Hausa traders, and Oriental words in the languages of East and Central Africa show by their shapes that they have come via Swahili. Many Afrikaans words in Shona have come in via Zulu. European words in Northern Central Africa have been brought by the Arabs, e.g. the French word *vapeur* (steamboat) became in Arabic *bâbûr* and this form has travelled up the Nile as far as the Zande language in N.E. Congo.

The second and perhaps the most important result of historical interest that we gain from a comprehensive study of loanwords in a large portion of Africa (for example Africa south of the equator) is that, if one maps the extreme extent of loanwords, one can show with fair precision the sphere of influence of the giver-languages. In this way we discover four main spheres of cultural influence in precolonial (that is pre-mid-nineteenth-century) Africa. Indian words extend from the East, brought by Swahili traders; in West–Central Congo, they meet the Portuguese words that travelled inwards from the West Coast. Afrikaans–Dutch words lead north from the Cape and stop at the Zambezi. But by far the largest cultural area of Africa is shown by long lists of loans from Arabic, extending in the West as far as Dakar and Sierra Leone and in the East as far as Madagascar.

We may safely assume that words did not travel without the objects they denoted. The Portuguese word *mesa* (table) is found over most of Central and East Africa as far north-east as Somali (*miis*). Some peoples preferred to create a word of their own, e.g. Herero in South West Africa has for 'table' *otyiriro* (a thing to eat from or at), side by side with *otyitafela* from Afrikaans *tafel*. But if the word is there in the language we can be sure that the object has arrived in the country, so that the lexicon of the language still gives us exact information on the stage of acculturation of its users.

How can we demonstrate that a word is a loanword? Similarity, close resemblance between two words in two otherwise unrelated languages, is not in itself a proof for borrowing. For instance, in Amharic and in Hindi the word for 'to be' is *hona*. A word of that meaning, however, is rarely borrowed and we can therefore exclude it from our list. In Swahili all words which contain one of the six phonemes *dh*, *gh*, *kh*, *q*, *th* and ʾ are borrowed from Arabic, these phonemes having themselves been adopted from Arabic. Words with two non-homorganic consecutive consonants (*m-* excepted) are foreign in most Bantu languages. For example, the Swahili *mstari* (a line on paper) is from Arabic *mistâr*; the Arabic *mi-* prefix derives nouns from verbs, but for Swahili speakers it creates the impression of being a class 4 plural prefix which was subsequently replaced by a class 3 singular prefix. I suspect that this is the origin of the Shona word *mutsara* (a line).

A further argument for the foreign origin of a word is its occurrence in unrelated neighbouring languages (note the plural). For example, the word *somo* (to read) in both Alur and Luo—two closely related Nilotic languages—might tempt the investigator to enter it in his list of proto-Nilotic starred forms. However, its presence in most other East-African languages, such as Luganda, Kikuyu, Sukuma and Masai, marks it out as a loanword from Swahili.

Obviously a loanword must retain a resemblance to its equivalent in the giver-language, or—if it does not—rules must be established to explain why it was altered, such as the reluctance of speakers to pronounce certain phonetic combinations, or their preference for monosyllabic words. The Luganda word *èm̀mûndú* (rifle) looks like a loan from Swahili *bunduki*, itself a loan from Turkish via Arabic. (The ultimate origin of this word is the Greek *pontikòn* (hazelnut), referring to the shape of a musket bullet.) The Luganda form of the word can be explained by Meinhof's 'law', which states that the first of two consecutive voiced pre-nasalized plosive consonants must become a nasal. The loss of the last syllable is also found in Luo *bunde*, the Nilotic languages preferring words of one or two syllables.

In spite of all our efforts to trace probable loanwords to their potential originals in the giver-languages, there is a large number of words the origin of which will remain undecided, or at least unproven. The Wolof word *frastu* (bottle) resembles sufficiently the Portuguese *frasco* to be acceptable as a loanword from that language. The Wolof *sondel* (candle) is close enough to French *chandelle* to be listed as a French loan. But can we equate Wolof *munas* (perfume) with Arabic *marash*? Is Wolof *gelem* (camel) from Arabic *gamal*? This last equation seems attractive but we still have to show that metathesis is a rule or at least a common phenomenon in Wolof. Similarly in Wolof *fas* (horse) and Arabic *faras* there are too many resembling features to discard borrowing, and too few to accept it. The Portuguese *manihoco*—one of the forms of the Brazilian (Tupi) word for cassava—must be the origin of the Swahili *mahogo*, but what happened to the syllable *ni*? In this case there can be little doubt about the question of borrowing, for extra-linguistic reasons, and we are left with the realization that loanwords may suffer a great deal on their long journeys from language to language.

The source of a loanword is sometimes obscured when the word is reanalysed in terms of a different morphological system. For instance, although the Tsonga word *xitimela* looks acceptable enough as a Bantu word, with a class 7 prefix and what looks like an extension *-ela*, yet it is a loan from English 'steamer' via Zulu. English and Afrikaans words with initial *s + consonant* are invariably remorphologized and assigned to the seventh class in Zulu, e.g. *isitolo* (from 'store'), *isipunu* (from 'spoon'), *isipinashi* (from 'spinach'), *isipanji* (from 'sponge'). When travelling northwards into other Bantu languages, these words retained their allegiance to the seventh noun class, and changed the prefix according to the prevailing sound-laws, so that the Shona word for 'store' became *chitoro*, which looks completely Bantu to the uninitiated, and is no longer recognizable as an English word. One may cite also the Swahili *vilabuni* (in the night-bars)—derived from English 'club'—which has been Bantuized to *kilabu*, plural *vilabu* and locative *vilabuni*, the last looking like an indigenous form.

The Luganda word *òbùsuùlu* (tax, ground-rent) has been wrongly connected with the Luganda verb *òkùsolooza* (to gather tribute, levy taxes) but, in reality, it is a loan from Swahili *ushuru* which is in turn from Arabic *ᶜushr* (tithe, tax), connected with Arabic *ᶜashara* (ten). It would be tempting to link the Afrikaans *kraal* (cattle kraal) with Luganda *èkìraàlo* (cattle kraal), whereas in fact the latter is connected with a pure Bantu verb *òkùlaàla* (to settle down)—note the conformity in tone pattern—while the Afrikaans word is from Portuguese *corral* (place to run about in), from the verb *correr* (to run). In the case of the word for tax the suggested Luganda derivation of the word was unsatisfactory, so that the word must be called a loan, whereas in the latter instance the Luganda derivation is the more likely one.

As with nouns, morphological problems arise also with borrowed verbs. For example in Arabic, we find *finishnâ* (we have finished) from *finisht*—from English 'finished'—which looks like a first person singular form of the perfect tense. Arabic *jiyb* (jeep) forms its plural inevitably as *juyūb*; *täksī* becomes *takâsî* (taxis), quite regularly, once one accepts the word as native Arabic. Parsons gives *sukurūderēbobi* as the plural of Hausa *sukurūderēba* (screwdriver). In Swahili I found *wamishe* (missionaries), plural of *mmishe* which is formed by prefixing from *mishe* (mission station), which is in turn formed from *misheni* (mission) by removal of what looks to the Swahili like a locative suffix *-ni*.

It will now be clear why loanwords must always be studied in groups *and* in groups of languages together. It is necessary to record all the intervening links in order to show why a particular word has adopted the form and meaning represented in the receiver-languages at the end of the chain.

These three criteria then—the shape of a word (its morphophonemic form), its meaning, and the extent of its distribution, i.e. the extent to which similar forms are found in neighbouring languages—help us to determine whether a particular word is a loanword. Two of these criteria are linguistic, one is geographical, *none* is cultural. We omit any cultural criterion because we wish to avoid the logical snare of first categorizing a word as a loanword because it denotes an object foreign to the 'pure' native culture and then later use this loanword to prove that the native culture did not have the object. In some cases 'neighbouring' may seem a rather loosely used term, as when a wide stretch of forest, a desert, a lake, or a mountain range separates two language areas. We may have to accept this until we have dictionaries of any intervening languages; in some cases these may be spoken by hill tribes or nomads who never participated in the exchange of culture that went on between the more powerful peoples. On the other hand, what may seem a barrier to us may not in reality have been one. Lake Tanganyika did not stop Swahili culture from spreading into Katanga, and the Sahara was crossed by several trade routes.

Sometimes it is obvious that a word under consideration is borrowed from a European language, most frequently English, French, Portuguese or Dutch (in order of frequency), but it is not always clear from which language. There are, however, linguistic criteria for ascertaining the origin, e.g. Malagasy *bénitra* (bayonet) and *bizimofo* (bismuth) must be from English and not from French because of the phonetic forms of the words in Malagasy. This is clear in spite of the fact that Abinal and Malzac rubricize these words as 'du français' in their dictionary.

In Luganda the word for 'blue' is *bbululû*, which looks like English, but which cannot have been borrowed directly because it has one syllable too many. The Swahili word is *buluu* which *is* directly from English; where Swahili has a double vowel, Luganda has the custom of inserting an extra *l*, cf. *kyoloòni* from Swahili *chooni* (latrine) and *èttaala* (lamp) from Swahili *taa.*

In the case of the English loans in Malagasy, these can be explained by two factors. In the first place a small group of English technicians, including an army officer, were in attendance at the court of the Hova king in the first half of the nineteenth century (see Hubert Deschamp's *Histoire de Madagascar*, Paris, 1960, p. 161). Secondly, a small group of English Protestant missionaries preceded the French Catholic missionaries on the island. It would be interesting in this connection to investigate the relationship between the occurrence of early European loanwords and the arrival of the first missionaries.

In Bemba, words like *ibotolo* (bottle) and *ibuuku* (book) could, for example, have been borrowed from either English or Afrikaans. However, as it appears that most European loans (not counting those from Portuguese) in Bemba are directly from English—as is indicated by their phonetic form—one is led to accept the English origin of these two words as well. The word for 'store' in Bemba, for instance, is *shitoolo* (not in class 7), so that the word did not travel all the way north through the other Bantu languages but was brought in direct from English.

Often the form of the loanword is so corrupted that only meticulous study will detect it as such. The Malagasy word for 'oil' is *diloilo*, which can only be understood if one remembers French *de l'huile.* Similarly we find *dipilò* (shot for a shotgun) from French *du plomb, dipoávatra* (pepper) from *du poivre, dité* (tea) from *du thé* and *diváy* (wine) from *du vin.* This latter word finally solves an old problem: what is the origin of the Swahili word *divai* (wine)? The answer is that it has not come in the long way from the Belgian Congo, where Europeans drink more beer than wine, but by dhow from Madagascar.

The Malagasy word *aràfana* (palmwine) puzzled me for some time. It looks like a passive verbal noun and could well be native from the morphophonological point of view. But it also looks deceptively like the Arabic *ᶜaraq*, Swahili *araki*, Malay *arak* (palmwine, gin)—yet how to account for the *f*! Finally I found Malagasy passive forms like *doafàna* (what has been beaten) from a basic form *doàka* (to beat). It follows that one can regard the Malagasy *aràfana* as a derivate from the presumed loanword **àraka* not now recorded in the language in that form.

We have seen that the largest part of Africa falls within the Arabic sphere of influence, the centre of which is Mecca. In the course of history three secondary centres have developed, no less important for our African studies, viz. Morocco, Egypt and South Arabia. From these, further tertiary foci of radiation of Arabic scholarship were created, such as Timbuktu, Kano, Khartoum and Mombasa. In contrast with the specifically technical influence exercised by some European languages, Arabic influence has gradually spread through all aspects of native culture. It aims at encompassing ultimately the total life of the community as well as that of the individual. On the outer fringes of this circle of radiation of Arabic influence, there live the peoples who have adopted only a few cultural objects with their names, such as 'money', 'gold', 'cotton'. They have received these items through the traders—who belong usually to particular tribes—chiefly the Swahili, the Hausa and the Manding, as well as the Arabs themselves.

The peoples who have had a more intensive contact with the Arabs have adopted a large number of loanwords, mostly in semantic clusters as—for instance—names for different types of cloth, the parts of a rifle, the objects connected with saddlery and words belonging to book culture, etc.

Finally, there are the peoples who live in the inner sphere of Arabic influence, and who have been largely converted to Islam. The best known examples are the Hausa, the Fula, the Manding, the Swahili and the Somali. With Islam, a flood of Arabic words comes into the language. A complete revolution has taken place and now there is only one step left to total assimilation—the adoption of the Arabic language, as we see it progressing in the Sudan and elsewhere.

In many ways the Arabs did not create the culture they brought to Africa. They merely handed on what they had previously acquired from other peoples, mainly the peoples of antiquity. That is why we find today in African languages words of such diverse origin as the words for pen, money, army and shirt from *Latin*; for philosophy, paper, diamond and list from *Greek*; for lead, temple, poor man and sulphur from *Babylonian*; for offering, angel, praise and prayer from *Syriac*; for soap, sugar, banana and musk from *Sanskrit*. Most of the words they brought are genuinely Arabic, however, such as grape (*zabīb*), copper (*sufūr*), cotton (*katan*), ink (*dawāt*), kettle (*ibrīq*) and gold (*dhahab*).

The second important area of foreign influence in Africa that is still discernible today is the Portuguese sphere which once extended along the entire coast from Cabo Verde in the west, via Cabo da Boa Esperança in the south, as far as Cabo Guardafogo in the east. The commonest Portuguese loanwords one finds are *mesa* (table) from Latin *mensa*; *sapata* (shoe) from Persian via Turkish and Italian; *chumbo* (lead) from Latin *plumbum*; *igreja* (church) from Greek *ekklesia* (this word now means 'prison' in Swahili); *ouro* (gold) from Latin *aurum*; *prata* (silver); *chapeu* (hat) from French, which travelled inland as far as Buganda (*èssèppeèwo*); and *carreta* (cart), which penetrated as far as Bembaland (*iceleeta*).

Perhaps the most valuable contribution of the Portuguese to the cultures of Africa was the importation of American fruits and other foods such as cassava, guava, pineapple (*ananas*), pawpaw (*papaia*), maize (*milhos*), chilli and cashew nuts.

Fruits were brought to Africa by the Indians too, mainly to East Africa. There is the mango (*embe*) and the custard-apple (*sitafeli*). The Indians brought cereals as well (white rice and wheat) and everything which appertains to curry, like pepper, chutney, pickles, etc. The Indians brought administrative terms (government, clerk), terms of trade (insurance, invoice), terms for travelling (carriage, litter), for betel chewing and all that is connected with its rites.

The Dutch occupied the Gold Coast in 1637 and South Africa in 1652 (in which year they abandoned Madagascar). In this island they left only the word for a musket (*basi* or *busi*), and in the Gold Coast the words for verandah (*stoep*), cloth (*doek/duku*) and a few others. The main impact of the Dutch language was felt of course in Southern Africa. A language like Shona, for example, contains several dozen Dutch words, most of which have been carried north through other Bantu languages. These comprise terms for the farm (donkey, ewe); household terms (pail, yarn and button); and words for clothes (trousers, shirt, handkerchief).

The two European languages which now have by far the most powerful influence on African languages—English and French—did not achieve their full impact before the nineteenth century was well under way, and the process of borrowing from these languages has been accelerated during the present century.

What we learn from such a study of loanwords can assist us considerably in the reconstruction of cultural history:

I. We can assess the level of civilization of a people before it came into contact with the giver-language culture. This assessment can, it is true, never be absolute, but it will always permit us to draw a fair overall picture of the 'native' culture of the people concerned.

For instance, the Swahili prefer to use the Arabic word for God *Ilahi* or *Allahu*. There is a word of Bantu origin—*Mungu*—which has been used exclusively by Christian missionaries, who naturally did not feel inclined to use an Islamic term. Mohammedans would point out, however, that *mungu* has a plural *miungu* (gods, i.e. idols). A plural of Allah is absolutely inconceivable and this may explain the preference of the Swahili Islamic writers for this word.

Another example is the Bantu word for 'boat, canoe' (**bwato*), not found in Swahili. The commonest boat on the Swahili coast is the *ngalawa*, the outrigger canoe, which is ideally suited for navigation on the Indian Ocean. The river canoe was discarded, together with its name. By this method of historical interpretation we can explain why a language has adopted a foreign word even though a native word was originally available.

II. The total body of loanwords in a language yields a fair picture of the material and cultural acquisitions of its speakers since they settled in that part of Africa, or became in any other way accessible to trade and the exchange of ideas. The linguist can usually establish the route which words have taken through Africa and also the relative age of loanwords, which often arrive in waves.

A few examples taken from Shona may help to illustrate the type of culture–historical evidence that we can draw from our collection of loanwords. Shona is particularly fortunate in that it is situated in Central Africa, literally on the crossroads of cultural influence. In Shona we find about 120 Afrikaans loanwords that have trickled in from the south, many of them evidently via Zulu. They denote in the first place articles of *clothing*, e.g. *bachi* (jacket), *bande* (belt), *burúku* (trousers), *chipereti* (pin), *nariti* (needle), *roko* (skirt), *makorosibandi* and *makurubandi* (braces), *fasikoto* (apron), *hembe* (shirt), *jasi* (coat), *kamu* (comb) and *konopera* (to button). The word *gumbeze* (blanket) is French *couverts* via Afrikaans. There are also words for *household articles* and *farming tools*, such as saw, hammer, sieve, kettle, knife, bolt, nail, scissors, spoon, rake, hoe; *textiles*, such as cloth, duster, cotton wool; *foodstuffs*, such as bread, salt, potato (*dapura*), tomato; *animals*, such as donkey, turkey, goose (*hanzi*); and *parts of the house*, such as brick, window. The words for window (*fasitera*), pan (*pani*) and mug (*bikiri*) are originally loans from Latin via Dutch and Afrikaans.

There are several hundred Shona words borrowed from English, and the number from this source is continually increasing as a result of the present sociolinguistic situation in Rhodesia.

There are sixty Portuguese words in Shona which refer to *smoking* (*fodya*, tobacco; *kasha*, snuff box; *fofo*, matches, ultimately from Greek *phosphoros*); *household goods* (candle, bottle); *metals* (*rata*, sheet-tin; *kobiri*, copper; *chumbu*, lead); and *dress* (*chapewa*, hat, itself a loan from French; *tsapato*, shoe, from Persian via Turkish and Italian; *samburera*, umbrella, via Afrikaans; *borusa*, pocket, from Greek via Latin). The word for rubber (*mupira*) is a loan via Swahili from Portuguese and, ultimately, from Latin *pila* (ball), which gave rise to Dutch *pil* (pill), diminutive *pilletje*, arriving in Shona in the form *piritsi* (pill)—so that the same Latin word has resulted in two Shona words of very different meanings, along different routes, many centuries after Latin became extinct.

Most interesting of all are the loanwords of Oriental and Swahili origin, including thirty from Arabic and ten from Hindi (which have all apparently entered via Swahili), and five from Swahili itself (incl. *ndege*, aeroplane, lit. 'big bird', *mupunga*, rice, and *muzinga*, cannon). The Arabs brought several words from Classical languages: *hanzu* (shirt, ultimately from Latin *camisa*), *ndarama* (gold, ultimately from Greek *drachma*) and *ngarava* (boat, ultimately from Greek *karabos*). Hindi gave hemp, chilli, rice. lemon and cloth (*pesa*): cloth is used for payment in many parts of Africa, esp. for bride-purchase, hence the change in the meaning of *pesa* from an original sense of 'money'.

III. Many of the examples cited in this paper have been loanwords of ultimate *non-African* origin, since more extensive documentation is available for these. The principles and techniques which have been illustrated by these loanwords are of equal validity, however, for the investigation of indigenous *inter-African* loanwords. This is a field in which a great deal of further research is still required, but from which it will ultimately be possible to reconstruct much of the detailed cultural history of Africa.

Africa and the Arab Geographers

JOHN WANSBROUGH

THOUGH some are of greater value than others, most medieval Arabic writers on Africa reveal certain basic weaknesses which may be ascribed, in my opinion, to two causes: the use by many of the same (limited) sources of information, and the shortcomings of Arabic orthography, especially for rendering non-Arabic words.

The first of these causes can be fully appreciated only by reference to the canons obtaining generally in Arabic literature for acknowledgement of sources and, as such, involves an examination of the Arabic concept of plagiarism, which need not be undertaken here.[1] Suffice to say that in Arabic literary theory plagiarism is treated as a rhetorical figure and, including many degrees of permissiveness in acknowledgement of authorities, is in no respect comparable to medieval European or modern notions of plagiarism. The consequence for our purpose is merely that it is not always possible to determine whether additional information in a text was derived from an independent source, or simply from the imaginative elaboration by one writer of material contained in the work of a predecessor.

The second cause, equally complex, requires some comment. The Arabic alphabet, closely associated with elaboration of the literary ('classical') language, is not really adequate even to the reproduction of Arabic words and especially of their inconstant spoken ('colloquial') forms. I refer to such general phenomena as vowel and consonant harmony, vowels in pause and in open syllables, and phonetic confusion between stress, quantity and gemination. Another problem is provoked by variant values across the entire range of dialectal Arabic for a single consonantal sign in the written language, with considerable overlapping of plosive and fricative, voice and voicelessness, as well as unpredictable fluctuation for such phenomena as velarization and palatalization. Problems arising out of phonological assimilation between languages and simple miscopying, as well as out of ignorance of the pace of linguistic change, are described by Dr. P. E. H. Hair in his contribution to this volume.[2] Each of these points must be taken into consideration in the examination of Arabic writing on Africa where the material in question is dialectal Arabic or lexica derived from an African language. It is important to bear in mind that Classical Arabic is not a valid standard of reference for such forms, or at least of no more value than is, say,

Biblical Hebrew in the attempt to isolate a Punic substratum in Maltese.

Occasionally the problem is more straightforward. Owing to the employment in literary Arabic of diacritical points in order to distinguish different sounds having otherwise identical signs, and to the carelessness of scribes in the use of these points, very elementary questions of decipherment arise. For example, the forms *merāq*, *muzāq*, *mezāta*, *merāta*, *merāqiya*, *buzāqiya*, etc. appear in the works of Arabic writers dealing with the Muslim conquest of North Africa. Because these forms, divested of diacritical points, are easily confused in Arabic script (مراٯىه), there has been some question as to whether this toponym was meant to indicate Marmarica (eastern Cyrenaica) or Byzacium (southern Tunisia).[3] Another example of this kind of problem is the identification of East African (?) *yūfī/nūfī* with Nupe, based upon two passages in Ibn Baṭṭūṭa's account. But without other evidence the proposal is not altogether convincing, and the consonantal skeleton (ٮوڡى) might be read in a variety of ways. In the second passage, dealing ostensibly with West Africa, Ibn Baṭṭūṭa mentions Nubia, which reflects the widespread confusion in Arabic accounts between Nile, Niger, and Senegal (all called *nīl*), and the general vagueness about African topography.[4]

Briefly, one could say that the failure of Arabic writers to specify their sources of information makes hazardous almost every attempt, on the basis of their writings alone, to date phenomena like the establishment of communities, movement of peoples, or volume of trade, while the ambiguities of Arabic orthography are a cause of serious confusion in identifying toponyms and anthroponyms and even more variable elements, like the commodities of trade. But the very abundance of Arabic writing on Africa would seem to make imperative some effort to establish criteria for evaluating the material found there. For North and West Africa this task may be more important than for East Africa. Owing, however, to a combination of more or less fortuitous circumstances, this paper is concerned almost exclusively with East Africa. To this end I have selected six terms about whose meanings there has been, to say the least, a notable lack of unanimity among scholars using the Arabic sources in which they appear. The terms are these: *sāḥil*, *jubb*, *sūsīyāt*, *karāzī*, *ka'bar*, and *zanj*.

Now, while I can hardly claim to offer definitive solutions to the problems provoked by these words, I hope that in the course of the following observations some of the causes of confusion will have become clearer. From a list of more than forty Arabic writers on Africa (including not only geographers and travellers, but also merchants, chancery officials, historians, and lexicographers, and to which can be added cartographers as well as compilers of astronomical tables and nautical handbooks) I have chosen the works of twelve as *loci probantes*.[5] Though in my belief these twelve writers, whose lives span the period 278/891 to 821/1418 and whose origins range from Persia to Muslim Spain, represent fairly the bulk of Arabic geographical writing in general and on Africa in particular, it may be reasonably objected that a satisfactory investigation of any single problem must be based on examination of every available source. But much of the Arabic material on Africa is still in manuscript, not always accessible, or at best in defective and uncritical editions. Responsibility for this state of affairs lies with Arabists, whose task it is to provide historians of Africa with critical editions of the relevant texts, ideally accompanied by translations but shorn of often misleading historical speculation. Ideally, too, the historian using this material must know as much as possible about the circumstances of its production, namely, who its authors were, where they lived, the extent and duration of their travels (if any), other sources of information, their methods of evaluating these sources, and even their purpose in writing at all. These points are elementary and it is regrettable to note that they are so frequently ignored by students having recourse to Arabic source material. There is another problem here, different from but related to the foregoing. It can be argued, and I think validly, that a sound understanding of geographical and historical literature in Arabic presupposes familiarity with other genres of Arabic writing. It is, in other words, not enough to read only the sources relevant to one's particular field of inquiry. Allusions there, whether conceptual or stylistic, can more often than not be understood only by reference to writing on other subjects, especially in Islamic literature, where the rôle of context and innuendo is so significant.

Most Arabic authors share two characteristics which for our purpose are of the utmost importance. The first is a conviction that all words employed in Arabic are Arabic by origin. The second has been described as a 'horror of anonymity', which necessitated provision of an etymology or history for every word or notion in the language. The former may be ascribed to the work of lexicographers, the latter to that of scriptural exegetes.[6] While discussion of neither falls within the scope of this paper, it may be remarked that both characteristics account for the extraordinary glosses appended by Arabic geographers to anthroponyms. For example, *afāriqa* are described as descendants of one Fāriq, a great grandson of Noah, or of Ifrīqush, a son of Abraha. *Barbara* (here spelled with *tā marbūṭa*) are said to be descended from one Barbar, or from Jālūt (the latter derived probably from Jewish traditions current in North Africa). The *anbāṭ* of the western Sahara are related to one Nabīṭ, whose name is synonymous with *aswad*, not, however, with reference to pigmentation but to a vocation as agriculturist. Similar popular genealogies grafted onto eponymous dynasts are also found for *qibṭ*, *nūba*, *ḥabas͟ha*, *buja*, *zanj*, etc.[7] This manner of thinking pervades a considerable portion of Arabic historical and exegetical literature, nowhere more than in the works of writers confronted by foreign words and unfamiliar practices.

I should like now to turn to the six terms selected here to illustrate the habits of Arabic writers dealing with things African. Very little can be said about the origins of these words, but their later evolutions appear to reveal different tendencies, i.e., from generic to specific but also vice versa, from geographical to ethnical and the reverse, as well as the phonetic and graphetic vicissitudes suffered by a word transmitted at different times, or perhaps simultaneously, in both speech and writing.

I. Ar. *sāḥil* is generally held to mean 'coast', in the sense of demarcation between land and water. As such, it is a synonym of *s͟haṭṭ* (cf. Mas'ūdī, *Murūj* III 35), and its originally adjectival function (*fā'il*) is preserved in its frequent appearance in *status constructus*. Thus, Ya'qūbī, Ibn Al-Faqīh, Iṣṭak͟hrī, and Abu'l-Fīda, amongst others, when referring to a seacoast tend to use *sāḥil al-baḥr*. But of course 'seacoast' is also rendered by *sāḥil* in *status absolutus*: thus Mas'ūdī (*Murūj* III 34) describing the land of Ḥabas͟ha: *wa-lahu sāḥil fīhi mudun kat͟hīra* ('it has a coast containing many cities'). Now Yāqūt (*Buldān* III 9) observes that *sāḥil* may be a place name without necessary relation to a coast, and one need only recall the metaphorical use of Arabic words like *jazīra* and *baḥr* ('island' and 'sea', as 'enclave', 'expanse', etc.). In a verse transmitted by Hamdānī (*Ṣifa* 216) appears this image: *fa'l-sāḥil min g͟hawrihā ḍabāb 'amā'* ('the border of its lowland is dark cloud'). In his description of a military expedition from Morocco to the Sudan in the late sixteenth century Fis͟htālī (*Manāhil al-ṣafā* 55) writes of *sawāḥil al-sūdān*, and here as in Hamdānī the word appears to signify 'perimeter', in the sense of topographical or jurisdictional marker.

Worth perhaps closer examination is the definition of *sāḥil* offered by H. A. R. Gibb in his translation of Ibn Baṭṭūṭa (II 379 n. 56): 'coastal entrepot for inland commerce'. Though it might, in the east African context, have been more apposite to cite, say, Ya'qūbī (*Ta'rīk͟h* I 219) on Ḥabas͟ha: *wa-sāḥiluhum Dahlak*, or Dimas͟hqī (Cerulli, *Somalia* I 44) on Mogadishu: *wa-laha sāḥil yusammā 'l-zanjbār*, Gibb refers to the material assembled by Dozy (*Supplément* I 636–7). A reading of these passages reveals that about three-quarters of them are ambiguous, i.e., that *sāḥil* could mean either 'coast' or 'port'. The others are, however, valuable, especially those from Bekrī (*Masālik* 69, 86, 87, 88, 153; 84 is not relevant), though they refer exclusively to North Africa. Usage varies: Ibn Al-Faqīh (*Buldān* 82) mentions *sāḥil Qurṭuba* (Cordova), which could be the Guadalquivir, while Iṣṭak͟hrī (*Masālik* 35) writes of *sāḥil al-ṣīn* (China) and *sāḥil tubbat* (Tibet) without complementary predicate. Hamdānī (*Ṣifa* 47) appears to mean 'port' when he writes *sāḥil Mekka* and *sāḥil al-Medīna*, though it may be that the operative factor is the use of a predicate. With regard to East Africa the problem will very likely be solved only by recourse to other than linguistic evidence. Based on an analogy to the Portuguese period, it has been argued that the coastal ports must have been serving inland commerce, since the kind of commodities ('Zeug') brought by the East Indian trade could never have found a market in the highly developed civilization of the East African coast. But such a description of the earlier period does not fit the evidence provided by the *Periplus*.[8]

II. Ar. *jubb*, like *sāḥil*, appears more often than not in *status constructus*. Thus, in Ya'qūbī (*Buldān* 342) *jubb al-'ūsaj* and in Idrīsī (*Nuzha* 136–7, 162, 164) *jubb al-raml*, both toponyms, of which the latter at least might suggest a synonym of *wādī/nahr/baḥr* ('river'). From the point of view of the classical lexicographers (Lane, *Lexicon* s.v.) and of western Arabic sources (Dozy, *Supplément* s.v.) *jubb* is a kind of well or pit, as in Qur'ān 12: 10, 15. Yāqūt (*Buldān* II 17; and the verse IV, 801) gives the meaning 'uncased or unpaved well', but goes on to say that *jubb* is also the name of a city near the Zanj country in the land of the Berbers (spelled with *tā marbūṭa*), from which are exported giraffes, whose skins Persians use to make sandals. In 1883 M. Devic (*Le pays des Zendjs* 70) rejected this item as a reference to the Juba River. In 1914 F. Storbeck (*MSOS* 17, 117, 128), identifying *jubb* with Jumbo, clearly wished to make the connection. The matter was further clarified, or complicated, by the appearance in the late (nineteenth century) *Kitāb al-Zunūj* of the terms *al-jubb* (var. *jub*) and *arḍ al-jubb*, which its editor identified with Giuba/Juba.[9] Now, the passage from Yāqūt (*Buldān* II 17) might have attracted less attention were it not for the juxtaposition there of *jubb* and *zanj*, which appeared to make of it a *locus probans* for the assertion that the Zanj were already (or still?) on the Juba River at the beginning of the thirteenth century. Apart from the impossibility of drawing any chronological inferences whatever from Yāqūt's work (a compilation of largely unacknowledged and certainly undated sources), the equivalence *jubb* = Juba, if it is a fact in *K. al-Zunūj*, is not proved for the earlier period. Devic (op. cit. 65 n. 2) observes that the Arabs call the Juba River 'Djoûb', which in standard transcription would give *jūb*. While I can hardly insist upon the canons of the literary language for quantity and gemination, it may be worth remarking that Ar. *jūba* seems to mean 'swamp', 'depressed or cleared land', or even a 'place for collecting rainwater' (Lane, *Lexicon* s.v. *jwb*; cf. Idrisi, *Nuzha* 147, with reference to the Fayyūm, and Mas'ūdī, *Murūj* II 370). This is incidentally a fair illustration of a lexicographical problem in

Arabic characterized by a high degree of coincidence of homonym with synonym. Yāqūt's *jubb* = *zanj* may anyway be of interest only to those who accept the second equivalence Zanj = Bantu (see VI below). To what extent this interpretation of Yāqūt has contributed to making an even more obscure passage in Mas'ūdī (*Murūj* III 6) evidence for the Zanj (Bantu) settlement of the Juba in the tenth century is indeed a problem.[10] It is true that the references in Dimas͟hqī (*Nuk͟hbat al-dahr* 23, 111; trans. 22, 139) are less ambiguous and could be of some value for the fourteenth century, though the editor may have been responsible for the final geminate (*jubb*). If it took place at all, the process by which a generic term became a specific toponym will not have been ubiquitously effective, and instances of *jubb*, as of *sāḥil*, must be handled with care.

III. Ar. *sūsīyāt* (sing. *sūsī*) seems to be the name of a textile, often but not always appearing as modifier to *t͟hiyāb* (sing. *t͟hawb*, 'garment'). The relative adjective *sūsī* is a normal formation from either Sūs or Sūsa, both of which toponyms are attested for various parts of the Muslim world. The latter appears, for example, in Ifrīqiya (Tunisia: Yāqūt, *Buldān* III 190–2) and must be Roman Hadrumetum, but also in Cyrenaica (Bekrī, *Masālik* 85), probably Apollonia. Sūs has a wider range of application: in K͟huzistān (Persia: Yāqūt, *Buldān* III 188–90), in Ifrīqiya (Yāqūt, loc. cit.) at Qamūniya, traditionally identified as the site of Qairowān (Bekri, *Masālik* 75),[11] and in southwest Morocco (Yāqūt, loc. cit.). Sūs in Ifrīqiya is generally but not invariably qualified by the epithet *al-adnā* ('nearer', but cf. Hamdānī, *Ṣifa* 40–1, and gloss, II 23). Ibn Al-Faqīh writes (*Buldān* 81, 84) that *sūs al-adnā* is beyond Tangier and that beyond that lies *sūs al-aqṣā* ('further', and thus in Ya'qūbī, *Buldān* 359–60, who mentions it together with Sijilmāsa; in Bekrī, *Masālik* 86, 160–1, 168; in Ibn 'Abd al-Ḥakam, *Futūḥ Miṣr* 198; in Balād͟hurī, *Futūḥ al-buldān* 232, etc.). Mas'ūdī (*Ak͟hbār* 63) equates *sūs al-aqṣā* with Azila, which is hardly southwest Morocco, while Ibn Al-Faqīh (*Buldān* 81, 83) names as capital of *sūs al-aqṣā* the city of Ṭarqala (cf. Yāqūt, *Buldān* s.v.), adding that both *sūs al-adnā* and *sūs al-aqṣā* are 2050 miles from Qamūniya. Balād͟hurī (loc. cit.) mentions a distance of twenty days or so between the two *sūs*, while Yāqūt (loc. cit.) gives a distance of two months.

It will be clear that Sūs in Africa was something of a problem. Sūs in Persia did not come into the topographical discussions but must be, as a centre of textile manufacture, taken into consideration for *sūsīyāt*. From his Geniza sources S. D. Goitein has concluded that the place in question is Tunisian Sūsa (Roman Hadrumetum).[12] Whatever the reasons for this choice, it is of interest to note the expression *sūsī rūsī* in a Geniza document dated 1098, translated by Goitein 'Sūsi linen produced in Russia'. It seems that here a transfer from specific to generic is exhibited, *sūsī* having evolved from its original role as designation of a Tunisian stuff to one denoting a kind, quality, or even colour of cloth. There may of course be some question about the meaning here of *rūsī*, since the cloth appears to have been used especially for turbans (cf. Dozy, *Vêtements* 317 n. 8). Both Idrīsī (*Nuzha* 125) and Zuhrī (*Jughrāfiya* fol. 93b) mention *thiyāb sūsīyāt* in connection with Ifrīqiya, but this might be interpreted as reference to either Hadrumetum or Qamūniya (and cf. the reference to export of *thiyāb al-ṣūf* from Barqa, Muqaddasī, *Aḥsan al-Taqāsīm* 239). More information is wanted on centres of textile manufacture, and particularly in Morocco.[13]

IV. Ar. *karāzī* (sing. *kurzīya*), like *sūsīyāt*, appears to be the name of a fabric (Idrīsī, *Nuzha* 3, 11, 39, 58, 78) and is even described by Ibn Jubair (ed. Leiden, 1907, 98; trans. Broadhurst, London, 1952, 93) as *ṣūf baiḍā' raqīqa* ('light white wool'). While *sūsī* is commonly described as linen (*kettān*) and *kurzīya* seems to be woollen, both were employed primarily for turbans, though probably only the latter could signify exclusively 'turban'. Indeed, Dozy appears inclined to derive the Arabic word from (Moroccan) Berber *terkerzit*, which has that meaning (*Supplément* II 455; *Vêtements* 380–2). Dr. J. Bynon tells me that *takerzit* is in fact attested in Morocco, and that a speaker's consciousness of the gender morpheme *ta*, together with substitution of (fem.) *īya* for *it*, might produce a form *kerzīya*.

But the etymological problem is not thereby solved. In Ottoman Turkish we find قرزيه, in medieval Hebrew קרימ׳יא, and in Venetian *carisea*.[14] The term is in various forms widespread in the commercial records of the later medieval Mediterranean world, and appears to be the name of a woollen cloth. For its ultimate origins an English toponym has been suggested: Kersey (Suffolk), which was of course a centre of the textile industry at that time and which has given its name to the material still known as 'kersey'. *Kurzīya*, attested by both Idrīsī and Ibn Jubair in the twelfth century, is very likely derived from *carisea*, whatever might be the etymology of that word.[15]

If this proposal is acceptable, it might be of some value in solving another specifically East African problem. Ibn Baṭṭūṭa's *qudsī* has been rendered by his various translators as 'Jerusalem stuff' (Defrémery–Sanguinetti II, 186–7; Gibb II, 376–7), rejected for good reason by R. B. Serjeant (*BSOAS* XXVI, 3, 1963, 656), who proposed reading *maqdashī* ('from Mogadishu'). On both paleographical and historical grounds this emendation is acceptable but, given the graphical possibilities of Arabic and the phonological possibilities among African speakers of it, I wonder whether we have not here another manifestation of *kurzīya*?

V. Ar. *ka'bar* (*ku'bar*) is one of several designations found in the works of the Arabic geographers for the capital of Ḥabasha. The major source is Mas'ūdī (*Murūj* III 34), while in a manuscript of Ya'qūbi the form كعبى appears (*Ta'rīkh* I 219 note c), though the text ,whose editor was probably influenced by the earlier edition of Mas'ūdī, has *ka'bar*. Efforts to identify this toponym have been numerous, and the present state of knowledge is summarized by C. F. Beckingham in the *Encyclopaedia of Islam* (2nd ed., s.v. Ḥabasha), The problem of identification is complicated, perhaps unnecessarily. by the appearance in contemporary and later writings of other names for the capital(s) of Ḥabasha, e.g., *jarmā/jarmī/jarma* (Isḥāq b. al-Ḥusain, *Aḥkām al-marjān* 409; Suhrāb, *'Ajā'ib al-aqālīm* 153; Yāqūt, *Buldān* I 29) owing possibly to confusion with *jarma* (Garama) in Fezzān, though Yāqūt distinguishes between *jarmā* and *jarma* (loc. cit. and II 65, resp.). Another proposal (Idrīsī, *Nuzha* 23–5; Ibn Sa'īd in Abu'l-Fīda, *Taqwīm* 158–9; trans. II 255–7) is the name *janbayta*, which, however, is not otherwise attested and may exhibit merely an arbitrary pointing of the consonantal skeleton حبسه (*ḥabasha*?). Further, Qalqashandī (*Ṣubḥ* V 303, based on 'Umarī, *Masālik al-abṣār*; cf. trans. M. Gaudefroy-Demombynes 22–3) has a more familiar احسم (Aksum?, with variants اخشم and احسوم in 'Umarī, cf. Gaudefroy-Demombynes, loc. cit.). Now, it may be that *ka'bar* was not meant to designate *the* capital of Ḥabasha, but rather, a provincial centre, and that the term in Mas'ūdī (and perhaps in Ya'qūbī) conceals another toponym.

In his description of Wafāt/Awfāt (Ifāt) Abu'l-Fīda (*Taqwīm* 160–1; trans. II 229) observes that that place is also called *jabara*, and that it is one of the largest settlements of Ḥabasha, located some twenty days inland (west) from Zaila'. This account appears later and substantially unchanged in Maqrīzī (*Ilmām* 26) who, however, also mentions *jarmā* (*Ilmām* 25), and in Qalqashandī (*Ṣubḥ* V 325, this time based on 'Umarī, *Ta'rīf*; cf. trans. Gaudefroy-Demombynes, *Masālik al-abṣār* 37–8; as well as on Abu'l-Fīda). There, Qalqashandī adds that *jabartī* is the relative adjective (*nisba*) of *jabara* (جبرة), a contention rejected on very good grounds (manner of dissolving final consonant clusters) by E. Ullendorff (*Encyclopaedia of Islam*, 2nd ed., s.v. *Djabart*).[16] If indeed *jabara* (جبرة) is an Arabic word *jabartī* is not a likely *nisba* formation. But the spelling *jabarat/jabart* (جبرت) is also attested (Maqrīzī, *Ilmām* 6–7; and cf. DeSacy, *Chrestomathie* I 457–8), for which a *nisba jabartī* is morphologically possible. Whether *jabara/jabarat* can be identified with Ifāt or with Zaila' is admittedly something of a puzzle. But because it appears to have been the name of an important centre in the Muslim inhabited portion of Ḥabasha, I am tempted to postulate an equivalence *jabara* = *ka'bar*.

Phonological difficulties abound and may prove sufficient to reject the proposal. Well known is the relationship in Arabic of *j* to *g*, rendered in the literary language by the same sign. Possibly less familiar is the alternation *j/k* attested for Yemen.[17] Of some relevance may be ʿUmarī's rendering of Ethiopian *agazen* by *ʿajaṣin* (Gaudefroy–Demombynes, op. cit. 8 n. 2). The second radical of *kaʿbar* is a problem, especially if *jabara/jabarat* is to be derived from Ethiopian *agbert* (cf. Ullendorff, loc. cit.), but here it may be worth noting that in another work Masʿūdī (*Akhbār* 67) has not *kaʿbar*, but *kafar*. One cannot of course be certain whether Masʿūdī read the word or heard it and, perhaps, imposed his own graphical interpretation upon it. J. Marquart (*Die Beninsammlung*, Leiden 1913, 304–5) advanced an argument based upon the assumption of graphical deformation, and made of both كعبر and كلغور a form كعسون, which was clearly Aksum. But this toponym appears in other, less recalcitrant, forms in the works of the geographers, whose identification of one capital of Ḥabasha with a centre of Muslim domination would seem at least to be a practical possibility.

VI. Ar. *zanj* (*zinj*) is in Cerulli's *K. al-Zunūj* (see II above) almost certainly an ethnic designation. The problem appears to be whether this is so in the earlier geographical literature. Some passages in Masʿūdī's *Murūj al-dhahab*, e.g., those describing physical features (I 163–6) and cultural phenomena (III 6–8, 26–31), could be so interpreted if the information there is corroborated by other sources. References to *zanj* in Masʿūdī's predecessors (e.g., Ibn Khoradadhbeh, *Masālik* 61; Yaʿqūbī in both *Buldān* 366–7, and *Taʾrīkh* I 219; Ibn Al-Faqīh, *Buldān* 78; Hamdānī, *Ṣifa* 4, 6, 32, 40, 52) are less conclusive, and the question arises whether the term is not geographical or even linguistic. For these writers, as for Masʿūdī, there appears to be a connection between *zanj*, *barbarā* (spelled with *alif*), and *aḥābish*, which could be set out as follows: *barbarā* are a subdivision of *zanj*, who in turn belong to *aḥābish*. Here, as in Yāqūt (*Buldān* II 967), there are differences, but all seem to be black (*sūdān*). Two contemporaries of Masʿūdī, however, distinguish between *zanj* and *sūdān*. Both Iṣṭakhrī (*Masālik* 36) and Ibn Ḥawqal (*Ṣūrat al-Arḍ* 59) report that in one (or some) region(s) of *zanj* country the climate is cold, the culture primitive, and the inhabitants white (*fīhā zanj bīḍ*).[18] While it is unlikely that we have here reports from two independent sources, the information may be of some value: Ar. *abyaḍ* need not be 'white' but it is surely something other than *aswad*. The distinction between *barbara* and *barbarā* is, moreover, blurred (cf. Yāqūt, *Buldān* II 17, IV 602), though Masʿūdī (*Murūj* I 231) appears to have been in no doubt about the difference. In this respect an item of linguistic data adduced by Ibn Al-Faqīh (*Buldān* 78) could be relevant: the names of God are given as *lumkulūjulū* (*biʾl-zanjīya*) and *m.dhīk.sh* (*biʾl-barbarīya*), respectively, the latter curiously reminiscent of Baraghwata (Moroccan Berber) *yākūsh* (Bekrī, *Masālik* 139), a similarity which would appear to weaken somewhat the distinction *barbara–barbarā*. Mas'ūdī's linguistic information is more detailed. God is called *m.l.k.n.j.lū*, glossed as 'the great master' (*Murūj* III 30, and cf. variants *m.k.liḥ.lū* and *m.k.liḵẖū*, III 445), while the ruler appears to be *waqlīmī/ā* (*Murūj* III 6, 29; and variant *f.līmī/ā*, I 371), glossed 'son of the great master'. I am unable to comment upon the significance of these terms nor of the cultural data given by Mas'ūdī (*Murūj* I 242, 333–4; III 6–8, 26–7, 30–1) except to recall that iron is employed for making ornaments among the *zanj*, and that cattle appear to play an important rôle in their economy. Can these features be reconciled with whatever other information there is for medieval East African society?

A century and a half before the appearance of *zanj* in the writings of the earliest Arabic geographers, the term was employed by Jarīr b. 'Atīya (d. 110/728) in a verse lampooning Aḵẖṭal and the rest of B. Taḡẖlib: *lā taṭlubanna ḵẖu'ūlatan fī taḡẖlibin; fa'l-zanju akramu minhum aḵẖwālā* ('seek not your uncles among Taḡẖlib, for the Zanj are more noble uncles than they').[19] The application is clearly pejorative, but not necessarily connected with anything African.

On the eve of the great Zanj revolt in lower Iraq appear a number of references to Zanj in the works of writers like Jāḥiẓ (d. 255/869) and Mubarrad (d. 285/898) which, because of the context in which they figure (literary and linguistic, but in relation to Classical Arabic), deserve a special study and will therefore be omitted here.[20] The revolt itself was described in great detail by Ṭabarī (d. 310/922; *Ta'rīḵẖ* 3/1742–87, 1834–80, 1898–2103), in whose account there is unfortunately very little information about the origins of the Zanj, though the scattered evidence for pigmentation may be useful.[21] The first efforts at recruitment by 'Alī b. Muḥammad, called 'leader of the Zanj' (*ṣāḥib al-zanj*), were among the slaves (Ar. *ghilmān*, sing. *ghulām*, not customarily applied to black slaves) belonging to various peoples who dwelt along the banks of the lower Tigris. These slaves were probably employed in a variety of ways, but Ṭabarī (3/1742) says only that they were 'clearing the salt flats' (*kānū yaksaḥūna 'l-sibāḵẖ*). 'Alī's first major assembly was in the mosque at Nahr Maimūn, where he preached to a large congregation of blacks (*sūdān*), employing interpreters for those who could not understand him (what proportion is not stated, though it seems to have been a minority) 'owing to their foreignness' (*min 'ajamihim*, 3/1750–1). It was just afterwards that 'Alī was approached by one Abū Ṣāliḥ Mufarrij Al-Nūbī, at the head of three hundred Zanj, offering his support (3/1751–4). Whether at this point of the narrative one might equate *ghilmān–sūdān–zanj* is not clear. Most interesting, however, is the simultaneous appearance with the Zanj of a man bearing the *nisba* Al-Nūbī (Nubian). In this connection it may be observed that one of the above mentioned *ghilmān* was called Sālim Al-Zaghāwī (of Zaghāwa; 3/1758, and cf. Yāqūt, *Buldān* II 932–3). After a further reference to the expectations of the *sūdān*, who feared being returned to their masters, appears this phrase: 'he separated the Zanj from the Furātīya' (3/1756–7: *wa-mayyaza 'l-zanj min al-furātīya*; with a proposed emendation *fazzānīya, Addenda* 787). *Fazzānīya* is, indeed, an interesting possibility in the light of both Zaghāwī and the following (3/1757): 'then he assembled the rest, consisting of Furātīya/Fazzānīya and Qarmāṭīyūn and Nubians and others who could speak Arabic'. The Qarmāṭīyūn may also have been of African origin (?),[22] and both Fezzānīs and Nubians would seem to suggest a connection with Africa. Further recruits to 'Alī's cause are often designated *sūdān* (e.g., 3/1759, 1763, 1764, 1767, 1771, 1773, 1774, 1775, 1776), though there may be one instance here of a distinction between *zanj* and *sūdān* (i.e., 3/1773), possibly (?) one of designation before and after recruitment to the movement. Another indication of this difference appears in the following statement: 'It was said of one of the black commanders of the Zanj leader called Raiḥān ...' (3/1766; *dhukira 'an qā'id li-ṣāḥib il-zanj min al-sūdān yuqāl lahu raiḥān* ...). There are one or two further references to individual Zanj as black (*aswad*), e.g., 3/1744, 1861, 2092, but also on 3/1861 *sūdān* is used not for the Zanj but for the black troops of the Caliphal army (and further 3/1864, 1903, 1905–6, 1911, 1920, 1965, 1977, 1995, 2003, 2020, 2024, 2047, 2056, 2080, 2091, 2096). These troops, who must have been very numerous and of whom many deserted to the Zanj, are apparently to be distinguished from *al-muqātila 'l-bīḍān* ('white troops'; 3/1866, 2083), also part of the Caliphal army. The reference 3/2080 is, incidentally, to the ethnic composition of Lu'lu's army, recruited in Egypt and Syria (?) and responsible for the final defeat of the Zanj. It consisted of Farāghina, Atrāk, Sūdān, Barbar, and Rūm. One further passage merits attention: after a defeat in the month of Ramaḍān 267/April 881 the number of Zanj requesting safe-conducts (*amān*) reached five thousand 'including black and white' (3/1993; *min baini abyaḍ wa-aswad*).

On the basis of this scanty information covering the years 255–70/869–83 it would be hazardous to guess at the meaning of Zanj. One might tentatively propose the following: many, but by no means all, of the early recruits to the movement were black and were slaves. These, *sūdān* and *ghilmān*, upon joining 'Alī b. Muḥammad, became Zanj. As employed by Ṭabarī, this term appears to be comparable to names like Furātīya/Fazzānīya, Nūba, and Zaghāwa, and perhaps to Qarmāṭīyūn.[23]

REFERENCES

1. See G. E. von Grunebaum, 'Der Begriff des Plagiats in der arabischen Kritik', *Kritik und Dichtkunst*, Wiesbaden, 1955, 101–29.

2. See P. E. H. HAIR, 'The contribution of early linguistic material to the history of West Africa', p. 50 ff. above.

3. These forms are found in e.g., IBN 'ABD AL-ḤAKAM, *Futūḥ Miṣr* 198; YA'QŪBĪ, *Ta'rīkh* I 215; DIMASHQĪ, *Nukhbat al-Dahr* 267. Cf. H. H. 'ABD AL-WAHAB, 'Du nom arabe de la Byzacène', *Revue Tunisienne*, 1939, 199–201.

4. IBN BAṬṬŪṬA, *Tuḥfat al-Nuẓẓār* II, 192–3, IV 395–6. Cf. H. A. R. GIBB, *Voyages*, London, 1962, II 380 n. 61.

5. YA'QŪBĪ (278/991), *K. al-Buldān*, BGA VII, Leiden, 1891–92; Fr. trans. G. WIET, Cairo, 1937.
IBN AL-FAQĪH (290/903), *K. al-Buldān*, BGA V, Leiden, 1885.
HAMDĀNĪ (334/945), *Ṣifat Jazīrat al-'Arab*, ed. D. MÜLLER, Leiden, 1884–91.
IṢṬAKHRĪ (340/951), *K. Masālik al-Mamālik*, BGA I, Leiden, 1870.
MAS'ŪDĪ (345/956), *Murūj al-Dhahab*, ed./trans. BARBIER DE MEYNARD–PAVET DE COURTEILLE, Paris, 1861–77.
IBN ḤAWQAL (367/977), *K. Ṣūrat al-Arḍ*, ed. J. KRAMERS, Leiden, 1938–39; Fr. trans. KRAMERS–WIET, Paris, 1964.
BEKRĪ (487/1094), *K. al-Masālik wa'l-Mamālik*, ed./trans. M. DE SLANE, Algiers, 1911–13.
IDRĪSĪ (560/1166), *K. Nuzhat al-Mushtāq*, ed./trans. (partial) R. DOZY–M. DE GOEJE, Leiden, 1864–66; Fr. trans. A. JAUBERT, Paris, 1836–40.
YĀQŪT (627/1229), *Mu'jam al-Buldān*, ed. F. WÜSTENFELD, Leipzig, 1866–73.
ABU'L-FĪDA (732/1331), *Taqwīm al-Buldān*, ed. M. DE SLANE–M. REINAUD, Paris, 1840; Fr. trans. M. REINAUD–S. GUYARD, Paris, 1848–83.
IBN BAṬṬŪṬA (770/1369), *Tuḥfat al-Nuẓẓār* (*Riḥla*), ed./trans. C. DEFRÉMÉRY–B. SANGUINETTI, Paris, 1853–58; trans. H. A. R. GIBB, London, 1929, 1962– .
QALQASHANDĪ (821/1418), *Ṣubḥ al-A'shā*, ed. Cairo, 1914–20.

6. See L. KOPF, 'The treatment of foreign words in mediaeval Arabic lexicology', *Scripta Hierosolymitana* IX, Jerusalem, 1961, 191–205; J. WANSBROUGH, 'Arabic rhetoric and Qur'anic exegesis', *BSOAS* XXXI, 3, 1968, 469–85.

7. Such can be found in e.g., YĀQŪT, *Buldān* I 324 ff.; ṬABARĪ, *Ta'rīkh* I 212; MAS'ŪDĪ, *Akhbār* 64; IBN AL-FAQĪH, *Buldān* 79, 83; YA'QŪBĪ, *Ta'rīkh* I 215–16

8. Cf. W. SCHOFF, *Periplus of the Erythraean Sea*, London, 1912, sections 14–18, and pp. 85–99, 284–5; the argument was advanced by F. STORBECK, 'Die Berichte der arabischen Geographen des Mittelalters über Ostafrika', *MSOS* 17, 1914, 119.

9. E. CERULLI, *Somalia* I, Rome, 1957, 233, 234, 237 and *passim*.

10. Cf. e.g., G. FREEMAN-GRENVILLE, *The East African Coast*, Oxford, 1962, 15; S. TRIMINGHAM, *Islam in East Africa*, Oxford, 1964, 6–7 n. 3, 61; R. OLIVER, 'The problem of Bantu expansion', *J. Afr. Hist.*, VII, 1966, 368.

11. Cf. also variant Qūnya and other references in G. MARÇAIS, *Manuel d'art musulman*, Paris, 1926, I 2 n. 1.

12. 'The working people of the high Middle Ages', *Studies in Islamic History and Institutions*, Leiden, 1966, 266.

13. Cf. J. JOUIN, 'Les thèmes décoratifs des broderies marocaines', *Hespéris* 15, 1932 and 21, 1935.

14. E.g., B. LEWIS, *Notes and Documents from the Turkish Archives*, Jerusalem, 1952, 38–9; Marino SANUTO, *Diarii* IX 536; Archivio di Stato, Venice, Miscellanea di Atti Diplomatici e Privati, no. 1630, part 5, art. 3.

15. On the other hand, a recent study brought to my attention by Dr. V. L. Ménage would appear to confirm an eastern Turkish etymology (*qars*), without however, shedding much light on the distribution and phonological changes exhibited by the word in its Mediterranean context (see James HAMILTON and Nicoară BELDICEANU, 'Recherches autour de *Qars*, nom d'une étoffe de poil', *BSOAS* XXXI, 3, 1968, 330–46).

16. Cf. also E. ULLENDORFF, *The Semitic Languages of Ethiopia*, London, 1955, 201–7; and S. MOSCATI (ed.), *Introduction to the Comparative Grammar of the Semitic Languages*, Wiesbaden, 1964, 60–1, 64.

17. Cf. H. KOFLER, 'Reste altarab. Dialekte', *WZKM* 47, 1940, 116, 120; C. RABIN, *Ancient West-Arabian*, London, 1951, 31. The *kāf* reported here may of course represent *gāf*.

18. Correctly read by DEVIC, *Le pays des Zendjs* 121–2, who did not consider it important, and by STORBECK, *MSOS* 17, 107 and 113, who proposed Kilimanjaro; misinterpreted by FREEMAN-GRENVILLE, *East African Coast* 18, and *Medieval History of the Tanganyika Coast*, Berlin, 1962, 39.

19. *In* Ṭabarī, *Ta'rīkh* 3/362; cf. J. Fück, *'Arabīya*, Paris, 1955, 31–2 for the rôle of ethnic designations in linguistic discussions.

20. Cf. Fück, loc. cit., and C. Pellat, *Le milieu Baṣrien et la formation de Ğāḥiẓ*, Paris, 1953, esp. ch. IV, but also the references to earlier appearances of the Zanj, 41–2.

21. See Aḥmad 'Ulabī, *Thawrat al-Zanj*, Baghdad, 1961; H. Halm, *Die Traditionen über den Aufstand Ali ibn Muhammads, des 'Herrn der Zang', eine quellenkritische Untersuchung*, Bonn, 1967.

22. Cf. Halm, op. cit. 58–70, esp. 67–8.

23. For the use of *zanj* in a later West African chronicle see J. O. Hunwick, p. 102 ff. below.

The Term 'Zanj' and its Derivatives in a West African Chronicle

J. O. HUNWICK

[The following paper was presented to the Seminar as a contribution to the discussion of the term *zanj*, arising from the above paper by John Wansbrough, and has been subsequently published in the *Research Bulletin*, Centre of Arabic Documentation, University of Ibadan, Vol. 4, 1968, 41–51.]

THE root *z.n.j.* occurs in the *Ta'rīkh al-Fāttāsh* in the following forms: *zanj* (as a collective), *zanjī* (masc. sing. noun/adjective), *zanjiyya* (fem. of the latter), *zanāji* (plural?), *zanājiyyūn* (plural of plural?), *al-zanājiyya* (collective). The Arabic broken plural *zunūj* is not found. The *T. al-Fattāsh* was written by several members of a Soninke family of scholars bearing the family or clan name Kati or Koti (Ar. *K't*) over three (or perhaps four) generations. The earliest of these was Maḥmūd, a contemporary and trusted friend of Askia al-ḥājj Muḥammad who ruled the Songhay empire from 1493 to 1528; the last of them, who probably put together the work in almost its present shape, is known to us simply as Ibn al-Mukhtār and was a grandson, or great-grandson of Maḥmūd Kati through his mother. He probably died during the latter third of the seventeenth century since, although the main narrative does not go beyond 1599, there are references to dates up to 1665.

The text we now have is not, however, uncorrupted; it was evidently tampered with by one or more interested parties at some later date. Seku Aḥmadu, the Pulo reformer of Masina (d. 1844) seems to have had a special introductory chapter written for the work, partly based on material which would logically come at a later stage in the work and incorporating a 'prophecy' made by al-Suyūṭī and others that the twelfth and final 'true caliph' of Islam would be a certain Aḥmad who would appear in Masina at the beginning of the thirteenth Islamic century.[1] Copies of this chapter alone were widely circulated in the Western Sudan.[2] Only one of the three manuscripts used by Houdas and Delafosse for their edition of the text includes all of this material and it is also the only one which includes the detailed material relating to the groups designated *zanj*; the other two Mss. include only one brief and insignificant mention. It is arguable, therefore, whether these passages formed part of the original work. However, in the preamble to the work (only contained in Ms. 'C', but clearly authentic) Kati states that part of his object in writing the work is to distinguish the genealogies of the servile from the free.[3] It seems to me more probable that persons belonging to the *zanj* (and other servile groups mentioned) later rose to become more prominent in Songhay society—perhaps following the upheaval caused by the Moroccan conquest—and were able to have the offending passages excised from the Mss. which were circulating at the time, or from most of them.[4] Seku Aḥmadu, on the other hand, would have had good reason to wish that these passages be restored and even included in the new first chapter which he was causing to be circulated, as the servile castes had traditionally been part of the inherited property of the rulers of Mali and Songhay. As claimant to the headship of the Muslim community in the area he would naturally hope to claim such ancient rights for himself.[5]

Having made this rather lengthy excursus into the textual problems of the *T. al-Fattāsh* for unavoidable reasons, I will now turn to an examination of the contexts in which the term *zanj* is used. The text bristles with problems of orthography and identification and at this stage I can do little more than present the material I have gleaned with some very tentative interpretations for linguists and historians to criticize.

Firstly, it is clear that the *zanj* we are dealing with have nothing to do with the *zanj* of the East African coast mentioned by Arab geographers.[6] The *zanj* of the *T. al-Fattāsh* are a servile caste or castes living in groups along the course of the Niger 'from Kanta (probably the old kingdom of Kebbi at about the latitude of modern Say) to Sibiridugu' (the area around modern Segu).[7] They were but one of the twenty-four servile castes which the Songhay Shi, or Sunni, dynasty 'inherited' from the rulers of Mali and which were later to be 'inherited' by the Askias. Twelve of these servile castes are enumerated in the *T. al-Fattāsh* and their occupations and levies listed. Two of these, the Sorko and the Arbi are designated as personal property of the Askia '*mamlūkāni lahu*'. The Arbi (Songhay *Aru bi*, 'black man') were domestic servants and bodyguards of the Askia.

In references appearing in the first chapter of *T. al-Fattāsh* (that emended by Seku Aḥmadu) there are two main references to the Sorko among servile castes; in parallel passages in the main body of the work the word *zanj* or the phrase 'of *zanj* origin' occurs. The modern Sorko are fisherfolk and boatmen of the Niger. In one of the later references[8] we are told that these *zanj* pay an annual tribute of dried fish and provide boats and crews for the Askia. The initial case for the identification *zanj* = *Sorko* looks simple enough at first sight. But further examination reveals that the term *zanj*, and indeed the term *Sorko*, had a wider significance.

Two parallel passages concerning servile castes of a certain locality given by the Askia al-ḥājj Muḥammad to the scholar Ṣāliḥ Diawara further illuminate the use of the term *zanj* and reveal a confusion over the word *Sorko* itself. At the end of chapter one[9] these castes are listed as '*Jaddādanke* [for *Ḥaddādanke*, I believe], *Fāl.n*, *Sarai* (?), *Bankan*, *Tumbā*, *Ḥardān* and *Balli*; the origin of all these is *S.r.k.*' In the parallel passage in the main body of the work (p. 71) they are listed as '*Ḥaddānk* [for *Ḥaddādanke*] *aghamm*,[10] *Fāl.n*, *B.l. kuku* [Songhay *kuku*, 'tall'], and *K.r.k.*'; their origin is *zanj*' (*aṣluhum min al-zinjiyya*). I believe that *S.r.k.* here does not refer to the Sorko fisherfolk, but rather is to be read *Surgu*,[11] the Songhay word for the Tuareg; *B.l.* would stand for the *Bela*,[12] sedentary slaves of the Tuareg living along the banks of the Niger, *Ḥardān* for *Ḥarṭānī* (Saharan Arabic), the negro populations of the Saharan oases, and *Ḥaddādanke* for the *ineden* (blacksmiths) who live among the Tuareg. (Ar. *ḥaddād*, 'iron-worker', with a Soninke (?) generic suffix *-nke*.) The other five ethnic terms used are not immediately identifiable. It is also possible that Sorko was originally a general word applied to royally-owned servile castes and only later used to denote exclusively a particular group of them.

A further use of the term *zanj* to include blacksmiths may be cited from two parallel passages, one immediately preceding the passage on p. 32 and the other following the passage on p. 71. They refer to servile castes of a certain area given by Askia Muḥammad to the scholar Muḥammad Tuli. P. 32 lists *Diam Tin* (elsewhere *Tana*), *Diam Wali* and *Surubannā* (?). P. 71 *lists Diam Wali*, the *Surubanna* and a '*zanjī* tribe' (*qabīla zanjiyya*) which presumably corresponds to the *Diam Tin* of p. 32. *Ẓam* (*dyam* in the Timbuctoo dialect) means 'artisan, forger of iron' in Songhay; the *Surubannā* were also blacksmiths.

Askia Muḥammad also made a gift of some *zanj* (either 1,700 or 2,000 of them) to Aḥmad al-Ṣaqlī, a charismatic *sharīf* who, with his descendants, haunts the pages of the *T. al-Fattāsh* after his dramatic appearance in the year 1519. He was given *zanj* in eight different localities, several of which were Niger islands (Songhay *gungu*). One group, called *K.r.bā* are said to have a Soninke (*Wa'kore*) ancestor and were called *Tunkara* (Soninke 'belonging to royalty'). The people (or rulers?) of Wagadu (*W.k/g.d.*) in the Sahel region around the area of Old Ghana[13] evidently had their own *zanājī/zanājiyyūn/zanājiyya/zinjī* (all four terms are used in the passage on p. 119) whom Askia Al-Ḥājj captured when he attacked Wagadu in 1583. They are specifically stated to be Soninke-speaking. The name of one of these *zanj* was Mami Gaw (*M.mī G(a)ū*), suggesting, perhaps an origin from the famous Gow hunters of the Niger; in another passage reference is made to a certain Ḥamad b. Diongo Gow, a so-called *Ẓanj-Bagaber* (a term I cannot comment on).

There is other evidence of people called *zanājiyya/zanājiyyūn* originating from Soninke-speaking areas. When, in *c.* 1580 Askia Dāwūd wished to make reparation to Ibn al-Qāsim (grandson of

Aḥmad al-Ṣaqlī) for the accidental killing of his father, Muzāwir, he offered him three localities complete with their *zanāji*, totalling some six hundred souls,[14] as follows:

(1) *Kadiel* (Fula 'little rock') in Burgu (central Masina flood-plain). These had been captured by Askia Muḥammad in a raid on Galambo, a Soninke populated area around the Senegal-Falémé confluence.[15]

(2) *Kiruni Balungu* in the area of Tiabugu (*Shāb.k/g.*), between Lake Débo and Bandiagara, according to Delafosse; they were from Kusāta, a Soninke clan of the Sahel raided by Askia Muḥammad,[16] which had earlier been dispersed at the break-up of the Ghana empire.

(3) *Bunyo-Bugu* (*Bū.y. B.k/g.*, Bambara 'plantation of Bugu'); they were the remnants of the booty brought by Askia Muḥammad from the Mossi country[17] and have no apparent Soninke connections. I am tempted from this evidence to suggest that the *zanj* concept, that of personal ownership of servile castes by a ruler, was not simply a Songhay institution taken over from Mali, but that it had existed in the Soninke empire of Ghana before that and that the Mossi rulers also had a similar system either influenced by it or, perhaps, independent of it. The fact that Kati, a Soninke by origin, is the only writer to use (or coin) the term is perhaps not without significance in this argument.[18]

To further complicate matters a case of even more distant ownership is cited. The *zanj* of Tombo (? *T.n.b.*—an island between Gao and Dendi) are said to be slaves of a certain Mulay Aḥmad, a *sharīf* of Marrakush. One of the members of this group (also called 'a Sorko') gives this information in a folkloric account of the origin of the name Tindirma when it was first being established as the seat of the Kanfari (or Gurman-fari) in about 1495. Later, between 1582 and 1586 Mulay Aḥmad's son 'Alī is said to have written to reassert his rights over this *zanj*'s descendants living at Tindirma. A remote, and purely hypothetical, explanation for this distant claim could be that the '*sharīf*' was in fact of Ṣinhāja ancestry and the ownership of the *zanj* was acquired when the Almoravids overran Ghana in the late eleventh century, the *zanj* being later acquired by a Songhay ruler who settled them at Tombo. But several other conjectural solutions to the problem are equally possible.

Finally we may note that the *zanj*, like all the other twelve (or twenty-four) servile castes, are to be distinguished from slaves in the normal sense of the term, although the word '*abīd* is also applied to them. They had never at any time, according to the *T. al-Fattāsh* been free men; their innate status was servitude (*qabā 'il ariqqā' lahu lā aḥrār usturiqqū*). Unlike slaves proper they could not be manumitted or purchase manumission. They were not allowed to marry 'free' (non-serf) persons and vice-versa; a special exception was made by Askia Muḥammad for the people of Mori-Koira (Songhay 'marabout's village'). Unlike slaves, the child born of a free man and a serf woman (from an illicit union? or from concubinage?) was still a serf. The issue of an (illicit) union between a free woman and a servile man was only free if the woman took the child back to her father's compound to be reared. If it remained with the man and learned his skills it reverted to serf status. This notion of the child's status being tied to that of the mother, associated with matrilocality, is curiously reminiscent of the Tuareg.[19]

The *zanj*, in common with other servile castes, were obliged to pay regular dues to the Askia either in kind or in service. Mention has already been made of Sorko groups paying in dried fish or by the provision and crewing of boats. Part of a group of *zanj* located at *Kūm*(*a*) (not identified) paid in ivory, again suggesting a hunting group; those of *Küynu* (somewhere between Timbuctoo and Dendi[20] paid 3,000 (measures of grain?—the commodity is not mentioned) per household per year. The remaining eleven servile castes consist of five groups of blacksmiths, one of leather workers (related to one of the blacksmith groups), one of royal grooms, one of royal domestic servants and bodyguards and three of agricultural serfs of pagan Bambara origin.

The Origin of the Zanj

The *zanj* of the Songhay empire appear to encompass a number of different groups associated chiefly with riverain occupations, iron-working and hunting. It may be suggested that they represent aboriginal groups who preceded the Songhay proper in the area of the Niger buckle. Possibly the fishers and hunters are to be identified with the groups whom Rouch calls 'masters of the water' and 'masters of the soil' or with the incoming Sorko and Gow whom the same author thinks may have come from the Chad area originally. Blacksmiths in Saharan societies and those in close contact with them along the periphery always have an 'untouchable' status which is at the same time lowly and elevated as they are held in fear on account of their reputation for magic but considered outsiders of obscure origin; the *ineden* of Tuareg society claim descent from King David.[21]

The traditions of the Muslim Songhay link the Sorko and four other servile groups with the legendary giant 'Ūj b. 'Anaq, a contemporary of Noah, and a mighty hunter and ravager of crops. By a process similar to that which modern science terms A.I.D. he fathered five sets of twins on five slave-girls of Noah. The five servile groups arise from the offspring of intermarriage between these twins.[22] Sorko, the youngest of the offspring of these unions, is represented as being extremely stupid and dull-witted. He was duped by two of his brothers into giving himself up as a ransom to a ruler of the Children of Israel who came to claim all three and their descendants. Sorko and most of his children were captured in this way; the few who escaped fled to the Niger.[23] This tale clearly shows that the status of the Sorko is both different from and lower than that of the other servile groups and that they are considered a dull and ignorant folk. Recalling Rouch's theory of the Chad origins of the Sorko, it is not without interest to note that the Kotoko fisherfolk of the Shari–Logon area south of Lake Chad are themselves said by tradition to be descended from a race of giants, the So.

It is not clear how the term *zanj* (and its various derivatives) came to be used in the *T. al-Fattāsh* with the meaning of 'servile castes who are the special and personal property of the ruler', which is, perhaps, as precisely as we are able to define it. No comprehensive Songhay term is apparent, except Sorko which is sometimes used as an equivalent. The term clearly had a technical significance for Kati and it may be that a parallel term does exist in Soninke. He himself may have coined this 'Arabic' term from reading of the revolt of the *zanj* slaves who worked in the saltpetre mines in southern Mesapotamia under the early 'Abbāsid rulers: black slaves, owned by the sovereign and employed to operate a specific sector of the economy. There the similarity ends, but it may have been great enough to suggest the coinage for a writer in Arabic in need of a classificatory term.[24]

NOTES

1. See O. Houdas and M. Delafosse, Introduction to French trans. of *T. al-Fattāsh* (*T/F*), Paris, 1913–14.
2. Both the Bibliothèque Nationale and the Bibliothèque de l'Institut de France, Paris, possess some examples.
3. *T/F* 11. (All page references are to the Arabic text.)
4. Félix Dubois quotes a Timbuctoo tradition that this was actually the case. (See F. Dubois, *Tombouctou la mystèrieuse*, Paris, 1897, Engl. trans. by D. White, London, 1897, 303).
5. This seems confirmed by a letter of Seku Aḥmadu preserved in copy in the Bibliothèque de l'Institut de France (Ms. 2406, pièce no. 46 (ii)) giving permission to enslave *zanj* and basing his authority on *T/F*. Barth also tells of Seku Aḥmadu threatening to sell the Sorko into slavery: see H. Barth, *Travels and Discoveries*, Minerva ed., 1850, II, 335.
6. See John Wansbrough, 'Africa and the Arab Geographers', p. 89 ff. above.
7. *T/F* 57.
8. *T/F* 57.
9. *T/F* 32.
10. Or *aghamman*. Delafosse translates this as 'long-haired'. If the term is indeed Arabic its meaning could just possibly be stretched to mean 'matted' (of hair). According to Dr. Nicholaisen *aghamman* means 'village' in Tamacheq (personal communication).
11. The letter *kāf* commonly represents the voiced velar plosive 'g' as well as the unvoiced 'k'.
12. They are considered related to the Sorko and do not intermarry with them: see A. Prost, *La langue Soṅay*, I.F.A.N., Dakar, 1956, 525 (under the entry *Sorko*).
13. Wagadu is the Soninke name for the area of the Sahel where the empire of Ghana once flourished. Mandinka: *Bāghana*, Berber: *Awkār*.

14. *T/F* 117.
15. In *c.* 1513–14, *T/F* 76.
16. *T/F* 39 Askia Muḥammad made several raids on Bāghana.
17. Raided in 1498–99.
18. It may not, however, be far-fetched to postulate that the term *zanāji*, etc. when referring to Soninke speakers from the Sahel in fact represents *znāga* (whence the arabicization *Ṣinhāja*). In parts of the Sahel region Azer, a Soninke–Berber hybrid tongue, was used until recent times by some sedentary groups of *znāga*.
19. But see J. Nicholaisen, *Ecology and Culture of the pastoral Tuareg*, Copenhagen, 1963, 22, for a modification of this over-simplified view.
20. *T/F* 23.
21. See J. Nicholaisen, op. cit., 18.
22. They are listed as Dienke, Bobo, Kuronkoi (Songhay, 'master of leather'), Korgoi (whose father was Tombo—see my remarks on p. 105 above) and Sorko.
23. *T/F* 26–8.
24. Askia Muḥammad was uncertain of his right to the twenty-four servile castes and required Islamic authority for their possession. *T/F* reports that he asked al-Ṣuyūṭī in person and al-Maghīlī by correspondence to rule on the matter and they both gave him permission to possess only twelve of them. In the existing texts of al-Maghīlī's *Replies* to the Askia a general question on inheritance of those termed 'slaves of the sultanate' is put and al-Maghīlī gives approval to this as a *ḥubs*, unless the inherited slaves were originally seized by force. Those who have always been in this condition (like the *zanj*) could be inherited.

The Historical Problem of the Indigenous Scripts of West Africa and Surinam

DAVID DALBY

THIS Seminar has considered a variety of themes in which linguistic data can contribute to the examination of historical problems. The problem considered in the present paper reverses the traditional symbiosis of the two disciplines, however, and it is the linguist who needs to consult the historian for assistance in the examination of a palaeographic problem.

The two oldest and best documented of the West African indigenous scripts, the Vai and the Bamum, have achieved some renown in the outside world—if only as two more interesting 'novelties from Africa'. Scattered reports have been published also on other indigenous scripts from West Africa, but without any adequate consideration of their historical and cultural implications. There has been no previous realization that the total of modern indigenous scripts recorded from that area has now reached sixteen—seven of which are syllabic—and that a seventeenth script—also syllabic—has been recorded among the Djuka Bush-Negroes of Surinam (the descendants of West African slaves). Data on five indigenous scripts of Liberia and Sierra Leone, a discussion of the inspiration and design of ten of the scripts, and supplementary data on six further scripts have been published by the writer in a series of papers in *African Language Studies*.[1] It is not the purpose here to duplicate the full details of this discussion, but rather to summarize the essential data on the scripts, together with the historical questions which are raised. Fuller details and bibliographical references are included in the three papers cited.

The basic data on each of the scripts are summarized below, with the scripts grouped into geographical areas (listed according to the date of the first known script in each area). The arrow indicates the direction of writing in each case.

A. LIBERIA AND SIERRA LEONE

(Vai, Mende, Loma, Kpelle, Bassa and Gola)

1. The VAI syllabary (with a total of up to 212 characters in its modern form) was devised in about 1833 by Mɔmɔlu Duwalu Bukɛlɛ of Jondu (near Cape Mount, Liberia), reputedly inspired by a dream and assisted in the design by a number of friends. The syllabary was standardized in about 1900, and its usage subsequently

SAMPLE CHARACTERS FROM THE INDIGENOUS SCRIPTS (Syllable *k*V)

ka
kɛ
ke
ki
ku
ko
kɔ
Vai (1849)
(1962)
Mende
Loma
Kpelle
Bassa
Bamum (1906)
kɛt
ket

The Bagam and Guro scripts (no record available), the Yoruba 'holy' script and the Gola script (both undeciphered) are excluded from this chart.

encouraged, by Mɔmɔlu Massaquoi. It has been employed for the writing of correspondence, records, original texts and translations from the Bible and the Koran. [→]

2. The Mende *Ki-ka-ku* syllabary (with a total of up to 195 characters) was devised in 1921 by Kisimi Kamara of Potoru (Sierra Leone), a Muslim tailor of Manding origin, reputedly inspired by a dream or vision and assisted in the design by two other tailors and a weaver. The syllabary has been employed mainly for correspondence and record-keeping. [←]

3. The Loma syllabary (with a total of at least 185 characters) was devised in the 1930's by Widɔ Zoɓo of Boneketa (Liberia), reputedly inspired by a dream and assisted in the actual design by Moriba, a local weaver and tailor. It has been employed for correspondence and record-keeping. [→]

4. The Kpelle syllabary (with a total of at least 88 characters) was devised in the 1930's by Chief Gbili of Sanoyea (Liberia), reputedly inspired by a dream. It has been little used, except perhaps for correspondence. [→]

5. The Bassa *Vah* alphabet (with a total of 30 characters and 5 tonal diacritics) was devised probably in the 1920's by Dr. Thomas Flo Lewis of Hodoahzon (Liberia), a native Bassa who had received medical training in the United States. According to local tradition, Lewis is reputed to have based his alphabet on a pre-existing (but undocumented) ideographic 'code'. The alphabet has been used for correspondence and translations from the Bible. [→]

6. The Gola alphabet (undeciphered, with a total of about 30 characters) has been described as a secret script of the Poro Society. This seems unlikely, however, in view of the fact that it is an alphabet. It has been used for correspondence, but the date of its invention is unknown (during the 1960's?). [→]

B. CAMEROUN AND NIGERIA

(Bamum, Bagam, Ibibio-Efik and Yoruba)

7. The Bamum syllabary (with 510 characters in its original, ideographic–pictographic form) was devised in about 1903 by Chief Nʒoya of Fumban (German Kamerun), reputedly inspired by a dream and assisted in the design by two companions, one of them a Fula; pictograms provided by Nʒoya's people also contributed to the design. Nʒoya progressively simplified and rationalized his script, until it had a final total of only 80 stylized characters. He prepared a large quantity of manuscripts in the script (including Christian texts), both in the Bamum language and in a secret 'court-language' which he invented himself. [→]

8. The BAGAM or EGHAP syllabary (with 'several hundred' characters) was devised in Cameroun before 1917, reputedly based on the Bamum script, although no details of its invention or the form of its characters have been recorded. [→ ?]

9. The IBIBIO-EFIK *Obɛri Ɔkaimɛ* alphabet (with 34 characters, plus 20 vigesimal numerals) was reputedly revealed in about 1930 to Michael Ukpon and Akpan Udɔfia of Itu Division (Eastern Nigeria) by SƐMINANT, i.e. the 'Holy Spirit'. The script has been used by members of the local 'Christian' Spirit Movement (*Obɛri Ɔkaimɛ*) for religious writing in their own 'revealed' language, but has not been used for the transcription of Ibibio-Efik itself. [→]

10. The YORUBA 'holy' alphabet (undeciphered) was devised between 1926 and 1928 by Josiah Oshitelu of Ogere (Western Nigeria), reputedly inspired by a dream or vision. The script was apparently used by him for religious writing in his own 'revealed' language, prior to his establishment of the 'Church of the Lord (Aladura)' sect, but was not—as far as is known—employed for the transcription of Yoruba. [←]

C. SURINAM (Djuka)

11. The DJUKA syllabary (with a total of 58 characters) was devised in 1910 by Afaka Atumisi, a Djuka 'Bush Negro' from the Drie Tabbetje district (Eastern Surinam), reputedly inspired by a dream. Afaka, an unbaptized Christian, composed religious texts in his script, which was used also subsequently by a Dutch priest for the transcription of the Catechism and other Catholic texts. [→]

A further example of 'revealed writing' in Surinam was noted by Herskovits in the late 1920's, consisting of undeciphered 'writing' revealed to a Paramaribo negro while in a state of spirit-possession (by a *winti* or 'familiar spirit', reputed to have come from West Africa with the man's ancestors).

D. GUINEA, SENEGAL AND MALI (Manding, Wolof and Fula)

12. The MANDING alphabet (with a total of 25 characters and 8 diacritics, including tonal diacritics, plus 10 decimal numerals) was devised around 1950, or earlier, by Souleymane Kanté of Kankan (Guinea). Kanté has produced a duplicated primer in the script and apparently other literature also. [←]

13. The WOLOF alphabet (with a total of 25 consonantal characters and 7 diacritics and vocalic symbols, plus 10 decimal numerals) was invented around 1960 by Assane Faye of Dakar (Senegal). Faye has produced a printed primer in the script. [←]

14. The Fula *Dita* alphabet (with a total of 55 characters in its earliest form and 39 in its current form, plus 10 decimal numerals) was devised between 1958 and 1966 by Oumar Dembélé of Bamako (Mali), inspired by the indigenous graphic symbols of the Kaarta region and by his grandfather's interest in Arabic and cryptic Arabic scripts. Dembélé has produced manuscripts in the script, including his own Fula poems. [→]

15. The Fula (Ba) alphabet (with a total of 29 characters, plus 10 decimal numerals) was devised probably in the 1950's by Adama Ba of Bamako (Mali). He has prepared at least two manuscript volumes in the script, including Fula poems. [→]

E. IVORY COAST (Bete and Guro)

16. The Bete syllabary (with 401 characters) was devised in 1956 by Frédéric Bruly-Bouabré, a native Bete from Daloa (Ivory Coast), inspired by the 'mysterious' shapes of certain mineral crystals and by a traditional children's game (in which a nonsense-language is 'read' from lines of stones or palm-nuts). [→]

17. The Guro script (syllabary or alphabet?) of M. Bébi-Gouré has been recently reported by G. Calame-Griaule and P.-F. Lacroix,[2] but no further data are yet available.

ACCOUNTS OF 'REVELATION'

It is notable that reference is made to an inspirational dream or vision in eight of the recorded accounts of invention (involving six of the eight syllabaries but only two of the eight alphabets). These accounts of 'revelation' may be summarized as follows:

1. Duwalu Bukɛlɛ, inventor of the Vai script, had a dream in which a white man told him he had been sent by other white men to bring him a book. After decreeing that no-one acquainted with the book should eat the meat of dogs, monkeys or unsacrificed animals, and that no-one should handle the book after touching a certain type of pepper, the white man revealed a number of syllabic characters to him. He promised to reveal the contents of the book itself on a later occasion, but never did so.

2. Kisimi Kamara, inventor of the Mende script, is reputed to have been inspired by a dream or 'vision', although no details of this have been recorded. He is known, however, to have been interested in the interference of spirits in human affairs and to have had a reputation for 'second-sight'.

3. Widɔ Zoɓo, inventor of the Loma script, dreamed that he was face to face with God. After being accused by Widɔ of leaving the

Loma in ignorance, God told him that he had feared the power of writing would cause them to lose respect for their traditional beliefs and customs and to become over-proud. Widɔ swore that the Loma would continue to live as in the past, that they would respect the 'secret of initiation', and that he would never teach the script to a woman. God then instructed him how to prepare ink from the leaves of a creeper.

4. Chief Gbili, inventor of the KPELLE script, had a dream in which an angel revealed the script to him; a variant tradition recounts that he invented the script during a seven year confinement, while thought to be suffering from a mysterious illness.

7. Chief Nʒoya, inventor of the BAMUM script, had a dream in which he was instructed to draw a hand on a wooden tablet, and then to wash it clean and drink the water. Next day he did this, and was inspired to start his work on the script (and subsequently on his secret 'court-language').

9. Akpan Udɔfia, one of the inventors of the IBIBIO-EFIK *Obɛri Ɔkaimɛ* script, had a series of dreams in which he was instructed in a secret language and informed that he was to be a teacher for *Sɛminant* (the 'Holy Spirit'). He subsequently had visions informing him that by drinking a certain potion he would receive knowledge washed from a great book written in coloured inks. He went into eight years' seclusion with his co-inventor, and other members of their religious sect, and during this period the script, secret language and religious texts were 'revealed' to them.

10. Josiah Oshitelu, inventor of the YORUBA 'holy' script, had a dream or vision in 1926, in which he saw an open book, written in 'strange arabic language'. It was immediately after this experience that he began the elaboration of his 'holy' script.

11. Afaka Atumisi, inventor of the DJUKA script, had a dream shortly before the appearance of Halley's Comet in 1910, in which a spirit sent by God appeared before him in the form of a white man. The spirit gave him a blank sheet of paper and informed him that a script would be revealed to him.

CHRONOLOGY

After the invention of the Vai syllabary in the 1830's (some twelve years after the North American invention of the Cherokee syllabary and about ten years before that of the Cree syllabary), no further initiative was taken in West Africa until the standardization and propagation of the same Vai syllabary almost seventy years later, from about 1900. The spate of other scripts then began, with the Bamum syllabary from about 1903 and the Bagam syllabary a few years later, roughly contemporaneous with the invention of the

Djuka syllabary in 1910, on the other side of the Atlantic. (It is of interest to note that the appearance of Halley's Comet in 1910 served to confirm the 'divine' nature of the Djuka revelation, and its previous appearance in 1835, immediately after the Vai revelation, was perhaps a factor in the establishment of that script also.) After an apparent pause, coinciding approximately with the First World War, the creation of new scripts seems to have reached a peak during the 1920's and 1930's: the Mende syllabary was devised in 1921, not only at about the same time as the Bassa alphabet but also only a year before the invention of an indigenous Somali alphabet, on the other side of Africa. Two further Somali alphabets were devised in 1928 and 1930, and four further West African scripts in the late 1920's and early 1930's: the Yoruba 'holy' script and the *Obɛri Ɔkaimɛ* alphabet in Nigeria, and the Loma and Kpelle syllabaries in Liberia.

The Second World War again coincided with an apparent pause in the elaboration of new scripts, but between the early 1950's and early 1960's there was a second spate of invention in western West Africa, involving the Manding alphabet,[3] the Wolof alphabet, the two Fula alphabets and the Bete syllabary. During the same decade, a further eight Somali alphabets were also devised, although the latest of these were stimulated artificially (by an official competition for a Somali script in 1961).

There is of course no reason to suppose that the above scripts include all those which have been devised in Africa in modern times.

HISTORICAL QUESTIONS TO BE CONSIDERED

The problem of the origins and possible inter-relationships of the seventeen scripts may be phrased in the following form:

> To what extent may the inspiration and design of the individual scripts be attributed to I. a stimulus from the Vai script on the inventors of the subsequent scripts, II. a common stimulus from pre-existing scripts or graphic symbols (either foreign or indigenous), or III. independent invention in similar social and cultural environments?

Notes on each of these three possibilities are set out briefly below.

I. It seems very probable that the inventors of the five other Liberian and Sierra Leonean scripts (Mende, Loma, Kpelle, Bassa and Gola) were aware of the neighbouring Vai script. This awareness may have been crucial to their inspiration, and to their design of a syllabic form of writing in three of the five cases. On the other hand, there is no evidence to suggest that the forms of characters used in the later scripts have been based upon or strongly influenced by the characters of the Vai script. There is likewise no apparent formal influence from the Vai script on any of the more distant scripts, although news of its existence might easily have reached the inventor of the Manding script in Guinea and the Bete script in Ivory Coast, and perhaps also the inventor of the Bamum script in Cameroun (the first in that area). In this connection, it would be valuable to know whether there is any record of Liberians—especially Vai-speakers—having visited German Kamerun around the turn of this century.[4] It is less easy, however, to conceive of any way in which the inventor of the Djuka syllabary in Surinam might have been inspired by news of the Vai syllabary (unless through the medium of a European missionary): the Djuka have had no known contact with West Africa since their ancestors fled from their slave-owners on the Surinam coast and settled in the forested interior at the end of the eighteenth century. There is also no formal resemblance between the Djuka and the Vai scripts, apart from the fact that both are syllabaries.

II. An influence from the Arabic alphabet is recognizable in the design of certain characters in the Mende syllabary and the Wolof alphabet, and there has been a similar influence from the Roman alphabet on the *Obɛri Ɔkaimɛ* and the Fula (Ba) alphabets. In general, however, the other documented scripts show remarkably little formal influence from either of these established alphabets, as reflected also in the predilection for syllabic rather than alphabetic forms of writing among the pre-1940 scripts.

The concept of a syllabary (in which a different symbol is used for each combination of consonant and vowel) is unlikely to have reached West Africa from Ethiopia, but it may have been transmitted from North America, where the Cherokee syllabary had been devised only a few years before the Vai syllabary—a connecting link might have been provided by American missionaries (and by the American Board of Foreign Missions in particular, which was active at the time among the Cherokee and was in the process of establishing itself in Liberia also).[5] On the other hand, the Vai and subsequent Liberian and Sierra Leonean scripts all show greater ingenuity and originality in the design of their characters than does the Cherokee syllabary (based largely on Roman letters and 'Arabic' numerals, with arbitrary syllabic values).

A number of similar characters—similar in both shape and value—occur in the Liberian and Sierra Leonean scripts and in certain pre-Arabic scripts of the Maghrib and Andalusia: the Neo-Punic script, the Iberian script, and the Libyan–Tifinagh scripts. With the exception of Tifinagh, there is no record of the usage of these scripts for well over a millennium, and Islam therefore represents the only medium which could account both for the partial survival of their graphic traditions and for their transmission to West Africa. A large number of cryptic and magical alphabets are known to have been associated with Islam, and the Hodh—on the Mauritanian fringe of West Africa—appears to have been one of the centres of these 'sub-Arabic' alphabets. One of the Hodh alphabets shows some striking formal similarities to the Mende script, and further research is needed to establish whether the 'sub-Arabic' alphabetic tradition was responsible for conveying a corpus of pre-Arabic graphic symbols to Liberia and Sierra Leone. The possible effect of cultural contacts during pilgrimages to Mecca also needs to be investigated.

Other characters in the West African and Surinam scripts appear to have a pictographic or ideographic origin (in which the relevant syllabic value has an appropriate meaning in the language concerned). In the case of these characters one may suspect an influence from indigenous graphic symbolism, and it is probably not a coincidence that the most extensive traditional graphic systems recorded in sub-Saharan Africa are those of the Bambara and associated tribes in Mali, and the *Nsibidi* system of certain Cross-River tribes in Eastern Nigeria. Linguistically, the Bambara are closely related to the Manding and the Vai (and a little less closely to the Mende, Loma, Kpelle and Guro) and have also been in cultural contact with the Fula; while at the other end of West Africa the *Nsibidi* system is employed in or near the areas where the Bamum, Bagam and *Obɛri Ɔkaimɛ* scripts have been invented. The Djuka of Surinam are likewise renowned for their preservation of traditional African graphic symbolism, as employed especially in wood-carving.

III. Several of the inventors are known to have been depressed at the inability of their peoples to write their own languages, and at God's apparent neglect of their race (to whom he had granted neither a revealed religion, nor the gift of writing). The various accounts of 'revelation' may well have arisen from this similarity of psychological pressure and cultural environment, and the circumstances and stimuli necessary for the invention and partial acceptance of new forms of writing may have been duplicated in several places.

NOTES

1. David Dalby, 'A survey of the indigenous scripts of Liberia and Sierra Leone: Vai, Mende, Loma, Kpelle and Bassa', *African Language Studies*, VIII, 1967, 1–51.
   ——, 'The indigenous scripts of West Africa and Surinam: their inspiration and design', ibid., IX, 1968, 156–97.
   ——, 'Further indigenous scripts of West Africa: Manding, Wolof and Fula alphabets and Yoruba "holy" writing', ibid., X, 1969, 161–181 (incl. postscript note on the Gola alphabet).
2. G. Calame-Griaule and P.-F. Lacroix, 'Graphies et signes africains', *Semiotica*, 1, 3, 1969, 256–72.
3. According to Calame-Griaule and Lacroix, however, the Manding alphabet was devised around 1930 to 1940 (op. cit., p. 258).

4. Since the presentation of this paper to the Seminar, Mr. Mark W. De Lancey of Indiana University has kindly drawn my attention to the fact that some Vai-speakers did visit Kamerun at this time. They were employed as guards, etc., on the expeditions of Zintgraff, and are known to have passed through the area of Fumban, the home of the Bamum script. Seven Vai are reported to have been left at Bali, some seventy miles from Fumban (and even closer to Bagam), in December 1899. See E. M. CHILVER, *Zintgraff's Explorations in Bamenda: Adamawa and the Benue Lands 1889–1892*, Govt. Printer, Buea, 1966, 21.

5. Dr. Svend Holsoe of De Pauw University, Indiana, has found record of an American, Austin Curtis, who was half-Cherokee and half-Negro, and who settled in Vai country in the late 1820's. There is no record of Curtis having been concerned with either the Cherokee or the Vai syllabary, but the date of his arrival in Liberia is suggestive (just *after* the invention of the Cherokee syllabary, and just *before* the invention of the Vai syllabary).

The Problem of the Nguni: An Examination of the Ethnic and Linguistic Situation in South Africa before the Mfecane[1]

SHULA MARKS AND ANTHONY ATMORE

THE term *Nguni* is now used to denote the peoples in the south-east coastlands of Southern Africa who speak similar languages and who share some aspects at least of a common culture. The Zulu are recognized to be Nguni when a term to include them and their neighbours in the Cape is required. The Swazi have been classified linguistically and culturally as Nguni but are even less frequently referred to as such than are the Zulu; being a relatively recent amalgam of Sotho and Nguni elements, they hold a somewhat anomalous position. The peoples of the Cape are recognized to be still politically, and to a slight extent linguistically, heterogeneous, and *Cape Nguni* is applied frequently to them as a generic term. Although in its strictest sense the term Nguni is a linguistic one, it is used far more widely. Murdock,[2] in classifying the 'Nguni', includes not only the Rhodesian Ndebele, who broke away from the Shakan kingdom of the early nineteenth century and who still speak an Nguni language, but also the Ngoni[3] groups of Malawi and Tanzania, who broke away at the same time but who no longer speak an Nguni language. The Transvaal Ndebele groups, too, of diverse origin and language, are similarly classified by him and others as Nguni. Although the present-day usage of Nguni has its inconsistencies, however, it is readily understandable. Likewise the term *Sotho*, which is now used to designate related languages (Tswana, Pedi and Sesotho) over a wide territorial area. This is an immense extension of its earlier meaning—the peoples, languages and country unified by Moshoeshoe in the early nineteenth century.

Nevertheless, the latter day inclusive use of the term Nguni may do much to distort the past. Recently historians have used the term rather freely of the peoples in the Natal–Zululand area, in an attempt to avoid the anachronistic 'Zulu' for the pre-Shakan period. In fact, it may be masking as great or even greater an anachronism. As we shall see, it should probably be used to designate only a few of the large numbers of peoples to whom it is now applied. The problem is that it is by no means clear just which groups were truly Nguni, and the picture is both complex and confused.

The political and military convulsions set in motion by Dingiswayo and Shaka greatly blurred, if they did not obliterate, previous ethnic and linguistic divisions. The advent of the white man, in Natal especially, only served in many instances to make confusion worse confounded. The powerful nation states which grew up out of the maelstrom of the *Mfecane* were able to enforce a measure of linguistic and cultural uniformity on their subjects which makes it extremely difficult for the historian to trace the pre-*Mfecane* situation. Yet it is only by reference to the earlier linguistic and ethnic patterns that any inferences can be made as to the possible origins of the various peoples in Southern Africa.

Clearly, the starting point in such an exercise must be the correlation of the available oral traditions with the slender fragments of archaeological information we have for this area. In South Africa most of the traditional histories were collected by gifted amateurs, both white and black, towards the end of the last century and the beginning of this. The most obvious difficulty with these collections is that their authors rarely cited the sources of their oral information and seldom made it clear in their narrative when they were retailing genuine traditions, or when they were allowing free rein to their not inconsiderable imaginations. But, for all their faults and their obvious need for reinterpretation, works like Ellenberger, *History of the Basuto*,[4] and Bryant, *Olden Times in Zululand and Natal*,[5] are indispensable, as they record information which, in the environment of twentieth century South Africa, has since passed into oblivion.

Bryant[6] and Soga[7] appear to be the first South Africans (either amateur—as they were—or professional) to make extensive use in English of the term Nguni. Previous writers had styled the Cape and Natal Africans (those living outside Zululand proper) simply, if inelegantly, Kaffirs. Bryant's works are themselves an interesting indication of how the use of the term Nguni developed in his thinking and experience. He arrived in Natal from England in 1883 and published his *Zulu–English Dictionary* in 1905. In the historical introduction to this dictionary, there is no mention of the word, although he is already concerned with the identification of the various layers of population in the Natal–Zululand area in pre-Shakan times. In the dictionary proper, he defines Nguni as 'the name by which the Tongas[8] call a Zulu–Kaffir, hence occasionally accepted by these latter themselves'. He adds that the word is also the *isitakazo* (praise name) of the Emanzimeleni tribe. By the time he came to prepare his next published works, Bryant was making wide use of the term. These were a series of articles published between 1911 and 1913 in *Izindaba Zabata*, a periodical of the Mariannhill Mission, and collected (in part) and reprinted by Struik in 1964 as *A History of the Zulu and Neighbouring Tribes*. In these articles he was beginning to use Nguni as a descriptive term in his researches into Zulu origins in such combinations as 'Pure' Nguni, Sutu–Nguni and Tonga–Nguni. The terminology and analysis is developed still further in *Olden Times*. In his last published work, *The Zulu People*, which was completed in 1935 (though not published until 1949) some of the excessive detail about the earlier history of the numerous tribes which encumber *Olden Times* is jettisoned, but in tracing possible origins and relationships elsewhere in Africa, his imagination soars to quite fantastic heights. Before examining his more pertinent theories of origin and migration, however, it is necessary to look briefly at other definitions of Nguni.

Dohne's *Zulu Kafir Dictionary*[9] contains no mention of Nguni; it does, however, make some interesting references to *amaLala* and other names used later by Bryant. In Kropf's *Kaffir–English Dictionary*,[10] *ubu-Nguni* is said to mean 'a neighbouring country, which possesses foreign commodities', but is used only in the locative *ebu nguni*, 'in the west, westward'. Interestingly enough, Bishop Colenso, in the first edition of his *Zulu English Dictionary*,[11] suggested that Nguni was 'another name for AmaXhosa'; but in the fourth edition in 1905, which had been revised by his daughter Harriette, Nguni had become 'another name for the amaXhosa, Qwabe and Zulu, and other kindred tribes'—a significant widening of the original definition. In this connection it is also relevant to note the rather curious and perhaps contradictory definition of the word given by Samuelson in his *King Cetshwayo Zulu Dictionary*:[12] 'a gentile, a foreigner; an ancient, a person belonging to an ancient stock'.

Neither Stow nor Molema[13] mention the word Nguni, although Stow[14] considers the term *Bakone*(*i*) as synonymous with Bakwena and quotes Moffat and his fellow missionary, Roger Price, as his sources; it has, he says, 'been considered by some as a term of reproach, and of Kaffer origin' and he quotes Arbousset[15] to the effect that 'the name *Bakoni* was applied without distinction by the Kaffers to all the coloured people they had known'.

Doke and Vilakazi add some interesting information in their *Zulu–English Dictionary*.[16] By 1948, of course, they were using Nguni in the accepted sense. They repeat Bryant's 1905 definition of Nguni as a Thonga name for the Zulu–Xhosa group (and the praise name of the Nzimela people) but add that *ebuNguni* (loc.) is the name the Zulu use for Zululand 'as they consider themselves to be the ancient stock of the group' and quote *Woza siya ebuNguni lapho abantu befa beluphele* (Come let us go back to Zululand where people die old), which they state comes from a Shangaan–Thonga song.

The only writer to rival Bryant in presenting a detailed account of the pre-Shakan situation in south-east Africa is Soga;[17] unfortunately, however, many of the details he gives flatly contradict Bryant. Soga, himself of mixed Xhosa–Scottish descent, considers that the term Nguni originated as a proper name (M)Nguni, the putative father of Xhosa. Only two great tribes, he says, 'are the people of Mnguni, the Ama–Xhosa and the Abe–Nguni of Nyasaland . . . by the other tribes of Natal, this tribe (the Xhosa) even to this day is more frequently spoken of as Abe–Nguni then as Ama–Xhosa', although among themselves Ama–Xhosa is more generally used.[18] Soga explicitly maintained that Kropf's translation of Nguni as 'in the west' was incorrect.

Soga therefore agrees with Bryant in suggesting that the Xhosa are Nguni, or, as Bryant would term it, 'pure' Nguni. About the Thembu he is not sure, and suggests a Lala or a Sotho origin, although Bryant considers the Thembu to be 'pure' Nguni. According to both Bryant and Soga, the Mpondo and Mpondomise are Mbo in origin, and both appear to follow Theal in suggesting a relationship between the Ama–Zimba and the Aba–Mbo.[19] On the other hand, Soga and Bryant are diametrically opposed to the origin of the Zulu themselves; here Soga commits what must be heresy to the confirmed Zuluphile by suggesting a Lala or even a Thonga origin. Bryant, as we shall see, actually relates the Lala to the Thonga, but Soga makes the significant point[20] that this term was applied to skilled workers in iron ore, and links the name with 'a large break away section of the Makalanga'; he also suggests that the Lala were the first people in the Natal area.

Like Soga, Bryant sees the migration of peoples into South Eastern Africa in three streams, all of which, however, he classes as Nguni because 'this was the name by which . . . these people generically distinguished themselves from the other two types [Sotho and Thonga] around them'.[21] This in itself marks a certain departure from his 1905 definition. He brings his wandering Nguni, 'the very first of the Bantu arrivals', 'from the north' into the Transvaal via the headwaters of the Limpopo:

(i) Here one group remained, to give rise to the 'local ba-Koni (Zulu, abaNguni) clans, the baHurutse, baKwena, ba-ma-Ngwato, baNgwaketsi and others', but not before a different Bantu element had fused with them. This new group, Bryant thinks, are 'Venda–Karanga', who mixed with the older baKoni to produce the Sotho, or, as he calls them, the 'Sutu–Ngunis'.[22]

(ii) Before the complete fusion of Koni/Venda–Karanga had been accomplished, a section of the baKoni whose language had been influenced to a certain extent, especially phonetically, by the Venda–Karanga, migrated eastwards. Bryant says these people were known to their 'kindred' as Tekela–Nguni (from the Zulu *uku-tekela*, to pronounce certain consonants in a peculiar fashion). Near the east coast, probably north of Delagoa Bay, these Tekela–Ngunis divided into (*a*) Mbo/Embo or Dlamini or

Swazi Ngunis, who moved southwards, towards Zululand and Natal, and (*b*) another group, which mixed linguistically with the Thonga (Gwamba) who were also moving southwards along the east coast. These mixed Thonga–Nguni also pushed southwards, bypassing the Mbo to become 'the head of the Bantu procession', through Zululand and into Natal. There were at least three different groups amongst the Thonga–Nguni, each with its dialect and customs: the Mtetwa, the Lala and the Debe. In this way, Bryant has his Thonga–Nguni and Mbo people coming into Zululand from the north (*eNyakato*), which he says in *Zulu People*[23] to be their traditional direction of migration.

(iii) Finally, Bryant posits a further group of the original Transvaal baKoni (Nguni who left the other groups before the advent of the Venda–Karanga) settling in the south eastern Transvaal. These were the 'pure' Nguni, whom he divided into two—the Ntungwa, from whom the Zulu were descended, and the Xhosa–Thembu. The Thembu reached the coast south of Durban, and then moved into what became the Cape; the Xhosa kept inland, close under the Drakensberg, and went into Griqualand East before reaching the coast to the south of the Thembu. Although at the time of separation the 'pure' Nguni spoke a single language, in time Zulu and Xhosa developed 'along different lines . . . until separated by a quite considerable extent of dialectal differences in speech'. By having his 'pure' Nguni come into the coastal area from the south-east Transvaal, Bryant explains the Ntungwa/Zulu traditions about an origin 'in the west', which, he maintains, the Xhosa have retained as an archaism. As we have seen, this is denied by Soga.[24]

Much of Bryant's argument depends on the identification of the term *Nguni* with the Sotho *Koni* and variants, and linguistically this is certainly feasible. There are groups of Koni people scattered widely through the Transvaal, and, to a lesser extent, Botswana and Lesotho. Many of these are now designated Transvaal Ndebele, but this would appear to be a European invented term. According to Ziervogel,[25] while one of these groups, the so-called Southern Ndebele, undoubtedly came from Natal originally, the Northern Ndebele (i.e. the Gegana, Mugombhane and Lidwaba groups) are said to have come from across the Limpopo to the north. One of his Lidwaba informants maintained that originally they were of 'Kalanga' speech, although this was later completely changed through contact with the Swazi.[26] Ziervogel classifies Northern Ndebele as part of the *tekela* sub-group of Nguni, together with Swazi, Bhaca, Phuti and Lala, and points out that while it is close to Swazi, as well as having been considerably influenced by Sotho, the Northern Ndebele 'also have some linguistic peculiarities of their own which have to be attributed to their origin in the north'.[27] It is significant that one section of the Lidwaba have a chiefly genealogy of well over twenty names.[28] The Northern Nguni therefore appear to lend some substance to part of Bryant's hypothesis, although clearly this cannot, and should not, be stretched too far. Van Warmelo[29] has described some of the tiny Koni groups scattered amongst the Pedi and Lovedu of the north eastern Transvaal. According to tradition, these were *in situ* when the Pedi first reached this area. On the other hand, the Phuti and other people in Lesotho whom Bryant designates Koni[30] are not so termed by Ellenberger;[31] indeed, the word Koni never appears in his work. They are, however, recognized to be from the Natal side of the Drakensberg, and to be the first Bantu inhabitants of present-day Lesotho.

Ellenberger[32] recounts an interesting tradition to the effect that a group of Fokeng (considered by Bryant to be Koni) intermarried with Bush women; the resultant Fokeng/Bush people were forced out of the country south of the Vaal, passed through Natal, and eventually arrived in Thembuland 'where they joined the Tembus, and became so completely absorbed by them as to lose their identity, and even their language'.[33] Ellenberger (in 1912) thought this 'disruption' of the Fokeng from the High Veld had taken place some 250 years previously. As we shall see, it has considerable relevance to the archaeological picture presented below.

This, and other evidence, is confused and conflicting. Some 'Koni' appear to have come from the coastal lands up on to the High Veld, whilst others travelled in the reverse direction. The chronological deductions of the recorders of these traditions vary enormously. Nevertheless, certain points do emerge from this mass of conflicting narrative. One is that the latter-day terms Nguni and Sotho are flags of convenience to describe the post-*Mfecane* situation and that their wide-ranging use is due to white intervention or invention, not least on the part of Bryant. In pre-*Mfecane* times they were either group names of local or at least limited application, or terms referring somewhat vaguely to foreign groups in general. What is not at all clear is exactly which groups owned these names, and other such as Mbo and Lala, and whether there were groups who may not have in fact fitted into any of the three categories—Lala,[34] Mbo or Nguni. Another conclusion to be drawn from the recovered traditional evidence is that the present day Zulu/Nguni and Sotho uniformity overlays a number of layers of languages and peoples. These layers are most apparent in the coastlands, but are also discernible on the High Veld. Is there any other evidence which makes the task of identifying these layers any easier?

Verifiable facts about the pre-*Mfecane* South African past are peculiarly few. Archaeology could give us our biggest lead. Unfortunately, the amount of excavation done on the south-east coast is meagre in the extreme, although the late J. F. Schofield's analysis of Natal coastal pottery is a useful beginning.[35] Schofield divided Natal pottery into four groups, which he labelled NC_1, NC_2, NC_3 and NC_4. Of these, only the first three are relevant, the fourth being modern Zulu pottery. NC_1 pottery, found with Late Stone Age or Khoikhoi (Hottentot) associations in the Cathkin Park area, is—according to Schofield—'undoubtedly Ronga ware from Portuguese East Africa'.[36]

NC_2 ware is particularly interesting. Found mainly around Durban and Durban Bluff, it has—according to Roger Summers—'so many features in common with Buispoort ware (ST_2) that [Schofield] . . . postulated intercourse between stone hut dwellers and those living at the foot of the escarpment'. Summers continues:

> There are however other features in NC_2 pottery which suggest an admixture from elsewhere . . .: the geographical probability is that 'elsewhere' was Mocambique, but at present we know nothing about its later prehistory.[37]

The trail of NC_2 pottery according to Schofield also continues into the Eastern Cape, where it is found amongst both the Mpondo and the Thembu people. Both Schofield and James Walton,[38] using the traditions recounted by Ellenberger, are inclined to associate NC_2 with the Fokeng—a Sotho group, whom, as we have seen, Bryant classifies as Koni. NC_2 pottery includes a large number of clay pipe bowls. Again in Schofield's view, which is in part echoed by Roger Summers,[39] it was made by people 'who used iron, but did not smelt it'. As no really large scale excavation has been done in this area, too much reliance cannot however be placed on this statement.

NC_3 pottery makers, on the other hand, clearly worked iron extensively. Their pottery is found mainly in the Tugela Valley and to the north of the river, although some sherds have been found at Weenen and Otto's Bluff near Pietermaritzburg as well as at Durban. On the basis of traditional evidence and the extensive iron slag, Schofield is content to identify the NC_3 potters as Lala.[40] Although oral tradition suggests that the Lala preceded the Mbo on the south-east coast, in the absence of carbon dating there is nothing in the archaeological record to support or refute this contention. Where NC_2 pottery precedes NC_3 as at Durban Bluff, tradition tells of a relatively short and late migration of 'Lala' from the Tugela Valley. It is thus conceivable that for a long period Lala and Mbo settlements were contemporaneous, but in different parts of the country.

At some stage, not necessarily a later one, there must have been the entry of yet another group of people—the Nguni. Unfortunately, for our purposes, none of the 'pure' Nguni groups have their own pottery tradition. According to Schofield, the Xhosa have adopted Khoikhoi pottery, whilst the Thembu and Mpondo have taken over the traditions of the Fokeng NC_2 potters. Amongst the Zulu, the women have adopted the wood-carving techniques of the men to decorate their pots.[41] All this suggests that the Nguni were pastoralists; it also makes their track particularly difficult to follow.

So far, the only other evidence of an archaeological nature we have is that of chiefs' grave sites and some Cambay beads and Chinese porcelain around Port St. John. According to Monica Wilson,[42] the burial sites of the Xhosa, Thembu and Pondomise ruling families were located in the Transkei for a considerable number of generations—ten at least in the case of the Thembu. Gervase Mathew has found some evidence—Ming china and red beads—around Port St. John, which suggests to him a pre-Portuguese, Swahili–Arab trading-site.[43] But systematic archaeological work, either here or elsewhere along the south-east coast is conspicuous by its absence, so that no firm conclusions can as yet be drawn from his finds.

Indeed, the Greefswald sequence[44] in the Northern Transvaal, the one really big Iron Age archaeological discovery in South Africa, tends to be used, as a result of the present poverty of evidence elsewhere, to interpret not only the High Veld but the whole South African situation. The earlier valley site, Bambandyanolo or K_2, is that of an Iron Age Community of cultivators and pastoralists. A burial site here has been dated to the mid-eleventh century and this ties up with other eleventh century sites in the central and southern Transvaal, although more recent work in the Eastern Transvaal (Phalaborwa) and Swaziland has turned up significantly earlier Iron Age dates. One of the features of the K_2 site is that the surviving skeletal material appears to be non-negroid and has been described as Khoisan (Bush/Hottentot). Physical anthropology is a notoriously difficult and contentious field, but it may be, as the traditional evidence also suggests, that the first Bantu-speakers in this area were tiny groups who infiltrated the Khoisan—and ultimately imposed their language and culture on some of their non-negroid neighbours. In view of the later genius displayed by the Khoikhoi at the Cape for assimilating other people's cultural apparatus, the possibility that the K_2 site was that of Khoikhoi influenced by Iron Age neighbours cannot be ruled out of court: linguistic, racial and cultural traits are independent variables.[45]

If the people of the High Veld in the first centuries of the present millennium were mixed Khoisan–Bantu pastoralists and cultivators —this dictated by the nature of their environment—what of the south-eastern coastlands? This fertile region was probably more suited to agriculture than to cattle-keeping, the more so in the early days of human settlement, when the valleys at least were heavily wooded,[46] although it should be remembered that the uplands of Natal and Zululand are now also excellent cattle country. Along the coast, it is conceivable that the earlier inhabitants were mainly agriculturalists who, in the course of several centuries of patient effort, cleared the forests and thick woodlands.

Even during the Portuguese period it is clear that much of the coast was still heavily wooded, although it is equally clear that the inhabitants from the Transkei northwards were both pastoralists and cultivators. From the records of survivors of Portuguese and Dutch ships wrecked along the coast in the sixteenth and seventeenth centuries, it appears that the Cape Nguni then occupied similar positions to those they held in the early nineteenth century.[47] Thus the northernmost people mentioned by the Dutch survivors of the *Stavenisse* in 1686 were 'Temboes and Emboes' (?Mbo), who lived behind the Natal south coast. These, or similar people, are still distinguished by the Mpondo—the next group to the south—as Abambo.[48] At Durban Bluff, sailors noted the smoking habits of the Africans, which again ties in with the archaeological evidence.[49] Similarly, in the Delagoa Bay area and its immediate hinterland, the Thonga tribal configuration remains remarkably unchanged.[50]

The Natal–Zululand coastal regions, however, present no such orderly pattern. Bryant,[51] apparently basing his views entirely on Theal,[52] suggests that although all the people in this area would today be classified as *Nguni*, their exact tribal configuration has changed considerably. As yet, however, no really thorough examination of the relevant Portuguese material, whether published or unpublished, has taken place for this section of the coast.

At this stage of the argument, it is necessary to try to fit these fragments of evidence into some kind of coherent framework. If we follow the traditions recorded by Bryant and Soga as well as the archaeological and other evidence, the picture seems to us something like this:

1. *Lala:* Iron Age cultivators, whom Bryant associates both with the Thonga and the Karanga, Soga solely with the Karanga. In support of the Thonga origin for the Lala, an entry in *The Natal Diaries of Dr. W. H. T. Bleek* seems relevant:

> I interrogated several Matonga ... I discovered that their language is the same as that in Peter's vocabulary of Lourenco Marques and seems to extend in the direction of Delagoa Bay. It is the language the Zulus call u Kutugeza, which the Mancolosi and other Malala tribes speak ...[53]

On the other hand, Schofield has suggested the affinities of some of the ancient ware of Natal–Zululand with Karanga pottery in Rhodesia. While this is tenuous, Bryant does link the Lala with the

Gwambe Thonga and possibly this is the clue: according to C. E. Fuller, the Gwambe resemble the Shona in many aspects of their language, proverbs, riddles, folk tales and omens.[54] Alternatively, it could be that the Lala were in fact the second and not the first layer of Bantu-speaking inhabitants, the first being represented by the NC^{1} 'Ronga type' pot.[55] If, as we suggested, the very earliest Bantu-speaking inhabitants were mainly agriculturalists, they would have had a culture similar to the various groups comprising the Thonga, and would have come from the same direction—north down the coast from the Lower Zambesi area. Baumann and Westermann,[56] writing in the early forties, considered indeed that from an ethnographic point of view the modern Nguni culture represented a fusion between an earlier agricultural way of life and a later pastoral way of life. It may therefore be that the term Lala is in fact disguising two (Karanga and Thonga), and perhaps more, distinct groups. This would also account for Bryant's three 'Tonga–Nguni' types.

2. *Mbo:* Mixed Khoisan–Sotho pastoralists and cultivators, who made the NC_2 pots and settled alongside, rather than mingled with, the earlier settlers. They came into Natal from the High Veld, avoiding the tsetse country to the north, and their route is fairly clear if they can be identified with the Fokeng. One must, however, be careful not to be led into thinking that *all* the Mbo are the result of the single recorded Fokeng migration. This would appear on the face of it to be most unlikely.

3. *'Pure' Nguni:* Probably pastoralists, who also appear to have entered from the High Veld. So far, the only possible clue to their presence there, apart from the Koni and perhaps the Northern Ndebele, relates to the Greefswald sequence and is of dubious value. There the Mapungubwe hill site itself was occupied later than the K_2 valley, in the late fourteenth or early fifteenth century, by people having a very considerably superior Iron Age culture to those in the valley. The skeletal remains are still predominantly Khoisan, but there are some negroid features. The evidence seems to suggest a new ethnic element and probably new linguistic elements also. Gardner, who excavated Mapungubwe, suggests a triple Nguni, Sotho and Venda peopling of the hill, but his grounds for suggesting the presence of the Nguni are never made explicit.[57]

In the absence of other evidence as to their origins and the tenuous nature of the existing material, in the case of the 'pure' Nguni the clues linguists may be able to provide could prove particularly valuable. Clearly, analysis of the various Nguni dialects of the south-east coast would be extremely useful, especially if the dialectal differences could be related to non-Nguni languages. An historical dimension could be added to this by the use of dictionaries and vocabularies which go back well into the nineteenth century. South African place names (many of the pre-European names for towns, villages and farms have been recorded) could well provide clues to the pattern of tribal migrations. Not only do we need to know far more about the relationship between Bantu and pre-Bantu languages, but also between present day Nguni, Sotho, Delagoa Bay Thonga, Venda and Shona.

Given financial support and encouragement, archaeologists could do much more to unravel these and related problems; further study of the Portuguese sources is also clearly essential. It seems to us, however, that linguists have a major role to play if progress is to be made in their solution.

NOTES

1. Unless quoting from earlier authorities, we have tried to use the current orthography for African words. For this and many other linguistic points we should like to thank Mr. David Rycroft of the School of Oriental and African Studies for his generous help. We should also like to thank Dr. Brian Fagan of the University of California, Santa Barbara, for helping us over some of the hurdles which lie in the path of the unwary historian tackling the writings of archaeologists. The paper has also benefited from the criticisms of members of the Conference on the History of African Peoples in Southern Africa before 1900, Zambia, July, 1968. None of the above, however, are responsible for the content of this paper.

   The term *Mfecane*, used here to cover the wars and resulting migrations of the Shakan and post-Shakan period, is discussed in the postscript note below.
2. G. P. Murdock, *Africa, Its Peoples and their Culture History*, New York, Toronto and London, 1959.
3. It should be noted that the term *Ngoni* may derive from the *isitakazelo* of the Nzimeleni clan who joined Nxaba and Zwangendaba on their migrations. For the Nzimeleni, see A. T. Bryant, *Olden Times in Zululand and Natal*, London, 1929 (repr. Struik, 1965), 276–81.
4. D. F. Ellenberger, *History of the Basuto*, London, 1912.
5. Op. cit. (note 3 above).
6. In addition to *Olden Times in Zululand and Natal*, Bryant also wrote of traditional history in his *Zulu–English Dictionary*, Natal, 1905; *The Zulu People as They Were Before the White Man Came*, Pietermaritzburg, 1949; and *A History of the Zulu and Neighbouring Tribes*, Cape Town, 1964.
7. J. H. Soga, *The South-Eastern Bantu*, Johannesburg, 1930; *The AmaXhosa, Life and Customs*, Lovedale, 1931.
8. I.e. the Delagoa Bay Thonga, as distinct from the Thonga/Tonga groups in Rhodesia and north of the Zambesi.
9. J. L. Dohne, *Zulu Kafir Dictionary*, Cape Town, 1857.
10. A. Kropf, *Kafir–English Dictionary*, Lovedale, 1899.
11. J. W. Colenso, *Zulu English Dictionary*, (1st ed.) Pietermaritzburg, 1861.
12. R. C. Samuelson, *King Cetshwayo Zulu Dictionary*, Pietermaritzburg, 1923.
13. G. Stow, *The Native Races of South Africa*, London, 1905 (repr. Struik, 1964); S. M. Molema, *The Bantu Past and Present*, Edinburgh, 1920 (repr. Struik, 1964).
14. *Native Races*, c. xxv.
15. T. Arbousset and F. Daumas, *Relation d'un Voyage d'Exploration*, Paris, 1842, 530. In a note on p. 269, the authors state: 'Les Bechuanas leur donnent [i.e. aux Zulus], le plus generalement, le nom de Bakoni.'
16. C. M. Doke and B. W. Vilakazi, *Zulu–English Dictionary*, Johannesburg, 1948.
17. *South-Eastern Bantu*, 83; 87.
18. Here Soga cites M. M. Fuze, *Abantu Abamnyama*, Pietermaritzburg, 1922. Magema Fuze was also among Bryant's and Bishop Colenso's chief informants.

19. The Vambe, Zimba, and Mumbo of the Portuguese accounts. See G. M. THEAL, *Records of South-Eastern Africa*, VII, Cape Town, 1898, which includes Dos Santos' account of these people further up the East coast. Apart from the similarity in name between the Mumbo and the Abambo, there is little evidence to link the two groups. As Monica Wilson has pointed out (M. WILSON, 'Early History of the Transkei and Ciskei', *African Studies*, 18, 1959), it is highly unlikely that there was a mass migration into South Africa as late as the late sixteenth century, in view of the complete absence of a record of this in oral tradition and the generally settled condition of life along the South East coast at the time of the Portuguese accounts.
20. *The South-Eastern Bantu*, 395.
21. *Olden Times*, 5–10; 232–3.
22. *Zulu People*, 6.
23. *Zulu People*, 11.
24. See p. 123 above.
25. D. ZIERVOGEL, *A Grammar of Northern Transvaal Ndebele*, Pretoria, 1959, 5.
26. Ibid., 180–3. Ndebele Text with English translation.
27. Ibid., 5, 13.
28. Ibid., facing p. 6.
29. N. J. VAN WARMELO, *Bakoni ba Maake*, Native Affairs Department, Ethnological Publications 12, Pretoria, 1944; and *Bakoni ba Mametsa*, N.A.D., Ethnological Publications 15, Pretoria, 1944.
30. *Olden Times*, 356.
31. *History of the Basuto*, 25.
32. Ibid., 19–20.
33. It may be on this tradition that Soga based his suggestion of a Sotho origin for the Thembu.
34. We have used the term *Lala* somewhat loosely for all the groups Bryant has termed 'Tonga-Nguni'.
35. J. F. SCHOFIELD, *Primitive Pottery*, Cape Town, 1948; 'Natal Coastal Pottery from the Durban District, a Preliminary Survey', Parts I and II, *South African Journal of Science*, 1935, 508–27, and 1936, 993–1009; 'A Description of Pottery from the Umgazana and Zig-zag Caves on the Pondoland Coast', *Transactions of the Royal Society of South Africa*, 1937–38, 25, 327–32. Citations below are to *Primitive Pottery* which in the main accurately reflects Schofield's earlier articles.
36. *Primitive Pottery*, 151; Dr. Fagan argues in favour of a Khoikhoi origin for NC1 pottery (personal communication).
37. R. SUMMERS, 'Iron Age industries of South Africa with notes on their chronology, terminology and economic status', p. 698, *in* W. W. BISHOP and J. D. CLARK, *Background to Evolution in Africa*, Chicago, 1967, 687–700.
38. James WALTON, 'Bafokeng Settlement in South Africa', *African Studies*, 1956, 37–40.
39. *Primitive Pottery*, 155. SUMMERS, op. cit.: 'Mining is likely to have been incidental to farming and specialisation is not indicated by the simple mining techniques employed'.
40. *Primitive Pottery*, 150.
41. Ibid., 157.
42. Monica WILSON, 'Early History of the Transkei and Ciskei', *African Studies*, 18, 1959.
43. Communication to the African History Seminar, Institute of Commonwealth Studies, December 1966.
44. L. FOUCHE (ed.), *Mapungubwe: ancient Bantu civilisation on the Limpopo. Reports on excavations at Mapungubwe . . . from 1933 to 1935*, Cambridge, 1937; G. A. GARDNER (P. J. COERTZE, ed.), *Mapungubwe, Vol. II: Report on excavations at Mapungubwe and Bambandyanalo . . . from 1935 to 1940*, Pretoria, 1963; B. FAGAN, 'The Greefswald Sequence', *Journal of African History*, V, 1964, 3.
45. The Bantu and the arrival of iron-working have generally been associated, but this hypothesis may well have to be reconsidered, both in the light of the findings at the Greefswald sequence and of recent discussions on the origin and expansion of the Bantu.
46. J. P. N. ACOCKS, 'Veld Types of South Africa', *Botanical Survey of South Africa*, Memoir No. 28, Pretoria, 1953.

47. M. Wilson, 'Early History of the Transkei and Ciskei', op. cit.
48. Ibid., 175. Both Bryant and Soga, as we have seen, classify the Mpondo themselves as Mbo, and relate them closely to the Dhlamini rulers of Swaziland.
49. Schofield, *Primitive Pottery*, 158.
50. C. E. Fuller, 'Ethnohistory in the Study of Culture Change in South East Africa', *in* W. R. Bascom and M. J. Herskowitz (eds.), *Continuity and Change in African Cultures*, Chicago, 1959.
51. *Olden Times, passim.*
52. G. M. Theal, *Records of South-Eastern Africa*, 8 Vols., London, 1898–1903.
53. O. H. Spohr (ed.), *The Natal Diaries of Dr. W. H. I. Bleek*, Cape Town, 1965, 77.
54. 'Ethnohistory in the Study of Culture Change', op. cit., 126–7.
55. Schofield, *Primitive Pottery*, 151. This perhaps also ties in with the recently reported carbon date of 410 A.D. ± 60 for an Iron Age site in Swaziland (*Journal of African History*, VIII, 1967, 3).
56. H. Baumann and D. Westermann, (French edition) *Les Peuples et les Civilisations de l'Afrique*, Paris, 1948, 124–5.
57. G. A. Gardner, *Mapungubwe*. See also the doubts expressed by Brian Fagan, 'The Greefswald Sequence', op. cit.

POSTSCRIPT NOTE ON THE TERM 'MFECANE'

The origin of this term seems almost as obscure as that of 'Nguni' itself. Bryant (*Olden Times*, p. 276) speaks of a clan *abakwaMfekane* (or *Mfekaye*), alias emaNcwangeni, but connects it rather with Zwangendaba and his people who moved northwards from Zululand, than with any of the refugee groups in South Africa. The word does not appear in the early Zulu or Xhosa dictionaries, but was used of, or by, the Natal–Zululand offshoots in the Eastern Cape: *amaMfengu* or *Fingo*. This seems to be the Sotho usage, i.e. it referred to refugee groups. Thus Nehemiah Moshweshwe wrote to J. M. Orpen about certain chiefs who had been ruined *ke Faqane*, i.e. 'by the Faqane' (Ellenberger papers, Lesotho, item no. 70A, letter 15 April 1905). The great Sotho historian A. Sekese similarly used the word in an article in the newspaper *Leselinyana*, in 1892. It was spelt *fangane*, but this was probably an orthographical mistake for *faqane*. Another Sotho writer, E. Motsamai, in the opening words of his *Mehla ea Malimo* (1912) wrote of *mehla ea khale, mehla ea lifaqane, mehla ea malimo*—'the times of old, the times of the *lifaqane*, the times of the cannibals'. Here the term is beginning to take on a more general meaning, i.e. Time of Troubles. The *q* in Sotho orthography represents a palato-alveolar click.

It is possible that the word was of Sotho origin, and passed from them to the 'Nguni'. Mr. D. Rycroft considers that the correct spelling in Zulu is Mfekane (no click), but Mrs. R. Jones-Phillipson informs us that in Xhosa there is a click (*c*). It is also possible that the term came into general usage in South African historiography through the writings of Europeans such as Orpen, Ellenberger and Macgregor.

I am grateful to Mr. Peter Sanders of Wadham College, Oxford, for supplying me with most of the Sotho information. (Anthony Atmore)

Internal Relationships of the Bantu Languages: Prospects for Topological Research

W. MICHAEL MANN

PROFESSOR MALCOLM GUTHRIE has put forward in his paper presented to this Seminar and elsewhere certain inferences about the prehistory of the Bantu languages which he believed could be drawn from his comparative data.[1] This paper is written in the belief that historians will wish to examine not only the conclusions reached, but also sufficient of the principles of comparative linguistics to enable them to distinguish data from hypotheses built on them, and to appreciate the nature and strength of the inferences leading from the data to the hypotheses. But beyond this: Guthrie's own conclusions are unlikely to exhaust the inferences that may be drawn from his data; and neither Guthrie's data, nor any additional data we have the prospect of assembling in the foreseeable future, can be regarded as adequate for unravelling the full prehistory of the Bantu languages. The first part of this paper treats in general terms the nature and limitations of historical inference from linguistic comparison. The second part describes topological approaches which have been used by Guthrie or which might be used by others to draw specific inferences on the prehistory of the Bantu languages.

One caution needs to be borne in mind in any application of linguistic data to prehistory. The people who speak one language are not necessarily the same as the group that employs one material culture or the group that recognizes one jurisdiction, although they may largely overlap; further, a group may adopt or borrow from the language of its neighbours or overlords without adopting their material culture, and so on. Linguistic data yields hypotheses about *speech* communities just as archaeological data yields hypotheses about cultural and physical communities. Subject to this caution, linguistic data could be used in confirmation of inferences drawn from non-linguistic data, and vice versa. However, we should be able to make safer use of this type of evidence if we knew more about the historical correlates of linguistic borrowing (and the parallel process of acculturation). Such knowledge could come from studies of better documented situations;[2] some light might also be shed by contemporary sociolinguistic studies of multilingualism.

Two languages may have points of resemblance (beyond chance resemblance) either because they have evolved from the same language, or because in some sense one has copied from the other (or both have copied from a third source); there may also be a combination of these factors. Historians have often concentrated, however, on the light that may be shed on the genealogical evolution of languages by the philological approach, to the neglect of the light that may be shed on language contact by typological comparison and other studies of the dispersion of linguistic features (which may be called topology[3]). At the same time some historians seem over-optimistic in their expectations of the philological approach.

The philological approach rests on a hypothesis about the universality of sound laws: whenever in a given language a change in pronunciation takes place affecting a sound or a sequence of sounds, the same change takes place uniformly in all forms of that language containing the same sound or sequence of sounds. Evidence for the hypothesis is provided by the possibility it affords of relating large numbers of linguistic forms, both in historical and comparative linguistics, by phonological rules or sound laws; the method evolved to exploit the hypothesis then entails setting up starred forms to symbolize these systematic correspondences between languages. However we cannot assume that all or only those forms that are systematically related in this way have been directly transmitted without the intervention of loaning. On the one hand, the philological method may catch in its net some indirect reflexes (i.e. reflexes whose transmission has involved loaning between related languages at some point),[4] especially where loaning took place at a time nearer to that of the proto-language; on the other hand, even in Indo-European studies a residue of clearly related forms (including 'basic' vocabulary) has remained intractable to the philological method—except for the sort that sets up rules to account for single forms. Historical interpretation has to proceed therefore either on the assumption that these discrepancies are likely to be statistically insignificant, or on a detailed assessment of the status of each putative set of cognates.

The philological method has generally served only to link documented languages directly with an inferred common ancestor, intermediate ramification being generally less easy to determine. Even in Indo-European studies there is no concensus as to intermediate ancestry above the level of language groups (Germanic, Indo-Iranian etc.), a level corresponding most nearly (in its remove from the documented languages) to the individual Bantu groups of Guthrie's classification (numbering over eighty).

It is possible, however, to seek a tentative intermediate genealogy by means of topology, i.e. by the study of recurrent patterns of distribution, especially patterns covering a limited part of the field only with minimal overlapping. A refinement of the method is to pay special attention to the distribution-patterns of the reflexes of synonymous starred forms.

The topology of entries attesting starred forms may also be analysed to reveal patterns of loaning. In this case account is also taken of skewed forms and osculant comparative series (e.g. where the starred forms can be related by mutation).[5] This application of topology is not confined to philological data; it can be applied to resemblances at all levels of language structure—sounds, morphology, syntax, tone-systems and so on.[6] But unlike vocabulary, points of comparison can no longer be quantified meaningfully, and it is not therefore possible to apply statistical methods.

When topology is used in this way, it may reveal not only the exclusive hierarchical relationships sought by genealogical classification, but also chain relationships (exemplified by the cline in which A is related to B, which is related to C, while C is minimally related to A) such as may have arisen from prolonged or intimate contact. The difficulty with topological resemblances is that it becomes very difficult to distinguish those relationships due to common origin and those due to loaning. One might devise a scale of probability for different types of feature according to their liability or resistance to loaning: phonological features, for example, are loaned very readily. But there is a suspicion that resistance to loaning at *all* levels may be generally weaker where languages display the degree of overall structural similarity possessed by the Bantu languages.[7]

Any picture that linguists can present of internal relationships among the Bantu languages is likely to draw a rather uncertain line between genealogical and contact relationships, particularly where the evidence is based on details of structural similarity, and very little impression of relative time-depth can be looked for. Nevertheless, the evidence is potentially very detailed, and every aspect and type of relationship requires historical explanation. It might be useful to look for a statement, for each Bantu language or language-group, of the depth and nature of its relationships with other Bantu groups, especially of any close relationship with groups that are disproportionately distant in geographical terms.

Topological examination of the distribution of the reflexes of starred forms and of other linguistic features reveals a vast number of patterns, and it is clear that no analysis would be possible without some attempt to classify these patterns.

The first step towards simplifying the topological statements is to list not the languages but the zones in which a feature occurs—the zones referred to being those of Guthrie's revised classification, numbering fifteen.[8] Guthrie uses two devices to classify the resultant patterns. The 'modulus of dispersion' measures the geographical extension of a feature, without reference to location, while the 'regional assortment' categorizes location, wherever the distribution belongs to a recurrent pattern.

Guthrie describes the means by which he calculates the modulus of dispersion in *Comparative Bantu*, I, Appendix 6/1. A modulus of between 0 and 7 (quoted as D:0, D:1, etc.) is assigned to each pattern, the highest numbers belonging to the patterns of greatest extension.

The regional assortment is in terms of six areas (three Western, three Eastern, distinguished in either case as North-, Central and South-). For Guthrie's statistical calculations to date[9] the classification has been as follows:

G (General): in at least four areas (two East, two West)
W (Western): exclusively or predominantly Western
E (Eastern): exclusively or predominantly Eastern
R (Residue): unclassified patterns

A more detailed classification is made in *Comparative Bantu*, I, para. 61. 71 ff., which might be used in future statistical calculations.

The basis for this classification of topological patterns is the frequent occurrence of patterns falling wholly or predominantly within one or other of the two regions (20% in the West, 39% in the East), in addition to patterns covering a large proportion of the whole field (23%).[10] No other way of classifying the topological patterns that has been tried leaves anything like so small a residue of unclassified patterns. This is not to say that after detailed analysis the present assortment might not be adjusted in some minor way, for instance by redrawing a zone or area boundary.

The recurrent Western and Eastern patterns argue for a division of Proto-Bantu into two dialects, Proto-Bantu A and B, just as the recurrent General patterns argue for a single ancestor-language, referred to as Proto-Bantu X. But this is not to say, for example, that comparative series (sets of reflexes attesting a starred form) with an Eastern distribution reflect source-items originating (or even occurring) in Proto-Bantu B. The only safe inference is that comparative series with a General distribution reflect source-items in Proto-Bantu X. Eastern comparative series may reflect a source-item in Proto-Bantu X subsequently lost in Proto-Bantu A or its descendents, or may reflect a source-item originating in some descendent of Proto-Bantu B. In all cases there is a danger that indirect reflexes may have falsified the regional assortment. There is a possibility of making a more reliable assessment of the origin of each comparative series, however, if its topology is considered together with that of synonymous comparative series and osculant comparative series (i.e. diverging slightly in form or meaning): Guthrie attempts this in the commentary of the forthcoming *Comparative Bantu*, II. Guthrie's inferences from vocabulary to the habitat and culture of the speakers of Proto-Bantu X were at first based on comparative series with General distribution (*JAH* 1962), but the approach may be refined by procedures of the kind described above (as Guthrie has exemplified in his paper presented to this Seminar), and the inferences extended to Proto-Bantu A and B.

Guthrie's statistical calculations are at present based not on the inferred origin of a given starred form in Proto-Bantu X, A or B, but on its topological classification as G, W or E. His inferences about earlier prehistory are drawn from items with the widest (i.e. General) distribution, while inferences about subsequent history are drawn from Common Bantu as a whole, or from items with low dispersion only.[11] Guthrie excluded for practical reasons putative starred forms with reflexes in less than three zones, but ultimately we may look to this source also for more detailed knowledge of recent ancestry.

For statistical purposes, Guthrie has selected twenty-eight sample or 'Test' languages. (It would not have been proper to have made statistical counts of features of *zones*, since Guthrie's zones are *not* genetic groupings—it never having been maintained that all languages in a zone share an exclusive intermediate ancestor.) One of the chief desiderata for an extension of Guthrie's work is to increase the number of Test languages, ideally to include one language from each *group*.

The most famous of Guthrie's hypotheses, relating to the Bantu 'nucleus', derives from a count of the number of General comparative series having reflexes in each Test language. The belt containing the highest number of reflexes includes Kongo, Lwena, Luba-Lulua, Luba–Katanga, Bemba, Ila, Rundi and Swahili in the presentation in *JAH* 1962, but Lwena, Ila and Rundi are excluded in *Comparative Bantu*.[12] In his paper to this Seminar and in *Comparative Bantu* he has introduced a refinement by counting up the sum of the moduli of dispersion of General comparative series having reflexes in each Test language, to yield a 'weighted coefficient of generalness'. This has the effect of giving greater weight to the most widely dispersed comparative series. The highest score is obtained by the two Luba dialects and Bemba; Guthrie refers to the area which includes them as the 'central nucleus area', while the languages of his original nucleus (with Sukuma but without Lwena) with their slightly lower scores form his 'extended nucleus area'.

Guthrie inferred from these data that the centre of Bantu dispersion was approximately in the Katanga woodland, the early Bantu-speakers expanding first east and west, and then north and south. While this may be likely, given the totality of the evidence, it is a little difficult to infer it directly from the statistical data referred to. All the Test languages are equally descended from Proto-Bantu X, so the difference shown up by Guthrie's figures is that some languages have changed faster than others (by losing inherited vocabulary and replacing it with new). Guthrie would then presume that the rate of change has been fastest among the pioneers, who would have been more constantly in contact with new populations. Unfortunately, we know very little about the correlates of differential rates of change, and among other factors that may be equally relevant are size of language community, political cohesion and range of regular communications.[13] To say this is not necessarily to dismiss the nucleus and the data behind it—ultimately we shall have to offer some explanation of the make-up of every language in terms of the extent to which it reflects the different sections of Common Bantu—but we should recognize that we may have to formulate more complex hypotheses, and seek analogies to support any correlations our hypotheses require.

The last approach to the analysis of Bantu relationships is a consideration of the relationship of the Test languages to one another in terms of their common entries from Common Bantu (i.e. how often a given pair of languages have reflexes of the same starred form). We need to take into account not only the number of reflexes in common but also the total number of reflexes in each language, since one hundred reflexes in common are more significant if only two hundred reflexes are present in each of the two languages than if each contains three or four hundred. For convenience of comparison it is useful to be able to reduce these figures to a single figure; Guthrie achieves this by means of an algebraic formula yielding an 'Index of Relationship' (*ALS* 1962; *TPS* 1964; *Comparative Bantu*, I, Appendix 6/3).

To illustrate some properties of this index we may introduce another device in which two languages are represented by diamonds proportionate in area to the number of reflexes in each, overlapping in such a way that the area of the overlap is itself proportionate to the number of reflexes they have in common. In this way an approximate scale can be given as follows:

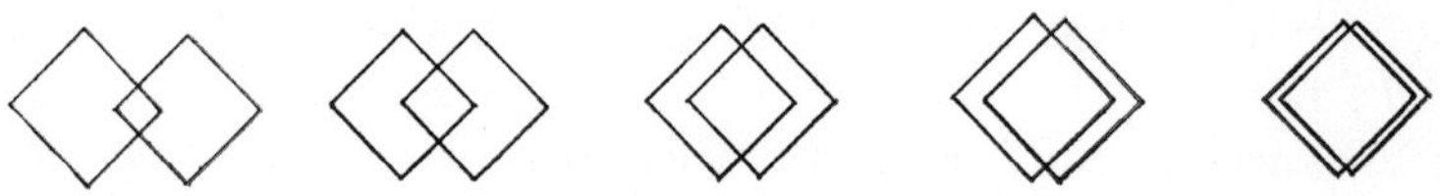

I.R.: 29 126 333 897 4091

If the aggregate of reflexes from the two languages remains the same, while the number of reflexes in each diverges increasingly, the index increases marginally to reflect the higher proportion of reflexes in the language with the smaller total:

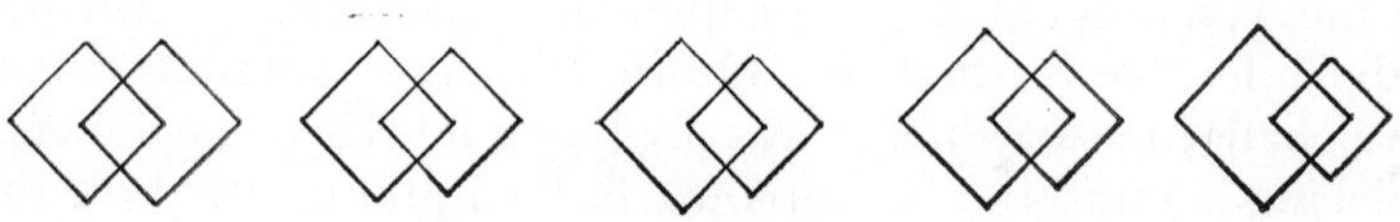

I.R.: 126 127 128 131 139

If the total of reflexes in only one language is varied while the total in common remains the same, the index rises or falls more sharply:

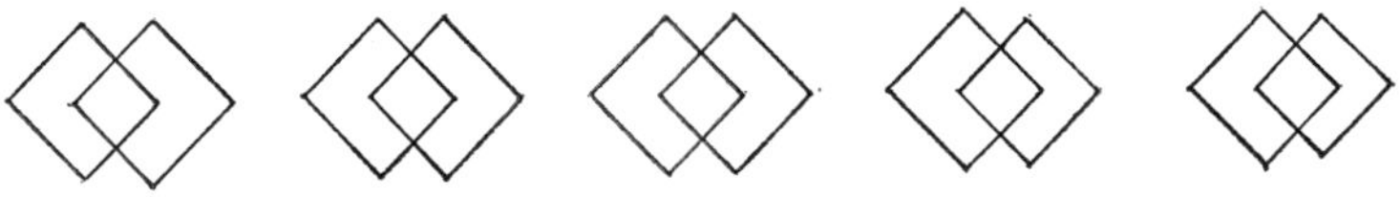

I.R.: 109 115 126 137 151 [14]

Guthrie gives a series of topograms in *Comparative Bantu*, I, Appendix 6/4, using contours to give approximate values for the Index of Relationship in the range 50–200 (other Indices being marked as '49 and under' or '200 and over'). This range reveals only the more distant relationships: closer relationships are illustrated for the languages of the North East in *TPS* 1964, where the figures quoted are in the range 140–2000.[15]

Guthrie, using the *full* data of his Indices of Relationship and many detailed inferences from the topology of individual comparative series, has formed conclusions about genetic relationships among the Test languages, which he set out in *JAH* 1962, p. 278, and in his paper presented to this Seminar. It is not possible to predict how the picture will develop when a larger number of languages is under review, but it does seem likely that careful examination of data of this kind will reveal a complex net of chain relationships alongside the strictly genetic relationships detected by Guthrie.

This paper has drawn attention to a number of factors that will have to be taken into account in evaluating the hypotheses about Bantu prehistory advanced by Professor Guthrie, and in exploring further hypotheses that may be extracted from current and future studies in comparative Bantu. It is hoped that it will both encourage historians to follow the detail of the argument, and endue them with a proper patience in their expectations of a study that in spite of present contributions has scarcely begun.

Professor Guthrie has kindly agreed to the publication of three diagrams, based on some of his unpublished figures. The figures used were not the final ones on which the topograms of *Comparative Bantu*, I, Appendices 6/2 and 6/4 were based; the diagrams are therefore presented for illustration only, and should finally be considered in conjunction with the detailed commentary of the remaining volumes of *Comparative Bantu* when these appear.

The area of each circle in Diagram 1 is proportional to the number of reflexes from Common Bantu in the language it represents. The circles are divided up according to the proportion of these reflexes that are assorted as General, Western or Eastern. Diagram 2 is drawn on the same principle, except that the area of the segments has been made proportionate to the sum of the moduli of dispersion (i.e. the 'weighted count') by varying the radius. (The segment representing the Residue has been left blank in this diagram for lack of data.)

These two diagrams have been drawn on the basis of substantially the same figures as Guthrie used for the calculation of his various 'co-efficients' (*Comparative Bantu*, I, Appendix 6/2), including the 'Co-efficient of Generalness', which suggested the hypothesis of the 'nucleus'. Figure 1 is related to the simple co-efficients, Figure 2 to the weighted co-efficients. The languages which make up the nucleus are those that have the largest black (General) segments in Diagram 1 (the nucleus as it was first presented in 1962) or Diagram 2 (the 'central' and 'extended nuclear areas' described in Guthrie's paper to this Seminar—cf. Diagrams 3 and 4 on p. 36 f. of this volume). The Co-efficients of Easternness and Westernness are in effect comparisons of the size of the corresponding segments, while the Co-efficient of Commonness is a comparison of the size of the complete 'pie' diagrams representing each language. (The weighted Co-efficient of Commonness cannot be deduced from Diagram 2 because the segment representing the Residue is blank.)

Diagram 3 shows the relationship between selected pairs of Test languages, using a logarithmic scale for the Index of Relationship —the more lines that link two languages, the more closely they are related. The pairs have been selected to display the degree of relationship within zones and across each zone-boundary.

KEY TO GUTHRIE'S TEST LANGUAGES

A.24	Duala	K.14	Lwena
A.74	Bulu	L.31	Luba–Lulua
B.75	Bali	L.33	Luba–Katanga
C.32	Bobangi	M.42	Bemba
C.71	Tetela	M.63	Ila
D.62	Rundi	N.31	Nyanja
E.11	Nyoro	P.21	Yao
E.13	Nyankore	R.11	Mbundu
E.15	Ganda	R.31	Herero
E.51	Kikuyu	S.13	Manyika
E.55	Kamba	S.21	Venda
F.21	Sukuma	S.33	Sotho
G.42	Swahili	S.41	Xhosa
H.16	Kongo	S.42	Zulu

NOTES

1. Malcolm Guthrie, 'Problèmes de génétique linguistique: la question du bantu commun', *Travaux de l'Institut de Linguistique*, 4, 1959, 83–92.
——, 'Bantu origins: a tentative new hypothesis', *Journal of African Languages*, 1, 1, 1962, 9–21.
——, 'Some developments in the prehistory of the Bantu languages', *Journal of African History*, 3, 2, 1962, 273–82.
——, 'A two-stage method of comparative Bantu study', *African Language Studies* 3, 1962, 1–27.
——, 'Some uses of arithmetical calculation in comparative Bantu studies', *Transactions of the Philological Society*, 1964, 108–28.
——, *Comparative Bantu: an Introduction to the Comparative Linguistics and Prehistory of the Bantu Languages*, Farnborough, 1967– (in progress). The first volume, the only one to have appeared at the time of writing, sets out and illustrates Guthrie's methodology; his conclusions for prehistory are contained in Part I, Volume 2. The data on which Guthrie has based his investigations is to appear in Part II (Volumes 3 and 4).
——, 'Contributions from Comparative Bantu Studies to the Prehistory of Africa', p. 20 ff. above.
The writer has had the benefit of much discussion with Professor Guthrie and access to unpublished material. He records his debt with gratitude.
2. A relevant study is L. F. Brosnahan, 'Some historical cases of language imposition', *in* J. Spencer (ed.), *Language in Africa*, Cambridge, 1963.
3. The term 'topology' is Guthrie's; see especially *Comparative Bantu* I, chap. 6.
4. Guthrie refers to 'indirect' cognates in his paper presented to this Seminar, but in the rather different sense of forms that are not fully regular in their systematic correspondences.
One has the suspicion that the open syllable structure attributed to Proto-Bantu and possessed by most modern Bantu languages may make it easier for indirect reflexes to escape notice, because of the high degree of phonological congruence that exists. (An open syllable is strictly one ending in a vowel; Common Bantu permits a syllable ending in a nasal—*m*, *n*, etc.—but there are no consonant clusters other than nasal compounds, i.e. nasal+consonant.) Guthrie's own impression (*JAH* 1962, 280) is that there has been very little contamination (inter-dialect loaning) since the formation of Proto-Bantu A and B (western and eastern dialects), although considerable contamination during the Proto-Bantu period. Whether this can be sustained in the light of the very diverse patterns of distribution and the possibility of undetected indirect reflexes might be disputed, however.
5. The terms are those used by Guthrie in *Comparative Bantu*. Skewed forms are forms that could be reflexes of a starred form but for a single irregularity in shape or meaning (para. 32. 61 ff.). If two starred forms differ only in one feature, they are said to be 'osculant', and may be derived from one another by 'mutation' (chap. 7). In his paper to this Seminar Guthrie used the term 'set of cognates' in place of 'comparative series' (the set of reflexes whose systematic correspondences are symbolized by a starred form).
6. It can be applied also to the sound-shifts established by the philological method, but such an application has no special status. Parallel sound-shifts frequently occur in neighbouring languages, even where the degree of relationship is slight or non-existent.
7. See U. Weinreich, *Languages in Contact*, New York, 1953 (reprinted The Hague, 1963), esp. 29 ff.
8. Stylized maps (topograms) showing the relative position of the zones appear in *TPS* 1964, 113, and in *Comparative Bantu* I, 65.
9. I refer only to Guthrie's published calculations. Guthrie has experimented with these and other statistics, but has presented only those that seem to show significant patterns. Where I refer to possible future calculations, I refer sometimes to ones suggested by Guthrie, sometimes to ones that I have devised.
10. 'Predominantly' is interpreted strictly as having reflexes in twice as many zones within the region as outside. The residue (18%) with unclassified distribution therefore consist of comparative series of more limited distribution, straddling the regional boundary without marked predominance on either side.
11. Underlying this course is the tenet that common innovations are more significant for sub-relationship than common retentions of earlier features. Innovations are likely to be more localized than retentions.

12. The figures quoted are at variance between the presentations; in the revised count, Guthrie counted as one some pairs or groups of related comparative series, and took account of some minor revisions in the comparative series.

It should be noted that in the visual presentation in *TPS* 1964 the difference in the number of reflexes between different languages is inadvertently exaggerated by making them proportional to the *side* rather than to the *area* of the diamonds representing each language.

13. Guthrie recognizes the break in the argument, but says that his hypothesis is offered in default of any better explanation of the statistical pattern.

For a study of the rôle of extra-linguistic factors in linguistic change, cf. the paper by Charles S. Bird, p. 143 ff. below.

14. Note that the Index of Relationship is a measure of proportion and not an absolute measure. It would be wrong to assume that the low Indices within the North West are due to the small number of reflexes from Common Bantu. The figures are in this case a genuine measure of the lack of homogeneity.

15. It is difficult using arithmetically graduated contours to display on the same topogram both more distant and closer relationships.

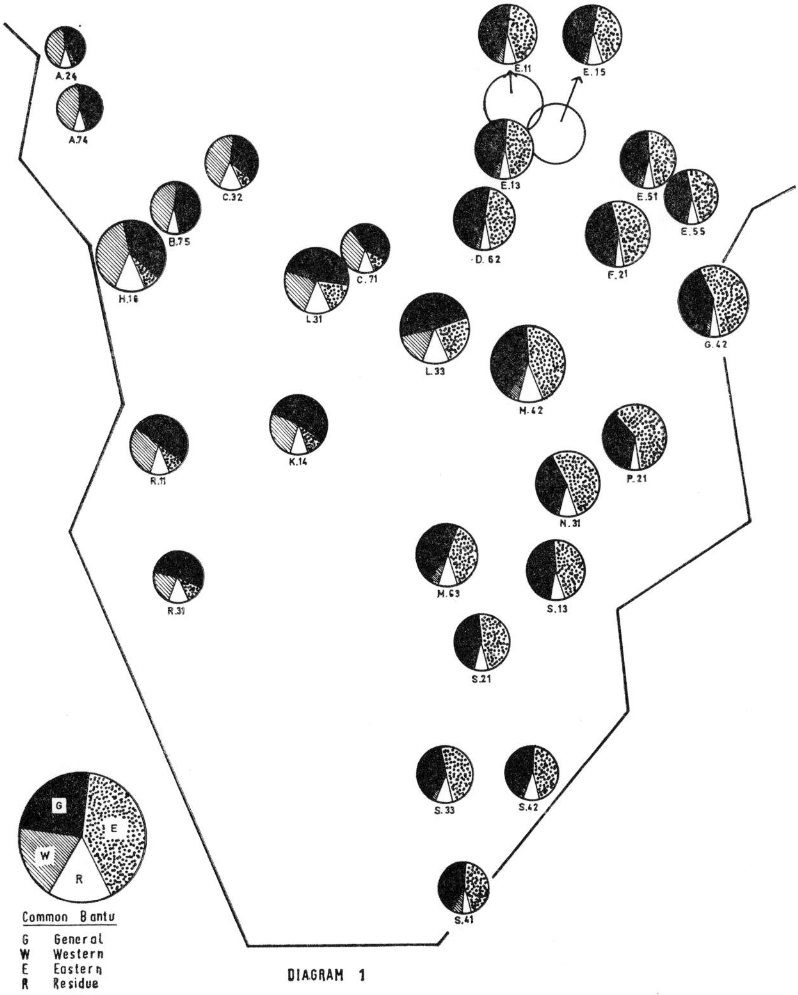

DIAGRAM 1

Common Bantu reflexes in the Test Languages: The regional assortment

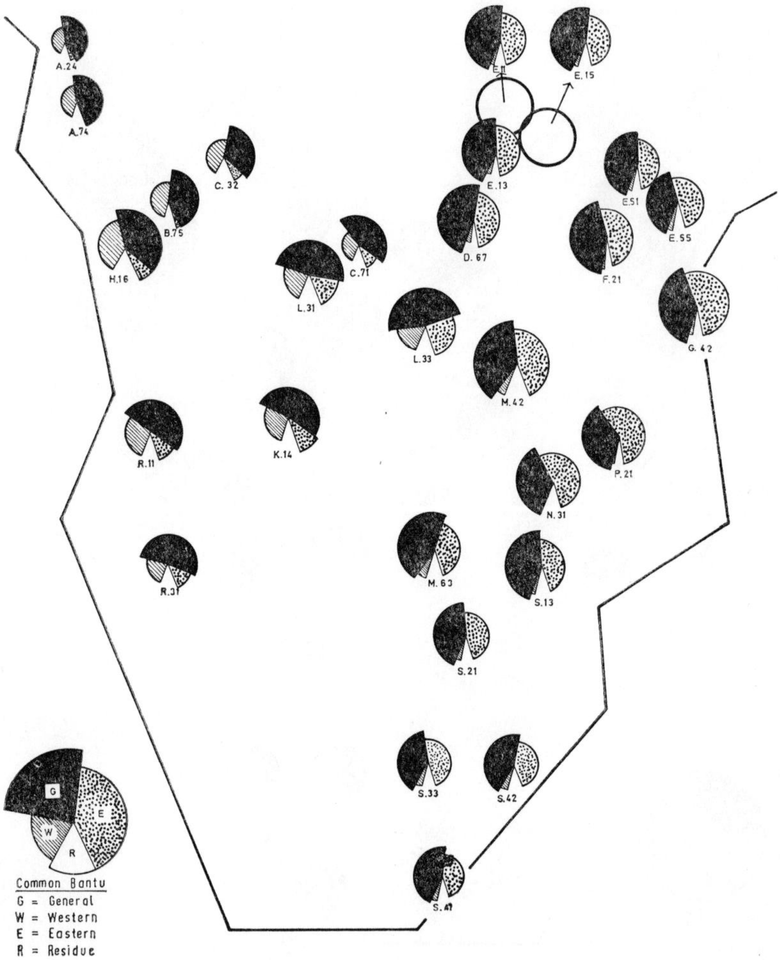

DIAGRAM 2

Common Bantu reflexes in the Test Languages: The weighted count

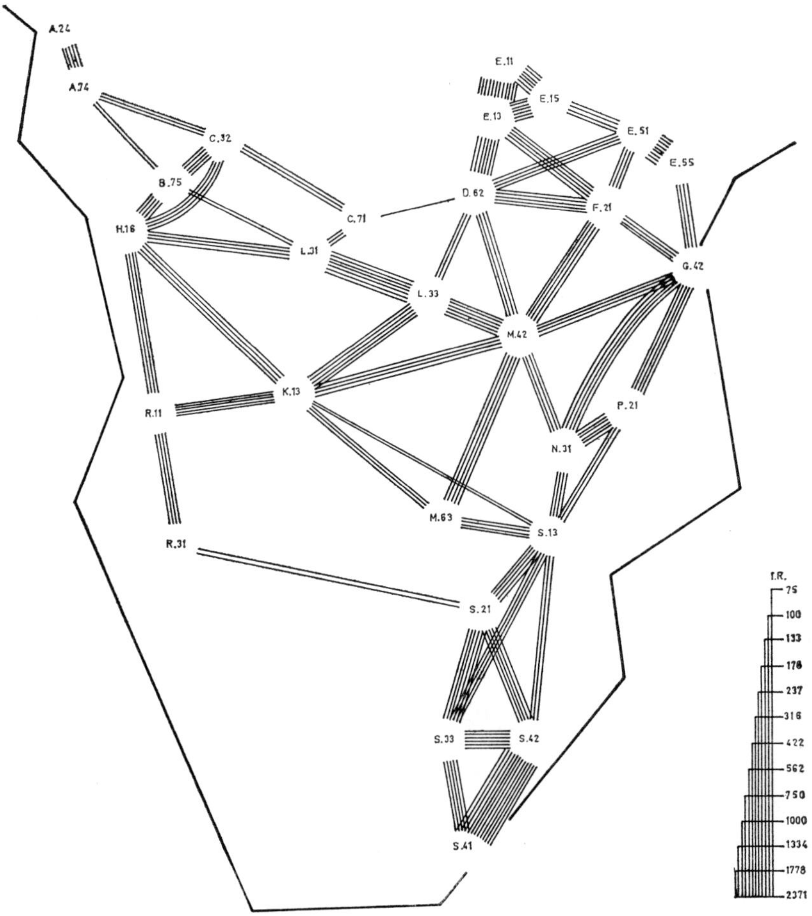

DIAGRAM 3

Index of Relationship between selected pairs of Test languages.

The Development of Mandekan (Manding): A Study of the Role of Extra-linguistic Factors in Linguistic Change

CHARLES S. BIRD

MANDEKAN is used here as a cover term for the various 'Manding' dialects known commonly as Bambara (Bamana), Màninka, Màndinka, Màndingo, Manya, Dyùla, Khasonke, Wangara and Marka–Dafin. The use of the term Mandekan for all of these dialects gains some support in the fact that, in the oral literature, all the people tracing their origin to the Mande,[1] call themselves *Mandekalu*, 'the people of the Mande'. Mandekan means 'the language of the Mande', from whence all of the above dialects have stemmed.

These dialects follow a rather typical pattern of language development described by the 'wave theory', i.e. neighbouring dialects are mutually intelligible, although speakers from opposite limits of the Mandekan area would probably have some initial trouble in understanding one another.

The geographical spread of Mandekan must be described in terms of a core area and an extended area. The eastern limit of the core starts in western Upper Volta. The western limit is found roughly in central Senegal, extending northward to the Mauretanian border and southward through central Guinea to the northwestern corner of the Ivory Coast. The southern limit may be roughly defined as the northernmost portion of the Ivory Coast, and the northern limit as the line running from Mopti in Mali across to the Senegal River (see Diagram 1). Mandekan is the principal mother-tongue throughout the core area.

In addition to this core area, roughly the size of France, there are sizeable Mandekan extensions to the west in Senegal, Gambia, Sierra Leone and Liberia. The penetration has been quite extensive to the south, Mandekan being the principal African trade language as far south as Abidjan. To the east, large numbers of Mandekan speakers are found in the north of Ghana and throughout Upper Volta.

Although the census figures for these areas are not too reliable, one could estimate the number of native speakers within the core area at around four million. The speakers outside the core, including first and second language speakers, surely double that figure. By African standards, the number of speakers and their geographical spread are both exceptional, and it is hoped to shed some light in this paper on the factors that have enabled Mandekan to achieve and maintain this exceptional status.

Before attempting to explain these phenomena, it may be well to place Mandekan in the general African language picture. Mandekan is a member of the northern sub-group of a major set of languages which has itself, unfortunately, been called 'Mande'. This northern sub-group includes Soninke to the north of Mandekan; Susu to the

DIAGRAM 1

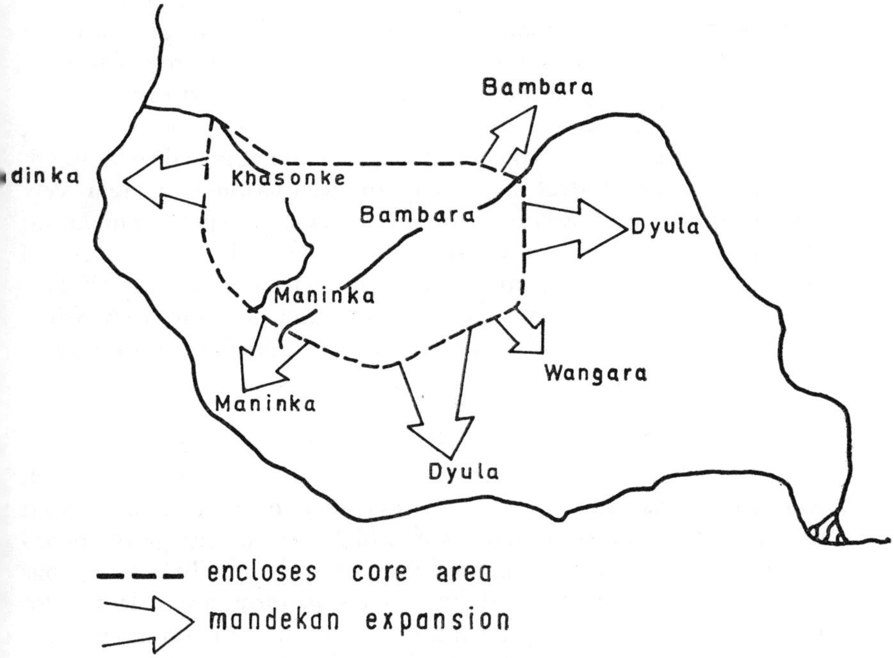

west; and Vai–Kono to the southwest. The southwestern sub-group of Mande includes languages such as Mende, Kpelle and Loma, spoken in Sierra Leone, Liberia and Guinea, and may well include a number of scattered smaller languages in the northern Ivory Coast. The southern sub-group comprises Mano and Dan and a few other smaller languages near the borders of Liberia and the Ivory Coast and the eastern sub-group includes a number of small isolated languages extending from the Ivory Coast to the western frontier of Nigeria. The manner in which these sub-groups are related to one another is at present subject to some argument and the inclusion of the languages found at the southern limits of Mande within one sub-group or another is also not finally resolved.[2] For the most part, scholars are only in complete agreement about what is and what is not a Mande language as opposed to the other major language groups in West Africa.[3]

Greenberg has classified the Mande languages as a 'branch' of his Niger–Congo family. This classification is, however, quite tenuous. Welmers[4] points out that the Mande languages, of all the major Niger–Congo branches, show the least relationship to the groups with which they are supposed to share a common origin. If the question is resolvable at all (a theoretical issue which will be discussed briefly below), it must in any case remain moot until a great deal more solid descriptive and comparative work has been done.

Returning to the Mandekan language itself, it is exceptional not only by its large population of speakers and their geographical spread, but also by its cohesiveness, i.e. the high degree of mutual intelligibility among all the dialects. One may contrast this situation with that of the Dogon language, on the eastern border of Mandekan, where, perhaps more typically of African language development, one finds a great deal of dialect differentiation over relatively short distances. Similarly, in Williamson's study of Ijo,[5] she mentions that, using the Swadesh 200-word list, she arrived at figures of 79·1%, 70·8%, 65·2% and 62·4% of shared 'basic' vocabulary between adjacent dialects. It is interesting to note that when similar tests were carried out using the Mandekan dialects from Segou, Kita, Gambia, Bobo–Dioulasso, Bouaké and Touba, we did not find any two dialects where less then 95% of the forms corresponded. It is of course possible that there are no clear linguistic boundaries between Mandekan and Vai–Kono, or even between Mandekan, Susu and Soninke. In this case, one would expect to find ambiguously classifiable dialects in which the percentage of correspondences would be considerably less. Unfortunately, no one has had the opportunity to work extensively in those areas. It should, however, be emphasized that dialects of Mandekan 800 miles apart still retain a high degree of mutual intelligibility.

In trying to explain these three exceptional features of Mandekan, i.e. the large number of speakers, its extensive geographical spread, and its relative cohesiveness, one might first hypothesize that the expansion of the Mande core was relatively recent. This hypothesis leads us into a number of contradictions with the historical evidence. We know that the Mande was one of the major parts of the Ghana empire, dating back a thousand years. We know from the oral literature that the Mande expansion into the Gambia took place during the reign of Sunjata in the thirteenth century and that the trade route settlements to the south date from the fourteenth century, if not before. In the legends referring to the establishment of the Mande, the only references made to the original inhabitants concern the 'little people' with whom the Manding people established a sort of symbiotic relationship, and from whom they learned to hunt. In contrast, we know that the Dogon people migrated from the Mande and established themselves in their present locale not much more than six or seven hundred years ago. We may certainly assume that whatever significant differences are found between Dogon dialects, the major changes took place after their establishment in their new home. If we are to give any credence to oral tradition at all, we must consider the more diversified Dogon dialects as the more recently established, but the more homogeneous Manding population as having been in place for a thousand years or more. There is little or no evidence which leads us to doubt that the proto-Manding core was an extensive area, stretching perhaps from Segou in the north down to the headwaters of the Niger in the south and across to the Faleme in the west. Whatever additional ramifications these facts may have, it is clear that time and space are not the only extra-linguistic factors that play a rôle in dialect diversification and linguistic change.

In order to show how these extra-linguistic factors can affect linguistic change, it will first be necessary to outline a model of language and linguistic change which can account adequately for the facts.

The development of generative grammar in the past fifteen years has led to a more formal way of looking at the structure of language. In the context of generative theory, a language is a set of rules which produce and interpret strings of symbols representing the structure of language. Transformational rules operate on items in specified contexts, permuting grammatical elements, deleting others, or adding new ones. There are, for example, rules of the sort:

1. *X* is rewritten as *Y* plus *Z*

Such a rule states that the category *X* is represented by or expanded into the categories *Y* and *Z*.

Some of the rules may be context-sensitive, e.g.

2. *X* is rewritten as *Y* plus *Z* in the context ____ *W*

Rule 2 states that *X* is expanded into *Y* and *Z* only when *X* occurs before *W*.

It is important to note that rule 1 is simpler than rule 2. The simplicity or complexity of linguistic rules has a very significant rôle to play in language change.

In addition to the above formalization of the notion of linguistic rules, generative grammar has also formalized the notion whereby it is not items such as the phoneme or the word that change, but rather features of these items that are involved. In standard generative theory, words can be defined as sets of three matrices of features: semantic, syntactic and phonological. Phonological features include terms of a finite universal set, such as +/− back and +/− high. Syntactic features are also of a universal and finite set and include terms such as +/− verb, +/− noun, and +/− adjective. Semantic features include those necessary to segment the continuum of the universe into relevant categories of time, space, colour, etc.

Given this view of language, it becomes apparent that it is not languages themselves that change, but rather rules of language or features of rules of language that change. This may at first seem to be a rather trivial distinction, but it has some far-reaching consequences. Since Mandekan may be considered different from Proto-Mande only by a number of modifications of the Proto-Mande rules, there is no definitive point in time where we could say Proto-Mande became or engendered Proto-Northern Mande, a part of which in turn evolved into Mandekan. Such an observation leads to the rejection of the familiar type of language-tree, which would, for example, depict the development of the Northern Mande languages perhaps as follows:

DIAGRAM 2

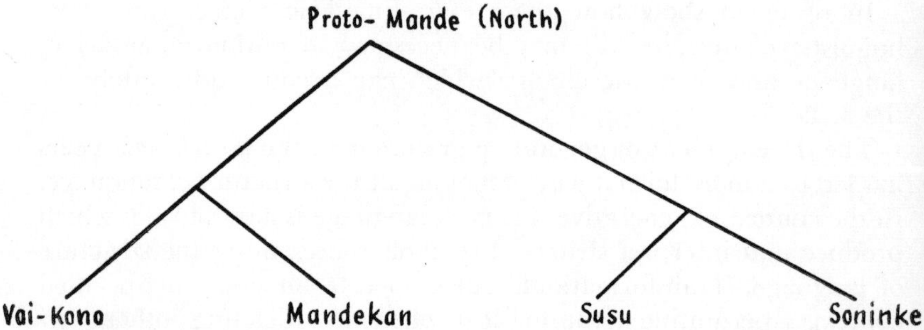

The tree implies that the four offspring arose from the mother proto-language at definable points in history, and were born perhaps of some massive social upheaval or catastrophe. Such a diagram does not allow any representation of the influence that non-related languages may have had on one or more members of the tree, and yet there is considerable evidence pointing to the modification of rules, or even to the borrowing of entire sets of rules, having been caused by the influence of neighbouring, but non-related, languages. Probably the greatest weakness in this sort of representation is that it does not allow an adequate characterization of perhaps the most common type of linguistic change, where no clear boundaries separate two adjacent and related languages. The languages may frequently be only part of a 'dialect chain', as is the case with French and Italian, with Baule, Asante and Fante, and perhaps with Mandekan and Vai–Kono.

The 'wave-theory' developed in the nineteenth century is a much more powerful model for the representation of language relationships. One of its most desirable features is that it eliminates many of the spurious distinctions between diachronic and synchronic linguistics.

In Diagram 3, the intersecting lines represent sets of rules shared by two or more languages. There are very strong arguments which illustrate that the intersecting lines represent historical-comparative isoglosses as well as synchronic language relationships.

DIAGRAM 3

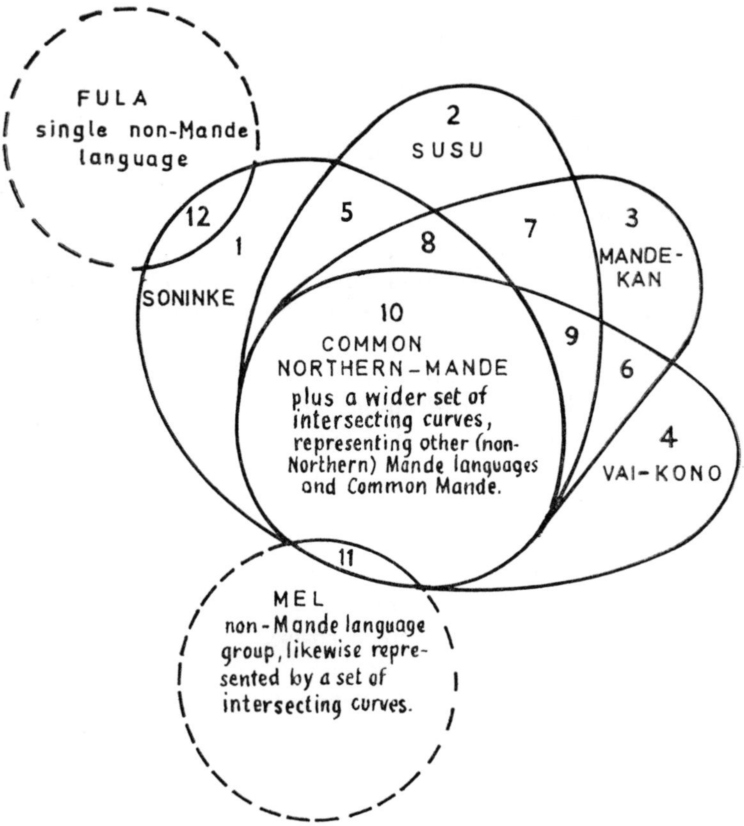

The power of this hypothetical depiction of Mandekan development can be illustrated by the number of claims made by the diagram; the numbered areas, for example, have the following meanings:

1. Rules[6] which distinguish Soninke from other Northern Mande languages.
2. Rules which distinguish Susu from other Northern Mande languages.
3. Rules which distinguish Mandekan from other Northern Mande languages.

4. Rules which distinguish Vai–Kono from other Northern Mande languages.
5. Rules shared only by Susu and Soninke.
6. Rules shared only by Mandekan and Vai–Kono.
7. Rules shared only by Mandekan and Susu.
8. Rules shared by all, except Vai–Kono.
9. Rules shared by all, except Soninke.
10. Common Northern Mande.
11. Rules shared by the non-Mande Mel languages, e.g. Temne, Kissi, etc., and by Common Northern Mande. If, in this hypothetical situation, further investigation showed that these rules were not part of Proto-Mel, we could safely hypothesize that they were borrowed from one or more Mande languages into one or more Mel languages. If, on the other hand, the rules were proven to be also Proto-Mel, there would be three possible alternatives: (*a*) a genetic relationship between Proto-Mande and Proto-Mel, (*b*) borrowing from Proto-Mande by Proto-Mel, (*c*) borrowing from Proto-Mel by Proto-Mande. There are no ultimate formal criteria for the resolution of these possibilities, and judgement would need to be made on the more or less aesthetically based principles of the nature and complexity of the shared rules.
12. Rules shared only by Fula and Soninke. In this case, since the shared rules would not form part of the set of rules which characterize Common Northern Mande, we could posit that these rules were borrowed by Soninke from Fula.

Such a model would serve to demonstrate that the rules which characterized Proto-Northern Mande are still largely operant today. It may be that the complex rules of Proto-Northern Mande have lost some of their restrictions or conditions on their operation and thus become more generalized, or—vice versa—that conditions or context-sensitive restrictions have been added to them to make them more complex. They are, on the other hand, recognizably the same rules.

The rules which characterize language are, as with other forms of social behaviour, idealized normative rules. They differ from many forms of social behaviour in that they are habitual and largely unconscious. Any form of habitual behaviour requires considerable and continual reinforcement of the rule which governs it. It follows then that if the reinforcing model is withdrawn, the behaviour is likely to change. In a hypothetical example, it may have been that there was at one time a Pre-Mandekan–Vai–Kono society that spoke mutually intelligible dialects. The society expanded towards the south, but as long as the lines of communication between the Mandekan and Vai–Kono areas remained open and as long as the southern extension still had its original cultural focus, there would be no reason to suppose that any significant change would have taken place. If, however, a hypothetical common empire crumbled, or if the lines of communication between the Vai–Kono people were cut by a subsequent expansion of neighbouring people, the Vai–Kono segment would have to reorient itself, finding a new cultural focus as a model for their behaviour. Rules from the adjacent and perhaps unrelated languages would come into conflict with Vai–Kono, which, having lost the reinforcing model of Pre-Mandekan–Vai–Kono, would add or subtract features of their linguistic and social rules to conform more closely to the new cultural focus.

Although in the Western world we tend to regard change as the normal state of affairs, it seems that stability and conservatism are the social ideals. Language behaviour is much the same. In the ideal state, there is no reason for language to change. It is only man's inability to achieve consistently the idealized norms and the interruption of communication between groups within a society that lead to change. The first of these factors is a constant, due to the natural imperfection of man's machinery. The second factor, however, is a variable and the situations which give rise to it are of some interest.

In discussing the uniqueness of Mandekan in relation to the majority of West African languages, it is more profitable to discuss those factors which have played a rôle in facilitating communication between extended branches of the society and which have thus acted as a conservative force on linguistic behaviour.

In an exhaustive study, one could mention facts about the climate, topology, geographic location, economic activity, social structure and numerous other factors which may play a rôle in increasing or decreasing social interaction and communication. I would like only to mention a few additional factors which seem to have had important effects on the development of Mandekan.

The first of these we will call the historical factor. The overall history of the Mande points to a general pattern which must have strongly influenced linguistic behaviour. The area has been, throughout its known history, incorporated within, or the centre of, large empires. One of the primary purposes of these empires was to stabilize the area in order to control and expand trade. Trade meant the movement of large numbers of people from town to town and the social interaction that resulted from this movement would certainly have led to the reinforcement of the linguistic norms of Mandekan.

A development that one might expect to find in a society engaged in extensive trade is the creation of a trade language. An interesting feature of trade languages in general is their high degree of syntactic regularity and simplicity. This also happens to be one of the most striking characteristics of Mandekan. The linguist would have to look a long time to find a case which requires an exceptional syntactic rule and we find that the conditions placed on the operation of certain rules common to other Mande languages have been lost in Mandekan. One might well hypothesize that a form of Pre-Mandekan came into being as a trade language and that, in a shift of cultural focus, the simplified rules of the trade language became the norms for the entire society. Here indeed we have an example of linguistic change, but one which, if our hypothesis is correct, affected the entire society and did not serve to differentiate one segment of the society from another. In any case, however the simplification did come about, the fact that Mandekan in its present form has very little syntactic irregularity and relatively little grammatical redundancy (such as noun class marking, case marking, etc.) leaves it practically devoid of those syntactic elements which are particularly subject to change.

To review our observations made in the above paragraphs, we have uncovered three factors which must be considered in any discussion of the development of Mandekan. These factors may be summarized as follows:

1. The historical factor: long periods of relative political stability over an extended area.
2. The communication factor: intensive interaction among extended groups through trade.
3. The linguistic simplicity factor: the generality and lack of redundancy in Mandekan syntactic rules.

In the general areas of social organization and values we find a number of other important factors which must have played a rôle in the development of Mandekan. One of the subjective observations that most visitors make about the people of the Mande is the great sense of pride and strong sense of identity which characterize them. It can certainly be argued that notions like pride and identity are not measurable and should thus not be brought into a formal argument. Whereas it is true that there are no units like foot-pounds or ergs of pride or social identity, it is equally true that these factors, subjective though they may be, do influence people's behaviour. It should follow then that language, being a form of behaviour, is equally subject to their influence.

One of the most obvious results of these factors is that the Mande is retained as the cultural focus by the most farflung of its members. The merchants who established trading colonies in Kong and Bonduku in the Ivory Coast, and those who colonized the Gambia sent their sons back to the Mande to learn the finer points of Mande culture and perhaps to return with a wife. Such a process served to cement the relations between the Mande heartland and its colonial extensions and in so doing aided in the conservation of the original linguistic norms and the moderation of the forces of linguistic change. It is interesting to note that the cultural focus of the Mande is still as strong as ever in spite of the efforts of the various governments to which the Manding now belong. The Mandekan broadcasts from Radio Mali and Radio Guinea are listened to wherever Manding people are found. It is also of interest to note that in a recent survey it was discovered that the Mandekan speakers on Radio Upper Volta and Radio Ivory Coast were recruited from southern Mali, the Mande heartland.

Manding society has a built-in mechanism for the reinforcement of this sense of identity and pride, as well as of its linguistic norms, in the form of its extensive oral literature.[7] There are three major types of oral literature in the Mande. There is what might be called 'folk literature' which includes the rabbit and hyena stories, love stories and burlesque and baudy tales of everyday life. Folk literature is distinguished from the other two types in that its performance or recounting does not require the services of the specialist. Each family or neighbourhood has its favourite folk story teller. It is due to the rather restricted range of these folk story tellers that we do not feel that they play any significant rôle in the process of linguistic change.

The second major type of literature in the Mande is what we will call the hunters' songs. The hunters' songs include ritual, as well as contemporary, songs and a number of works in the 'heroic' epic tradition. These works are performed by a specialist, called the *dònso-jeli*, or griot of the hunters. There is little information currently available on either the *dònso-jeli* or his songs, but preliminary research has shown that these artists travel widely, and in so doing are likely to have an important effect on linguistic behaviour.

The third type of oral literature characteristic of the Mande is what we shall call the literature of the courts. It is this literature that contributes the most to the Manding sense of identity and it is this literature that is the exclusive property of the casted griot, or *jèli*.

The casted griot is a rather enigmatic feature of West African society. His functions are many and varied. He is the preserver of many of the historical traditions and the royal genealogies. He is the seer and magician, reading omens, both good and bad, to predict the course of the future. He is the emissary and porte-parole from one court or family to another, and his casted status has guaranteed his safety from enslavement or execution, regardless of the message he transmitted. He is both composer and performer of a great store of oral literature.

Each griot clan is attached by tradition to a noble clan. For example, the griot clan Diabaté is attached to the noble Tarawele family and the griot clan Kuyaté is attached to the noble Keita clan. As well as serving the extended clan at major life ceremonies, such as births, deaths and weddings, the griot travels widely, exercising his trade and bearing news from one town to another.

The griot begins to learn his trade as a small child within the family. He frequently serves as an apprentice to one of the older members of his immediate family, or is sent to do his apprenticeship at one of the griot training centres, such as Kangaba or Keyla in southern Mali. During his apprenticeship, he masters an instrument such as the *nkɔ̀ni*, a two to seven stringed instrument similar to the guitar; or the *kɔra*, a twenty-one stringed lute-harp. He gradually masters a vast set of oral themes and perfects the rapid and dramatic style characteristic of the griot's recitation.

The important thing to note in the griot's training is that no matter where the griot may have been born, he will at one time or another train in the same place as all other griots. In addition, the griots come together for important ceremonies, such as the changing of the roof of the sacred hut in Keyla and the important life ceremonies of great nobles. Not only does this interaction and continual communication help to preserve the nature of their message, but it also helps to standardize the very language that they use. Given the rôle of the griot as the guardian of speech and the ready-made prestige that they draw from their manner of speaking, it is not difficult to see how the griots have functioned as an informal 'Academy', exerting a normalizing force on the society's linguistic behaviour. This is not of course a claim that all griots speak in the same way. Such a claim could easily be shown to be fallacious. It is, however, the case that griots borrow freely from one another and it can be claimed that this borrowing and interaction temper the forces of language change.[8]

The kinds of literature that the griot performs are quite varied, but they are all characterized by an epic type of structure, interspersed with a series of songs. Research is currently being conducted to determine the formal elements of the griot's verbal art. Our information points at present to an abstract form which could be described in terms similar to those used by Lord in his investigation of Serbo-Croatian epics and their relation to the songs of Homer.[9] The songs, as do many of the formulae in the epic, contain a rich poetic form, full of highly abstract symbolism and imagery, as well as syntactic deviations and a large number of relatively archaic syntactic and phonological forms.

The most striking piece of this literature is without doubt the Sunjata epic. Sunjata was the Mande king who ruled around the middle of the thirteenth century. The epic may run for upwards of thirty hours of recital time or may be told in the course of an evening, depending on how the griot decides to edit his performance. The epic consists of three major parts: the miraculous birth and youth of Sunjata, his adolescence in exile, and his return and victory over the Susu king, Sumanguru. In the course of the story, the audience learns how the Keita dynasty was established and how the other principal families of the Mande allied themselves to the Keitas.

There are other epic style pieces, such as that of the seventeenth century king of Segou, Da Monson, and there are hundreds of songs of praise devoted to the major noble families of the Mande. These songs are sung for the families to whom they pertain at each important life ceremony. It is clear therefore that the population has ample opportunity to hear the griot many times during the course of the year and to appreciate his language and his art.

Given this fairly high degree of exposure to the speech of the griot, and the fact that the griot's language is rich with borrowings from a number of dialects as well as numerous archaic forms, and accepting our assumption that the knowledge of dialect variations and historical forms, abstract though they may be, serve to temper change, it follows that the griot's very language has been an active force in shaping the development of Mandekan.

When we speak of 'tempering' linguistic change, we are in reality referring to a situation where there is an oscillation between diversification and reorientation to the old norm, or, more concretely, between two pronunciations, one a regional diversification and the other, the original form, maintained through the efforts of the griot. A good example of this phenomenon is found in a sound change that took place in the northern area of the Mande, stretching from Segou across to Kolokani. In this particular case, the original phonological sequence *-ɔgɔ* was shifted to *-wa*, e.g.

original	new Northern	
tɔgɔ	*twa*	'name'
dɔgɔ	*dwa*	'younger sibling'
kɔ̀gɔ	*kwà*	'salt'
nyɔgɔn	*nywan*	'together'

We know from texts written early in this century[10] that these two forms must have been in competition for at least two or three generations. Although the original form may have lost ground in terms of the number of speakers who used it, it never disappeared. The fact that it did not disappear can be accounted for by the griot's tenacity and his deprecation of the new northern form as 'bush talk'. The great amount of population movement from the northern region to the southern region, where the original form was still in use, must also have played a significant rôle in retaining the original form. It is interesting to note that today, with the new economic and political focus on Bamako, the original form is regaining lost ground, a process that would not have been possible had it ever been lost entirely.

In this discussion of the griot and his art, we have uncovered two more factors which should be considered in a serious discussion of language development in the Mande:

4. The cultural focus factor: the retention of the original cultural focus through nationalism and family ties.

5. The oral literature factor: the retention of archaic and dialectal forms in the griot's oral art.

In looking once more at the Mandekan and Dogon situations we may, in summary, postulate that extensive linguistic change may take place over a relatively short period of time, as in the Dogon case. There are, however, numerous extra-linguistic factors which inhibit or retard change, as in the Mandekan case. In our discussion of these factors, only one, the complexity of linguistic rules, is quantifiable, and it is clear that the four remaining variable factors cannot be used to quantify linguistic change. On the other hand, their rôle in decreasing the rate of such change cannot be denied, and we are forced to accept the fact that the rate of linguistic change is itself not quantifiable in any regular way.

NOTES

1. 'Mande', with the definite article, is used in this paper to denote the Mande heartland on the Upper Niger ('Mali'), in distinction to the wider use of the term to cover the whole 'Mande' language family. 'Manding' is used as a cover term for the whole cluster of ethnic groups and their culture, by analogy with French 'mandingue' (and in keeping with the procedure adopted by this Seminar).
2. For further details concerning the classification of the Mande languages, see:
   Wm. Welmers, 'The Mande Languages', *Georgetown Univ. Monograph Series*, 11, 1958, 9–24.
   A. Prost, *Les Langues Mandé–Sud du Groupe Mana–Busa*, IFAN, Dakar, 1953.
   J. Greenberg, *The Languages of Africa*, The Hague, 1963.
3. Prost, however, has suggested that Sonrai may actually be a Mande language (oral communication).
4. Welmers, loc. cit.
5. K. Williamson, *A Grammar of Kolokuma Dialect of Ijo*, Cambridge, 1965.
6. We consider the notion 'rule of language' to include rules of the following type:
   Concept X is represented by the phonological form Y
   This rule is more or less the basic postulate which all comparative linguists accept as primitive to their investigations.
7. 'Oral literature' is so contradictory a term that the conscientious linguist cannot help but wince when using it. It would seem that oral or verbal art would be better terms. Since 'oral literature' is already established for this aspect of verbal behaviour, we shall bow to tradition, but continue wincing.
8. The claim made here is abstract and somewhat delicate. It does however seem the case that, when the speaker is exposed to dialects which diverge from his own speech, he either adds transfer rules to his own grammar which enable him to convert the divergent forms back into the ones he is more familiar with, or he modifies his own grammar by making the rules more abstract to account for the conflicting forms. In the first case, the speaker is unconsciously doing the work of the synchronic

comparativist. In the second, he is unconsciously reconstructing a common form for the two dialects. For example, eastern Mandekan is distinguished from western Mandekan in that it includes a rule which changes *t* between two vowels to a flapped *r*, e.g.

Eastern	Western	
jàra	*jàta*	'lion'

Obviously the eastern form predominates in the eastern region, but the western form is heard frequently in the oral literature and from various travellers and visitors from the West. The speaker knows that there is a relation between *t* and *r* between vowels, and perhaps at a higher level of abstraction, he may consider them to be the same.

It is our claim that this sort of knowledge, unconscious though it may be, has a conservative effect on the forces of language change.

9. A. Lord, *The Singer of Tales*, Cambridge (Mass.), 1965.

10. See, for example:
M. Travélé, *Petit manuel francais-bambara*, Paris, 1910.
——, *Proverbes et contes bambara*, Paris, 1923.